MORMON CHRISTIANITY

MORMON CHRISTIANITY

What Other Christians Can Learn from the Latter-day Saints

Stephen H. Webb

OXFORD
UNIVERSITY PRESS

OXFORD

UNIVERSITY PRESS

Oxford University Press is a department of the University of Oxford.
It furthers the University's objective of excellence in research, scholarship,
and education by publishing worldwide.

Oxford   New York
Auckland   Cape Town   Dar es Salaam   Hong Kong   Karachi
Kuala Lumpur   Madrid   Melbourne   Mexico City   Nairobi
New Delhi   Shanghai   Taipei   Toronto

With offices in
Argentina   Austria   Brazil   Chile   Czech Republic   France   Greece
Guatemala   Hungary   Italy   Japan   Poland   Portugal   Singapore
South Korea   Switzerland   Thailand   Turkey   Ukraine   Vietnam

Oxford is a registered trademark of Oxford University Press
in the UK and certain other countries.

Published in the United States of America by
Oxford University Press
198 Madison Avenue, New York, NY 10016

Library of Congress Cataloging-in-Publication Data
Webb, Stephen H., 1961– author.
Mormon Christianity : what other Christians can learn from
the Latter-day Saints / Stephen H. Webb.
pages cm
Includes bibliographical references and index.
ISBN 978-0-19-931681-6 (cloth : alk. paper)   1. Church of Jesus Christ of
Latter-day Saints—Theology.   2. Mormon Church—Theology.   I. Title.
BX8635.3.W43 2013
230'.93—dc23
2013006034

1 3 5 7 9 8 6 4 2
Printed in the United States of America
on acid-free paper

CONTENTS

CONTENTS

ACKNOWLEDGMENTS

Studying Mormonism has made me a better Christian, which is why I am eternally grateful for the teachings of Joseph Smith as well as all those scholars, church leaders, and everyday believers who have labored to maintain those teachings as a living tradition. I have lectured and visited classes at Brigham Young University (BYU) three times now, so I cannot even begin to thank all the people I have met. BYU is a thriving, Christ-centered, and intellectually exciting place and should serve as a model for how Christianity and the academy can be productively integrated. I am especially grateful to the philosophy department for hosting me, including James Faulconer, Dennis Packard, James Siebach, and Roger Cook. Richard Williams, the director of the Wheatley Institution, invited me to deliver the 2012 Truman G. Madsen Lecture on *Eternal Man* on November 15, 2012, and I am grateful for that opportunity as well as his warm hospitality and his thoughts about Mormonism and free will. Emily Reynolds made my visit a very enjoyable experience and I felt like I got to know her father, Truman Madsen, through her generous and welcoming spirit. Others at BYU whom I want to thank include Paul Kerry (and his splendid Fidelio students), Alonzo Gaskill (a wonderful writer on Mormonism), Scott Peterson (a truly entrepreneurial thinker), Jacob Baker, Jack Welch (one of the first explorers of the amazing textual complexity of the Book of Mormon), Charles Randall Paul (founder of the Foundation for Religious Diplomacy), Sandra Rogers, Gordon Daines, Robert Millet, Fred Woods (who is the best interviewer I have met), and Roger Terry (for very helpful advice). I was also blessed by conversations with BYU President Cecil O. Samuelson and his predecessor, Elder Jeffrey R. Holland.

Of all the people at BYU, I am most in debt to David Paulsen, a fearless metaphysical pioneer who amiably opened the door for me to the richness of Mormon thought. He is truly a lover of wisdom, my mentor in Mormon studies, and an elder to me in the Christian faith.

Phil Barlow, now the Arrington Chair of Mormon History and Culture at Utah State University, is a man of winsome and gentle piety. Many years ago he planted a seed of curiosity about Mormonism in me and it is no fault of his own that it has taken a long time to come to fruition.

I am grateful to Ian Markham for inviting me to the Virginia Theological Seminary to share some of my work on Mormonism with his colleagues and students on November 8, 2012. He has been an important source of support even if, as he often points out, he rarely agrees with me on theological issues!

My former student and research assistant Adam Brasich, who is now a promising scholar in his own right, stepped through the door of Mormon studies just before I did, and I am happy that I had his company in my early explorations. Hal Boyd has played a special role as encourager and sponsor—he seems to know everyone in Salt Lake City and I am grateful for all of his introductions—and for that, as well as the gift of a Bob Dylan album cover, I am very glad to know him. Benjamin Brown, whom I have not met, kindly read every page of this book, and his feedback made it a much better final product. He is a student at the University of Chicago Law School, where I am sure he missed some study time due to his diligence on my manuscript, but I have no doubt that he did not get behind. If he decides not to practice law, he can always be a very good editor.

John Morehead, the editor of *Sacred Tribes Journal*, gave me the opportunity to respond to two scholars who wrote about my book *Jesus Christ, Eternal God: Heavenly Flesh and the Metaphysics of Matter* (New York: Oxford University Press, 2012), which includes a chapter on Mormonism. I am grateful to him and to Francis J. Beckwith and Charles Randall Paul. For their essays and my responses, see *Sacred Tribes Journal* 7, no. 1 (Spring 2012), available on the Web at http://www.sacredtribesjournal.org/stj/. Some of the material in Appendices B and C is taken from my responses to Beckwith and Paul.

Jack Welch invited me to revise the chapter from that book for the journal he edits, published as "Godbodied: The Matter of the Latter-day Saints," *BYU Studies* 50, no. 3 (2011): 83–100. I enjoyed working with the entire staff of the journal. Jack and his wife also hosted me for the BYU Studies Academy meeting on Feb. 9, 2013. The word *meeting* does not do justice to the wonderful conversations I enjoyed.

Finally, my editor Cynthia Read was a model of patience and encouragement. I am very fortunate that she believes in my work.

I wrote this book during a time of transition, and I want to thank my wife, Diane Timmerman, for her love, patience, discipline, and courage. While I was finishing this book, we welcomed the newest member of our family, my son, Teka. He could not figure out what I was doing at the computer all day, but someday, when he is old enough to understand, I will tell him everything about this very eventful year.

MORMON CHRISTIANITY

Introduction: The Mormon Ecumenical Moment

Governor Mitt Romney's campaign for the presidency in 2012 inspired many observers of religion in America to talk about a Mormon moment. Books, articles, and websites abounded with discussions of the meaning of Mormonism. When Romney lost to President Obama, many of those same observers announced that the Mormon moment was over. I think that is shortsighted. Far from waning into insignificance, the interest in Mormonism sparked by Romney's campaign has the potential to open up a Mormon moment of much greater duration and lasting consequence. This longer moment is what I call the new Mormon Ecumenicism.

Ecumenical means "of worldwide scope or application," and Mormonism, with its impressive overseas growth, is clearly ecumenical in that sense. But ecumenicism also means the attempt to restore unity to Christian churches separated by doctrine, history, and practice. At its best, the ecumenical movement tries to show how the various branches of Christianity are all nourished from (and contribute to) the same root. The ecumenical movement, unfortunately, has fallen on hard times. Old theological battles have not been won or lost, and little progress has been made by replacing theological dialogue with social engagement. Christianity remains divided and fragmented.

Nonetheless, there is reason to suspect that Christianity is on the verge of potentially radical transformations. The rise of a truly global Christian community is breaking down not only geographical barriers but also doctrinal walls that have kept churches divided for centuries.

What better way to revisit Christianity's past and reenvision Christianity's future than to examine one of the youngest branches on the Christian tree? The Mormon branch of Christianity is young, but it is also gnarled with the wisdom of the past. Scholars categorize Mormonism as an example of a nineteenth-century movement in American Christianity known as restorationism. As politicians were busy building a new country, many church leaders wanted to build a new version of Christianity. Restorationists had an ambitious and idealistic dream of establishing Christian unity by "restoring" the church to its New Testament form. Democracy was a form of government that tried to put political power in the hands of the people; restorationism followed a parallel path for the church. By organizing Christianity according to a few New Testament principles, restorationists hoped to bypass centuries of divisive theological debate and ecclesial rivalry.

Many of the early leaders of and converts to Mormonism were inspired by Joseph Smith because they did not find what they were looking for in any other church. They were not alone. Lots of people on America's frontiers shared this general dissatisfaction with the state of Christianity. American democracy guaranteed religious freedom, but the prohibition of a nationally established church resulted in a free market for religious ideas and institutions. Religious competition led to theological and organizational innovations that energized many Christians but left others confused or disenchanted. Even at its best, the growing religious diversity was messy and complicated. Some churches dug in their heels by claiming to offer the one and only true way to worship God. Others appealed to individual religious experience in the hope that shared emotions could replace theological consensus. Restorationists offered a relatively simple solution for those who wanted a better way to cope with so many religious options. In the land of freedom, equality, and opportunity, restorationists urged Christians to start afresh by getting back to the basics. There was much religious work to do, and restorationists hoped to inspire individuals to take ownership over their own theological education.What better place could there be to build the kingdom of God than on America's wide-open frontiers?

I grew up in a church that traces its roots back to the same restorationist spirit that animated Mormonism. It was part of the Campbellite-Stone tradition, named after Alexander Campbell (1788–1866) and Barton Stone (1772–1844), who were contemporaries of Joseph Smith (1805–1844). Campbell and Stone merged their groups in 1832, two years after the Book of Mormon was published and Joseph Smith founded his own church. One of Mormonism's most important early members, Sidney Rigdon, was originally a friend and follower of Campbell. The Campbellite-Stone movement eventually developed into the Churches of Christ, Disciples of Christ, and various independent Christian churches, while Smith's church, first simply called the Church of Christ, became known by 1838 as The Church of Jesus Christ of Latter-day Saints (LDS).

For the Campbellite-Stone tradition, restoration meant going back—by means of common sense and elementary logic—to the primitive church that can be found in the New Testament. My childhood church, for example, taught me that Christians should have no creed but Christ. We rejected all creeds because we thought that they were the product of philosophical speculations alien to the biblical narrative. Religious practices not found explicitly in the Bible might be well intentioned, we argued, but they inevitably create more problems than they solve. The hard-fought theological battles that left so many scars throughout church history are best covered up with a healthy dose of indifference. We intended to rise above the contentious history of denominational differences and the scholarly obscurities of ecclesial dogma by burrowing into the safe and narrow confines of the earliest years of the church. Theology works best when it is boiled down to the bare minimum of what is essential for salvation. Everything else is mere clutter and distraction from the task of winning souls for Christ. The result was a theological minimalism that could easily slip into biblical literalism.

Mormon restoration is unlike this or any other version. Smith agreed with other restorationists that Christianity had lost its way, but he disagreed with them about what exactly it was that Christianity had lost. Most restorationists wanted to strip Christianity of all of its historical baggage. Smith wanted to sort through that baggage to see what was worth retrieving. He thought that the fullness of the Gospel was discarded in the early church's struggle for institutional stability and doctrinal consensus. Smith's most important intellectual virtue, it seems to me, was an ability to look into the past with an utterly fearless and therefore expansive rather than contractive imagination. Consequently, Mormon restoration requires an arduous task of reconstruction that leaves no room for a nostalgic view of the past. Rather than abridging the Gospel, Mormonism dares to maximize it in all of its lush density.

Early Mormon leaders—men like Brigham Young and the Pratt brothers (Orson and Parley)—were drawn to the speculative prospects of Smith's big ideas. They were intrigued by the thought that we could share in God's power in heaven (a process that theologians call divinization). They were empowered by Smith's insistence that the spiritual world is composed of its own kind of matter and is, therefore, as real as anything we experience here on earth. They were humbled by the possibility that God was still choosing individuals to receive new revelations about sacred mysteries and God's mighty acts in history. And they were inspired by the notion that the core of our identity, whether it is called a soul, spirit, or intelligence, existed with God in heaven long before we were born. The excitement of exploring these new intellectual vistas strengthened them in the many trials they underwent for their faith. Mormons were persecuted, hounded, ridiculed, and ignored, but they were consoled by the tight bonds of their community and the sheer elasticity of their theological beliefs.

Mormonism spread far and wide, but many of its most important ideas about God did not sink very deeply into America's theological soil. Perhaps the most striking Mormon theological proposition is the idea that God has a body. Traditionally, Christians have believed that God is pure spirit, and spirit (or God's spirit, anyway) is defined in terms of its absolute difference from the material world. The traditional view, which is often called *classical theism*, holds that God is utterly unique. God is not one of the things of this world. He is absolutely transcendent, and as such, God is utterly beyond the stretch of our imagination, let alone the range of our knowledge. We can know God only if and when God reveals himself to us, but even then, we do not know God's substance (or essence). Our finitude gets in the way of his infinity.

Much of this book is nothing more than an attempt to take seriously the possibility that God has a form or shape that is something like what we call a body. Classical theists think the idea that God is embodied is nonsensical. It is like saying that squares are round. If it is the nature of God to be pure spirit, then by definition God cannot have or be a body. Classical theism was slow to develop in the church and did not receive its most systematic treatment until the work of Thomas Aquinas (1225–1274), but most Christians today share its assumption that God is immaterial. Christians, of course, believe that God in the form of the Son (the second person of the Trinity) assumed a body during his incarnation, but those who follow the logic of classical theism also believe that the Son was from the beginning every bit as immaterial as the Father and the Holy Spirit. Because God created the world out of nothing (a doctrine, as we will see, that Mormons reject), the eternal God exists before, beyond, and above the existence of the material world.

The proposition that God is embodied was especially unappealing to America's emerging class of professionally trained theologians in the nineteenth century. Eager to find their place among the cultured elites, they wanted to prove that they were the match of their European peers. Many Europeans already thought that Americans were crude and anti-intellectual. What could be more anti-intellectual than projecting flesh and bone onto the divine? Isn't this what children think, and doesn't growing in faith mean leaving behind such crude caricatures of the divine? Moreover, Christian leaders were anxious at the end of the nineteenth century to salvage the moral ideals of Christianity from Darwinian materialism. Most people then, just like most people today, equated materialism with atheism. *Christianity* and *materialism* were treated as two words that could not be brought together—as in Christian materialism, which sees the spiritual as a higher form of matter—without violating the basic grammatical rules that prevent us from talking nonsense. One could be a Christian or a materialist but not both. Arguably, choosing between religion and materialism is the great social and cultural decision that sets the modern period apart from the ancient and medieval, and many people of faith thought that this decision was forced on the world by godless ideologies such as Marxism, secularism, and Darwinism.

Some scholars think that modernity is over and that we now live in a postmodern period when the boundaries separating science, philosophy, and theology have dissolved, leaving the truth about the world up for grabs. That is probably an exaggeration, but it is true that much has changed since the days when Christians saw themselves fighting a war against the forces of materialism. Marxism is dead, and even many secularists avidly seek spiritual meaning in their lives. Most biologists still reject any trace of design in nature, but philosophers of science puzzle over how novel properties can emerge from the interactions of relatively simple physical systems, and many scientists wonder at how the laws of the universe could have been perfectly coordinated to permit the development of living organisms. More importantly, scientists have demonstrated that the nature of the material world is much more perplexing than anyone could have imagined prior to the twentieth century. Scientists keep discovering new forms of matter with strange names like quark-gluon plasmas and Bose-Einstein condensates, and nobody knows what dark matter is, even though it constitutes more than 80 percent of the mass of the universe. Physicists have poked so many holes in the atom that there seems to be little left of our common-sense preconceptions of what matter is. The world all around us is not as solid as it once appeared to be.

Scientists have changed their minds about matter, but have theologians? And if theologians did change their minds about matter, wouldn't they have to change their minds about God? Not every Christian doctrine is implicated in theories about matter, but what about those that are? I can think of two areas where theologians have responded creatively and constructively to new scientific approaches to matter. First, holistic medicine has convinced many people that the brain and the body interact in ways that blur the boundary between spirit and matter. Mental states have physical consequences just as much as chemical processes shape how we think, feel, and act. Whether or not the soul is the same thing as the mind, if the mind is intimately related to the body, then it is likely that the soul is as well. Christians believe that the soul is the source of our identity as individuals (it stays the same while our bodies change) as well as the reason for the uniqueness of the human species (we are more than animals because we are ensouled). They also believe that the soul is immaterial. Yet if the soul is purely immaterial and the body is merely material, then soul and body have little if anything in common. How, then, can they interact? Against soul–body dualism, theologians have recently become interested in thinking about new ways to analyze the human person. Hypothesizing a material soul does not mean that we are nothing but chemical processes and thus everything we do and think is determined by causes beyond our control (this is the version of materialism, often called reductive materialism, that truly is opposed to Christianity). Instead, it means that the spiritual and material worlds are much closer to each other than the assumptions of classical theism would lead us to believe. Matter is imbued with spiritual potential, we could say, while the spiritual has physical reality and power.

Second, ecologists and other scientists, in the light of various environmental disasters, have demonstrated just how fragile, as well as singular, the earth's environment is. Our planet is uniquely constituted for the emergence of life (a phenomenon called the Anthropic Principle), but it is also incredibly vulnerable to human use and abuse. In this context, theologians have been eager to reconsider God's relationship to the world as well as the ultimate value of nature. Many traditional theologies of nature portray the world as a mere backdrop to the drama of salvation. God created the world, from this perspective, to provide a place where human souls could be tempted in order to test their obedience to him. In much of traditional theology, then, God and the world are held apart as definitively as the soul and the body. By contrast, theologies of nature informed by ecology strive for a more holistic understanding of God's relationship to the world. When God pronounced creation good in Genesis, God meant that creation is good apart from any role we play in it. God delights in nature, and we are meant to enjoy nature too, but only as responsible caretakers of what God has given us. Nature is more than the setting for moral combat, like stage scenery that can be discarded after the play is over. Nature, in fact, is the name not only for everything that is not God but also for everything that will be united to God when purified of the effects of sin. So construed, God and nature are mutually related to each other in ways that classical theism could not imagine.

Yet, for all of these reconsiderations of God and matter, the suggestion that God is material (or, more precisely put, that matter can be attributed to the divine; that is, matter, in its perfect state, can be considered one of God's predicates or perfections) still strikes many traditional Christians as absurd if not downright horrifying. To classical theists, matter and God do not mix because matter is the source of decay, disease, and death. Matter changes, while God does not. Matter is dead, while God gives us life. Matter limits us, while God sets us free. Those are obvious truths if matter is the inert stuff that is destined to disappear when our souls enter into the afterlife. But what would happen to these assumptions if we thought that matter is more like the fields of energy that animate the whole cosmos rather than incredibly small particles held together by external forces? What would happen if we thought of matter as the stuff that makes relationships possible, including our relationship to God? What would happen if we thought that matter and spirit are just different names for the same thing, depending on how you look at it?

And if we thought about matter in all of these ways, what would happen to our understanding of God? Is it really bad theology to imagine that we will see God face to face one day? Is it really childish to think that God can actually speak as well as feel, think, and act? Is it nothing more than vanity to suppose that, since God created us in his image, our existence, including our bodies, is the best clue we have to figuring out what God is like? If God looks like something (rather than being completely without form), doesn't it stand to reason that he looks like us?

And here is the biggest "what if" question of all: What if Joseph Smith's vision of God really does have something important to say to all Christians today? What if his insight into the materiality of the divine is what the world today most needs to hear? And what if Christian unity can be achieved by recovering the physical power and presence of the divine?

Mormonism is about much more than matter, of course. A strong case can be made for the importance of other Mormon teachings in the revival and reunification of Christianity today. In this book I will examine Mormon teachings on scripture, postmortem salvation, pre-mortal existence, baptism, communion, and the history of the church. I will focus mainly, however, on what I call Mormon metaphysics, which could also be called the Mormon worldview, because I think that Mormon metaphysics provides the best gateway into the whole range of Mormon religious beliefs and practices.

Those who think that a material view of the divine is crude and simpleminded will be surprised to find that Mormons have a very sophisticated and radical metaphysics. By arguing that only the physical is real and that the divine is physical in ways that we can only glimpse in this world, Mormon metaphysics actually has some advantages over more traditional metaphysical schemes that emphasize the immateriality of the divine. Most significantly, Mormonism can address directly and sympathetically the question of materialism that lies at the heart of modern atheism. Indeed, atheism has been in the news in recent years almost as much as Mormonism. Claiming to have their own history of facing stereotypes and prejudices, some atheists have mounted an aggressive campaign to gain social respect and cultural validation. Atheism is widespread and growing because so many of our cultural elite think that every aspect of human existence can be reduced to a closed set of physical causes and that this worldview is clearly superior to any supernatural alternative. Atheists embrace the physical world as the only possible reality, even while scientists keep pushing the limits of our ability to imagine what matter really is. Traditionally minded theologians need to push the question of what matter is too, and in doing so they will find that their Mormon colleagues have already been there and are farther along the path in envisioning just how much matter can be said to extend to the divine.

The Mormon imagination is solidly grounded in material reality, but it takes the physical world to new and unheard-of heights. That is why Truman Madsen (1926–2009), perhaps the most prominent and influential Mormon writer of the twentieth century, could say, "I am with those who wish for a larger cup to grasp the ocean." The ocean is a wonder to behold. Standing in front of it or diving right in can be a sublime experience that is hard to put into words. But the ocean is more than just a prod to our imagination or a limit to our descriptive talents. It is also something we can feel, play in, and, yes, dip a cup into. Trying to grasp the ocean with a cup is a potentially comical endeavor, since the ocean will overflow even the biggest container, but that is no reason to go into it empty-handed. If God is physically real, then we need an approach to physical reality that can do God justice. To that end, Mormonism just might provide a very large cup for tapping into the divine.

Chapter 1

Mormon Envy

I am not a Mormon, but sometimes I wish I were one. I grew up in a tight-knit religious community that shaped every aspect of my life. My church was a world set apart, not unlike the way Mormonism has chosen for much of its history to stay on the sidelines of the American mainstream. Many aspects of Mormonism take me straight back to the powerful experiences I had in the evangelical church of my youth. Indeed, Mormonism cultivates a sense of belonging, purpose, and focus that is not easy to find in many churches today. Mormons, for example, do not play soccer on Sundays. That is, they honor the Sabbath, which is something my church emphasized when I was growing up. Mormons have a strength of religious character that helps them to put religion ahead of popular culture, and that is no easy task.

In fact, Mormons can be so intense about their church that some Protestant fundamentalists call them a cult. This accusation is ironic, because Mormons and fundamentalists have a lot in common. They share a commitment to absolute truths, the sacredness of the family, the need for strong moral communities, and a reverence for the King James Version of the Bible. Like fundamentalists, Mormons know how to draw a sharp line between who they are and what they do not want their children to become.

I had to become a parent before I could begin appreciating my own quasi-fundamentalist upbringing (the distinction between evangelicals and fundamentalists was only beginning to be made when I was growing up). The sharp line my church drew between truth and falsehood felt more imprisoning than protective when

I was a kid. Especially when I started high school, the intensity of my church experience was so all-encompassing that it felt suffocating. I thought that my church was not big enough to accommodate my spiritual needs and theological explorations, but now that I have children of my own, I have more sympathy for what my ministers, parents, and Sunday school teachers were trying to do.

My church had plenty of reasons to separate itself from secular society. After all, the seventies, which exactly matched my second decade of life, from age ten to twenty, can lay claim to being the most socially tumultuous period in American history. When the radical sixties spilled over the borders of college campuses, the suburbs went wild, and it was not a pretty sight. A decade that began with the sappy sounds of soft rock and ended with the awkward gyrations of disco, with escalating rates of divorce, drug usage, and urban decay in between, was as culturally confusing as it was economically stagnant. My church reacted by condemning popular culture, but it did not have enough culture of its own to provide an engrossing alternative. Its theological architecture was too weak to withstand, at least for me, the power of the world outside its doors.

Once I got some distance from my church, I found it impossible to return. For years I felt like a spiritual exile, trapped by a religious past that would not let me go. In a way, the intensity of my religious upbringing ruined my search for a new church home. I was so used to an all-consuming tradition that every church I visited seemed like playacting by comparison. I was like a young man whose first love was so passionate and turbulent that I doubted I would ever fall in love again. I could not go forward, but I also could not go back.

As it turns out, my situation was pretty typical for the period. The seventies was a time of incredible transition for evangelical Christians. The age of heavy-handed fundamentalism, with all of its alarm about the coming end of the world and its denunciations of godless, secular society, was drawing to a close, but the era of evangelical self-confidence, when conservative Christians made their peace with popular culture by flexing their political muscles and creating their own media presence, was still on the horizon. The megachurches that evangelicals now attend are designed to keep their young people engaged and occupied. The Sunday morning praise music is a slightly gentler version of Saturday night rock, and the big screens make the worship as familiar as a sports bar and grill. Nowadays Christian teenagers can have it all—that is, they can be plugged into Christ and the Internet, often at the same time. They are not forced to choose between being Christian and being cool.

I found my own version of a megachurch—a church big enough to let me affirm the goodness of the world without becoming mired in worldliness—in Roman Catholicism. After attending a series of Protestant churches, I became Roman Catholic six years ago. I love the spaciousness of Catholicism, the way it seems to float above time, making it a depository of all things eternal, but as much as my Catholic parish is now my church home, the evangelical world still tugs at my soul. When I think about what Christianity is, or should be, my mind returns there to survey its dense religious landscape. I forget the weeds I had to pull and the thorns I had to avoid. The church of my childhood looks lush and full in my memory, even if it was enclosed by a pretty high wall.

I tell this story because becoming a Roman Catholic opened the door for me to begin appreciating Mormonism, while becoming immersed in Mormonism has helped me to retrieve the value of my evangelical youth. That sounds like a much more complicated "hermeneutical circle" than it really is, so let me explain!

Many Christians think that Mormonism is not really a part of Christianity, but if forced to identify what style of Christianity Mormons most resemble, most people would probably choose conservative Protestantism. That is because Mormons have strict moral values and put churchgoing at the center of their lives. They also tend toward a literalistic reading of the Bible, even though, much to the dismay of traditional Christians, they add to the Bible another testament to Jesus Christ called the Book of Mormon.

I can relate to this connection. When I talk to Mormons, visit a Mormon church, read Mormon books, or spend time at Brigham Young University, I feel like I am reentering the evangelical-fundamentalist world of my youth. Mormonism seems to me to be a comprehensive form of Christianity. By that, I mean that Mormonism is a variation of Christianity that wraps its arms around the whole person, giving members a strong worldview as well as an institutional belonging that sets them apart from the world at large. Mormons have their own language, outlook, history, and style. The way they talk and act reminds me of the people I grew up with.

Being with Mormons makes me feel right at home. Indeed, it was only *after* I began studying Mormonism in earnest that I fell in love all over again with the evangelical tradition of my childhood.

I was not able to appreciate Mormonism on an intellectual level, however, until I became Catholic. I had studied Mormonism for years, but I needed to become immersed in the theological breadth and sacramental depth of Catholicism *before* I could begin appreciating the intricacies of The Church of Jesus Christ of Latter-day Saints (the official name of the Mormon Church, commonly abbreviated as LDS). Before I became a Catholic, Mormonism was just too exotic for my Protestant sensibilities. Mormons worship in temples, wear sacred garments, submit to an elaborate religious hierarchy, pray for the dead, and ordain young men to the priesthood. By making me alert to the beauty of ritual and the necessity of solid structures of authority, Catholicism erased my prejudices about the peculiarities of some Mormon practices and let me appreciate it as a branch of Christianity with its own strengths and advantages.

Some readers will think that the two parts of my story contradict each other. I have recounted how Mormonism has helped me to appreciate my evangelical youth, and I have related how Mormonism started to make sense to me only after I became Roman Catholic. It is certainly possible that my spiritual journey has been merely eccentric and unusually befuddling! Nevertheless, I think that my experiences have put me in a theological place where I can see something about Mormonism that even some Mormons might miss. Mormonism is not just a variant of Protestantism. True, it emerged in the early nineteenth century when there were few Catholics in America and Protestant prejudices against Catholicism were popular and pervasive. Early Mormons shared many of those prejudices, so it might seem odd to suggest that Catholics are in a better position to appreciate Mormonism than Protestants. Yet throughout this book I will argue that Mormonism has a deeply Catholic sensibility. Of course, it combines elements of Protestantism and Catholicism in a way that is more than something that simply adds them together. But that is just the point: It strives for a philosophical richness, organizational coherence, and ritual completeness that is typically associated with Catholicism, not most forms of Protestantism. Perhaps the moral of my story is that it takes a special spiritual journey for non-Mormons to begin appreciating what the Latter-day Saints are all about.

Perhaps, too, the best conclusion to draw so far is that Mormonism is hard to classify. That does not mean, however, that Mormonism is a confusing set of beliefs with arbitrary religious practices. Mormonism is hard to classify in part because it transcends the standard debates in America that differentiate Protestants and Catholics (and one Protestant denomination from another). Some scholars argue that Mormonism is so different from traditional strands of Christianity that it constitutes a new religion altogether. Other scholars have even compared it with the way Islam is both related to and distinct from Judaism and Christianity. I disagree with both of those views. By providing an alternative to current forms of Christianity that nonetheless does not fit into any conventional classificatory scheme, Mormonism can seem like it does not even belong on the Christian map. In fact, for many Christians Mormonism does not feel like a part of Christianity because it is terra incognita, an unknown land that cartographers are unable to document because nobody knows what is really there. That means to me that studying Mormonism should be an exciting theological adventure. It is also possible that those willing to explore Mormonism will be inspired to revise their maps of what they think they already know about Christianity.

As an exercise in religious mapmaking, I will identify three basic strategies that churches of all traditions and denominations use to secure their institutional identity and foster their growth. These categories will help generate some sociological observations about why Mormonism is so hard to compare with other Christian traditions.

The first strategy is what I call *the ethics of exclusivity*, typically associated with fundamentalist churches. The second is what I call *the exhortation of the emotions*, and it is the strategy of evangelical churches like the one I grew up attending. The third is what I call *the ethos of elasticity*, and it is standard in liberal churches. (I am not trying to be polemical or political in using the much debated term *liberal*. I mean *liberal* in its best sense—nonjudgmental, open, and tolerant. I also mean *liberal* in its technical theological sense, which means a rejection of the doctrine of original sin and thus a relatively optimistic view of human nature, as we will see.)

These categories are in part a product of the way Protestant churches have been forced to compete against each other in the religious market for a shrinking share of the church-attending pie. I am not suggesting that any individual church or entire denomination fits neatly into only one of these categories. Roman Catholic, Eastern Orthodox, and Pentecostal churches (churches that emphasize the charismatic gifts of the Holy Spirit such as tongue speaking and faith healing) are especially good at straddling these divisions. Nonetheless, I think that these categories will be valuable to the extent that they help shed light on how Mormonism demands a rethinking of every aspect of Christian history and tradition.

First, the ethics of exclusivity. A tradition can try to hang onto its young people by policing contact with the outside world and disciplining those who cross the boundary between "us" and "them." Churches that pursue this strategy are known as fundamentalist, because they have a set of beliefs and behaviors that are not negotiable. They grow by being exclusive, which might sound paradoxical but for the fact that many people want (and need) to be part of a community that provides well-defined rules and high moral expectations. I call this strategy an *ethics* of exclusivity because it puts so much emphasis on the moral decline of the modern world and thus the need for clear and consistent rules of behavior. "The world" is just a name for everything that fundamentalists think people need to be saved from. That is why fundamentalist churches have preachers, not ministers (preachers proclaim the Gospel, while ministers meet spiritual needs as a therapist might do). The same basic message can be repeated every Sunday, and the same call for repentance can end every service, because faith is a gift that sin keeps preventing us from receiving.

Second, the exhortation of the emotions. Evangelical churches like the one I grew up in are different from fundamentalist churches precisely because they put more emphasis on the subjective than the objective. We still had our core set of beliefs, and our leaders taught us to be wary of the ways of the world, but church was essentially about cultivating certain kinds of religious experiences. Emotion, by which I mean everything from strong passions to sentimental thoughts and warm feelings, is by nature temporary, which is why the emotions need to be exhorted on a regular basis. Most evangelical preachers are experts at cajoling, motivating, exciting, and redirecting the emotions of those in the pew by appealing to the personal aspects of salvation. Evangelical churches are less concerned about trying to reform the world (which is a task pursued by liberal churches) or separating themselves from it (a goal of fundamentalism) than establishing an experientially deep relationship to Jesus Christ. What has really set evangelical churches apart from their fundamentalist cousins, however, is their more positive appreciation for popular culture as well as a more holistic view of salvation. Evangelicals have expanded the personal relationship to Jesus in fundamentalism to include a social outreach that attends to the recreational, educational, and social—as well as spiritual—needs of the community.

Third, the ethos of elasticity. Exclusive churches take the risk of providing their members with too little room to grow, while elastic churches go in the opposite direction. Elasticity is an ethos because it is more of a mood, or state of mind, than a set of rules or beliefs. Traditions are elastic when they are able to stretch into new shapes with each succeeding generation. The obvious problem with elasticity is that traditions that are stretched too far might not be able to return to their original shape. Of course, that is just the point for elastic institutions: they welcome substantial change as the means for adjusting to new situations. Nonetheless, even the strongest material can be deformed and even destroyed by being subjected to too much external pressure. Mainline Protestant denominations that tend to be theologically liberal are acutely aware of this problem, since they have been losing members by the millions in the last several decades. That does not mean that elasticity is a bad trait for churches to exhibit. It just means that it can be hard for elastic traditions to find new durable shapes after being pulled in so many disparate directions. Traditions have to be big enough to grow into, but if they are too loose-fitting, they will not provide the warmth and protection that make them worth wearing in the first place.

All of these strategies have implications for how churches should relate to (and how they will be perceived by) the non-Christian world. Fundamentalism is especially attractive to families, because it promises parents that it will protect their children from worldly temptation and social turmoil. In modern America, however, when young people have the whole gamut of popular culture at their fingertips—and in their ears—just saying no to the world at large is not enough. Liberal churches tend to accept contemporary social changes while putting their energy into alleviating poverty, promoting peace, and providing the contemporary world with a deeper and better way to understand itself. Meanwhile, evangelical churches have set out to create their own group activities and cultural means of expression in order to provide an alternative to the social status quo. To do so, of course, they inevitably borrow from the wider culture that surrounds them. Churches compete not only with each other but also with the sports and entertainment industry, and when they beat popular culture on a level playing field, they can end up resembling their opponents. Victory turns into defeat when the result is a style of worship that blurs the boundaries that fundamentalists worked so hard to erect and maintain. Indeed, the rise of an entertainment culture goes a long way toward explaining why the influence of fundamentalism in America has been eclipsed by evangelical styles of worship. It is hard to compete with churches that mimic American consumerism by promising to satisfy our desires for exciting and emotionally satisfying personal experiences.

These are socially stressful times, and any church that recharges peoples' spiritual batteries and replenishes their emotional resources is going to go far in keeping a hold on its members, young and old. When I went off to college, however, a focus on the personal and the subjective was insufficient to keep me returning to my evangelical roots. I needed ideas worth defending and ideals worth sacrificing for. I found Roman Catholicism attractive in part because it was so alien and challenging to my Protestant upbringing. Catholicism, in fact, blurs my three categories in interesting and challenging ways. Catholicism is *exclusive* in a very literal way since it excludes non-Catholics from participating in the Eucharist (what Protestants tend to call the Lord's Supper) during Mass. Catholicism is also *elastic*, with plenty of variety in beliefs even if its liturgical practices are orderly and uniform across the globe. After all, some of the greatest minds in Western history have debated every aspect of Catholic belief without coming to a final consensus on many theological questions. Catholicism honors and preserves the whole history of Christian theology and practice for individual appropriation, but it avoids the dangers of moral relativism, where one person's opinion about the issues of faith is just as good as anyone else's. By treating theological truths as part of the Sunday liturgy (the Nicene Creed is recited at every Mass), the Church invites meditative explorations and philosophical interepretations of what its doctrines mean. Finally, Catholicism is *emotional* in a very specific sense of that term. What is at stake in Catholic worship is not a feeling you get from the songs or the sermon (both of which can be restrained and dull, admittedly) but the visceral (sensory, physical) knowledge that, aided and abetted by a variety of ritualized word and actions, you are becoming one with Jesus by consuming the consecrated bread and wine, which have been transformed in a deeply mysterious way into the body and blood of Jesus Christ.

Catholicism, of course, has its own challenges in making its message relevant to its youngest members as well as new converts, and I am not writing this book to proselytize for Catholicism (or Mormonism, for that matter). Nor is my treatment of churches meant to be exhaustive. I have not discussed Pentecostal churches, which constitute one of the world's fastest-growing Christian traditions. Pentecostal churches are often accused of being overly emotional, but they actually combine an appeal to emotion with very elastic theological beliefs as well as social and cultural codes that maintain a high degree of separation from the world. Nonetheless, Catholic and Pentecostal traditions are much easier to locate on the religious map I have drawn than the Latter-day Saints.

Mormonism's similarity to Catholicism can be found most prominently in the category of *the ethics of exclusivity*. Both traditions reserve the heart of their rituals for members alone—and not just ordinary members but members in good standing. Mormonism's exclusivity, however, is located in temple ordinances, while Catholic exclusivity is focused on the Eucharist. That can make comparisons of Mormonism to Catholicism confusing, since Mormons have a Protestant view of the Lord's Supper, treating it rather informally, but a Catholic view of temple rites. Arguably, Mormonism does a better job of establishing ritual boundaries than Catholicism, since after Vatican II an increasing number of Catholics receive communion without going to confession, while Mormons must pass a worthiness interview with their bishop or stake president to be admitted to the temple (they receive a "temple recommend").

In terms of *the exhortation of emotions*, Mormonism appeals to the passion of testimony rather than the feeling of being born again that is cultivated in so many fundamentalist and evangelical churches. The distinction is an important one. Mormon Sunday worship (in contrast to its temple rituals) is plain and simple compared with the High Church liturgies practiced by Catholics, Orthodox, Episcopalians, and Lutherans (with their formal prayer books, religious art, and many rituals). There are no icons or statues and no professionally trained preachers reading a sermon in liturgical vestments. Yet their Low Church ways of worship show little of the charismatic gifts such as speaking in tongues that were so prevalent in Mormonism's early days. Mormon worship is neither revivalist nor contemplative. People with no special theological training do the speaking (Mormons call these sermons "talks"), members are asked to give their testimonies, songs are sung with piano or organ accompaniment, and the sacrament of bread and water is distributed. Testimonies are the heart of the gathering. Sincere expressions of trust in the validity of the Book of Mormon and other revelations received by Joseph Smith as well as the divinity of Jesus take the place of Catholic sacraments or Protestant sermons as the primary means of mediating the presence of God. Testimony of this kind is significantly different from someone recounting a conversion experience. Conversion looks inward and usually focuses on guilt and inadequacy as well as a dramatic change. Testimony looks outward at someone who is the object of trust and confidence. Mormon testimonies can be very emotional, but they are also expressions of an unwavering certainty. They often include statements like "I know Joseph Smith was a Prophet" or "I know the Book of Mormon is true." Such testimonies rely on the emotion of conviction rather than the feeling of being saved from sin so typical of most conversion narratives.

Perhaps most surprisingly, Mormonism also has traits in common with *the ethos of elasticity*, which sets it apart from the dogmatic commitments of Catholicism and the practice in much conservative Protestantism of distilling theology into a set of rigorously argued propositions. Mormonism is like many liberal churches in downplaying the importance of creeds and dogmas, and though the Saints have a lot of beliefs, they are reluctant to transcribe those beliefs into a long list of propositional truth claims. Mormonism is also remarkably open to changes and developments in its own theological positions. There are reasons for this. Mormonism, for example, does not have a professional class of priests trained in seminaries, nor does it have officially recognized church theologians. This absence means that there is no authorized body of intellectuals analyzing, explicating, and refining official Mormon positions. It does have a religious hierarchy, but this leadership exercises a pastoral role that tends to emphasize the practical over the speculative. The Mormon hierarchy also safeguards the dynamic character of Mormon theology, since the church president, in continuity with Joseph Smith, has the authority to interpret past teachings and issue new ones, based on personal revelations from God. Needless to say, liberal churches do not accept the idea that God still speaks to prophets, and Mormons are not social activists who treat human failings as a product of environmental conditions. Nevertheless, Mormonism definitely has a liberal side, which will surprise those who think that intellectual flexibility is a function of not having too many beliefs. Mormons help us to see that elasticity actually has to do not with the number of ideas a tradition teaches but with how traditions allow those ideas to evolve and mature. In that respect, Mormonism is more elastic than those liberal churches that strictly enforce their unwavering commitment to progressive politics, even though liberal churches have few formal doctrinal commitments and make openness and change a part of their official policy.

The idea that Mormon beliefs are elastic requires the most explanation because it is probably the sociological observation that my readers will resist the most. Calling Mormon beliefs expansive is a way of clarifying my point in the introduction about the bigness of Mormon ideas. This contention will sound strange to many of my readers because Mormons tend to be biblical literalists (a trait they share in their own distinctive way with many conservative Christians), and most people do not think that biblical literalists are sophisticated enough to have many ideas, let alone big ones! Moreover, there is a growing gap in American society between those who have firsthand experience of what it is like to belong to a religious tradition with strong communal bonds and those who do not. This lack of experience with how ecclesial authority actually works can lead to a lot of prejudice and misunderstandings. All institutions, from colleges to corporations, have mission statements, but most of them are broad, open, and inclusive in order to reach out to the world for the largest possible audience. Consequently, it is quite natural to assume that religious traditions that restrict their members' interactions with the secular world must have a rather narrow set of beliefs.

Mormonism is especially vulnerable to these kinds of conjectures and suppositions. Mormon theology is sufficiently different from what most Christians believe that skeptics can be tempted to reduce it to a simple set of claims for quick criticism and polemical rebuttal. North American Mormons are also geographically concentrated in the state of Utah (or, more precisely, in what is called the Mormon corridor, which extends from California to Arizona and northward to western Wyoming and eastern Idaho). This has changed in recent years with an "outmigration" of Utah Mormons to other states,but there are still many Americans who do not know any Mormons personally and thus might be inclined to think that the stereotypes about them are true. Due in part to its social isolation, Mormonism has produced its own distinctive culture, which includes a prohibition against alcohol, a 10 percent tithe to the church, bans on tattoos, the encouragement of large families, and strict enforcement of chastity before and outside of marriage. In addition, a long history of prejudices and even persecution has led many Mormons to be wary of how outsiders perceive them. All of this adds up to the fact that trying to understand Mormonism is a demanding task. Rather than look at Mormon spiritual life as a whole, it is easier to make a list of Mormon beliefs and dismiss them without putting them in their cultural and historical context.

In spite of the obstacles that keep many people from even trying to understand the basics of the Mormon faith, Mormonism keeps growing. In the early twentieth century, there were about three hundred thousand Saints. (*Saints* is a common abbreviation of the church's official name, Latter-day Saints, and many members prefer it to the name Mormon, which began as a nickname based on the Book of Mormon.) By 2010, that number had climbed to fourteen million members. Mormonism's early growth was fueled by the migration of overseas members to the United States, many from England and Scandinavia. In the nineteenth century, all Mormons were encouraged to gather with the main body of Saints first in Kirkland, Ohio, then Nauvoo, Illinois, and finally in Utah, but by the twentieth century, foreign converts were urged to remain in their homelands, giving Mormonism a truly global presence. Churches are more than just their theological ideas, of course, but the statistics suggest that what Mormonism offers is big enough to accommodate converts who come from a variety of cultural backgrounds and have traveled diverse spiritual paths. Far from having a simpleminded theology, the Mormon worldview is rich in nuances and full of the kind of complexity that gives the Saints a lot of room for intellectual and spiritual growth.

That Mormon theology is often crudely caricatured is ironic, given how complex it can be. Mormonism defies theological categories as much as sociological maps, but for that very reason it is intellectually challenging to both outsiders and insiders. Indeed, even when it comes to having elastic beliefs, Mormonism is elastic in its own unique way. I have already mentioned one reason why Mormon elasticity is different. Mormonism, like all religious traditions, holds central beliefs that are nonnegotiable (like trusting that Joseph Smith was a true Prophet), but since the President of the Church is considered a living Prophet who is empowered to receive divine revelations, even central beliefs are subject to clarification and reinterpretation. Another reason is that Mormons do not have a closed canon (canon is the theological term for a set of books that constitutes a religion's sacred scripture). Mormons affirm the Old and New Testaments of the Bible but add to it another testament of Jesus Christ, namely, the Book of Mormon. Critics sometimes claim that ongoing prophecy (linked to a doctrine of continuing revelation) and an open canon make Mormonism unpredictable and confusing. That might be true if the Saints did not have a stable foundation for their theological worldview. I will examine that foundation throughout this book, but I should point out that some Mormon scholars agree with those critics who say that they do not have anything like a systematic theological worldview because they delight in the intellectual freedom that is the result. These anti-foundationalist scholars celebrate Mormonism as a uniquely fluid and flexible Christian tradition that is unconstrained by doctrinal principles and philosophical commitments. I think that they are wrong, but the reader should be aware that I am offering an interpretation of Mormonism that emphasizes its philosophical consistency and logical coherence, while some Mormon scholars would argue that Mormonism does not have (and should not have) methodical and metaphysical ambitions.

A more precise term for the foundation of any worldview, indeed, a more precise term for the study of "big ideas," is *metaphysics*, and the thesis of this book is that Mormons have an original, fascinating, and provocative metaphysics. Admittedly, *metaphysics* is not a word commonly associated with Mormons. It was definitely not a word I heard in evangelical circles when I was growing up, although in the past few years evangelical theology has become extremely sophisticated in its use of metaphysics to defend and elaborate Christian truth claims. Before proposing my own interpretation of Mormon metaphysics, it might be helpful to think carefully about what metaphysics is.

Metaphysics is a word that means different things to different people. To some, it refers to anything having to do with the spiritual or supernatural. To skeptics who do not believe in the supernatural, *metaphysics* is just a fancy word for all things hokey and absurd. To others it refers to a very specific way of thinking about the supernatural, namely, the magical or the occult. Walk into any bookstore and look for the section on metaphysics. You will find a wall of books about everything from quantum physics to positive thinking (and even books about how quantum physics is the foundation for positive thinking). I am using the word in a more technical sense—but not so technical that it gets lost in the maze of modern philosophy.

For those who have had an Introduction to Philosophy class in college, metaphysics means something entirely opposed to magical thinking or speculation for the sheer fun of it. There they probably learned that the word is much misunderstood and maligned. It is from the Greek language, and it means after or beyond (*meta*) physics. Literally, then, it can be taken to mean the science of everything beyond the physical world. That, however, is a mere accident of history. Metaphysics got its name because anthologies of Aristotle's works actually put it *after* his works on physics. Aristotle did not think of metaphysics as the study of the supernatural. Instead, he called it "first philosophy," and for him and philosophers ever since, metaphysics is nothing more than the study of the fundamental nature of all that can be known. If that sounds a lot like what scientists do, it should, since philosophy and science were essentially the same kind of activity in the ancient and medieval periods.

Metaphysics as first philosophy is more respectable than metaphysics as the occult, but even in its more sophisticated guise, it still has a bad reputation among many people today. That is largely the fault of professional metaphysicians, who have turned the study of the nature of things into a branch of philosophy with its own specialized terminology, untranslatable jargon, obscure puzzles, and hypothetical questions that nobody really asks let alone wants to answer. Originally, beginning with Aristotle, metaphysics was born out of a sense of wonder, not a drive to master logical minutiae. Most people have paused at some point in their lives to think about why there is a universe rather than nothing at all and what the most basic stuff of the universe is. These are fundamental questions that can be asked by anyone at any time, but the answers to these questions also supply the building blocks for philosophical and theological constructions about what all of this stuff means for us human beings.

Metaphysics can mean the study of the universal nature of reality, but it can also mean examining (for the purposes of clarifying or criticizing) the logical assumptions and rational principles that support and sustain particular views of the world (whether they be religious, political, or economic). Those two meanings are related but separable. Indeed, as we will see, modern philosophy is largely the story of their separation. Modern metaphysicians are passionate about trying to construct an objective view of the world, but they are less interested in particular worldivews, which they see as subjective and arbitrary and thus resistant to logical analysis.

A worldview is more than just a personal point of view. Worldviews enable individuals or groups to make sense of their lives on an intellectual level. They provide a cognitive orientation that often stays in the background during everyday activities but nonetheless guides decisions and actions big and small. Worldviews explain what things mean, but they are also dependent on metaphysical assumptions about what things *are*. Sometimes the term *worldview* is treated as just another name for metaphysics. Technically speaking, however, metaphysics studies the nature of the world, not any particular view of it. The two terms overlap, however, because every metaphysical system is itself a worldview, even if it is kept at a very abstract level of discourse, while every worldview includes metaphysical assumptions. It is thus too simple to say that worldviews provide answers while metaphysics probes questions, because metaphysicians try to answer their own questions, while worldviews teach their adherents what kinds of questions are most meaningful to ask. Still, worldviews include a lot more than metaphysics, no matter how tightly bound they are to their own metaphysical assumptions. In any case, the term *worldview* is helpful because it highlights the fact that all systems of belief have assumptions and arguments about what kinds of things exist in the world and what kind of substance those things share. First principles give coherence and consistency to our most fundamental ideas about reality.

Worldviews are grounded in first principles, but that does not mean that adherents to a worldview are always aware of their own first principles. Indeed, first principles are usually assumed rather than made explicit in carefully worded statements. People argue about first principles when worldviews clash or a worldview is experiencing growing pains and needs adjustment or correction. Think of metaphysics as the frame and the worldview as the picture inside the frame. When you look at a picture, you do not think about the frame, but without the frame, there would be no picture. Different worldviews, like paintings in a gallery, can have a lot in common, but their frames set them apart. For example, all Christians have a view of the world that sees it as fallen and in need of redemption, and all Christians view the world through the salvific significance of Jesus Christ. Not all Christians, however, share the same assumptions about what the pre-fallen world would have been like (what its goodness must have been), what the fall did to the world (what constitutes a sinful nature), and what salvation means (what the nature of perfection is).

Metaphysics has lost its connection to worldviews because many professional philosophers treat metaphysical questions as elaborately complicated conceptual puzzles rather than the most basic expressions of human curiosity as well as the essential ingredient in any coherent and organized way of life. Philosophers in the ancient and medieval periods were absolutely clear that the most abstract ideas should arise from the most concrete and common experiences. They treated metaphysics as the foundation, not a branch, of philosophy because it addresses the most basic issues that all people who seek wisdom want to understand (*philosophy* means the love, *philo*, of wisdom, *sophia*). By identifying all knowledge with the pursuit of wisdom, the ancients avoided the modern prejudice of treating religion as if it belongs in a compartment far removed from philosophy and science. To the ancient mind it would have been obvious that philosophy, science, and religion alike generate wonder about the cause of all things and and raise the question of whether that cause is ultimately different from other causal forces in the world. Science too was a matter of wisdom and contemplation. For Aristotle and company, for example, questions about the nature of things were different from the explorations of physics due to their level of generality, not their subject matter. Metaphysics and physics are both concerned with the world as we know it, but physics (and the other natural sciences) takes a close look to get at the details, while metaphysics takes a big step back in order to look at the whole picture, frame and all. Still, there is something intuitively correct about distinguishing metaphysics from physics proper by the preposition *beyond*. From the Greek philosophy of Plato and Aristotle to the Christian theology of Augustine and Aquinas and right up through the more empirical outlook of the Enlightenment, philosophers have argued that whatever is true and worthwhile is unchanging and immaterial. Things made of matter are constrained by time and place, and while there are truths about contingent things, which we call facts, metaphysical truths pertain to the way things have to be in order to be at all, regardless of their location or history. If this higher form of truth cannot be found in material things, then it must be looked for in the ideas and concepts that belong to logic and metaphysics. Truth, beauty, and goodness, it follows, lie beyond this world of fleeting appearances. This philosophical position originated with the ancient Greeks, but most Christian theologians were only all too happy to affirm it as well. Indeed, nearly all philosophers, until atheism became intellectually acceptable in the twentieth century, took it for granted that truth is ultimately to be found in the perfect nature of God.

God can be identified as "the truth" because God never changes and, being immaterial, God is not limited in any way. That God is not one of the objects of the world is the core assumption of the classical theism that I discussed in the introduction. God is not a being like us. God does not even "have" being. God simply is—but he is (he exists) in a way that is utterly unknown to us. In fact, he does not really exist at all, since he is not one of the existents of the known world. To say that he exists implies that he might not exist, but his existence is necessary, not conditional. It follows that he is beyond existence (or being) altogether. He is not nothing, but he is not something either. He is, in the popular phrase of immaterialists, *Wholly Other*. In order to know this God, we have to be wholly other than the material world in which we exist.

Materialistic explanations of how our minds work are now the norm in philosophy, natural science, and the social sciences, but those theories are a very recent phenomenon. Most of Western history treated the mind and the soul (the two were often conflated) as immaterial substances, just as God is an immaterial being or spirit. From this perspective, our bodies are like the objects in the world that we see all around us, but our souls are like the divine, and the soul is what lifts us above the other material objects of this world. The human soul is the source of our reason and freedom (which are interconnected because we can reason about the world only when we are free from material influences and constraints) and makes us different from every other kind of living creature. God is even more different from us than we are from nonhuman animals, but we share with God this one trait: the essence of our identity is not composed of matter.

If perfection belongs to the immaterial realm, then matter is mired in imperfection. That is also something philosophers and theologians could agree about through most of Western history, although the traditional Christian position was more complicated than simply identifying matter with evil. Christians taught that the material world was created good but had fallen along with human beings, so that nature is now at war with itself as well as with us. Some theologians went so far as to argue that nature is in need of restoration to its original condition, drawing from the words of the Apostle Paul: "We know that the whole creation has been groaning in labor pains until now" (Rom. 8:22). The idea that all of nature will be redeemed from its fallen state, however, was often marginalized and overshadowed by Christianity's emphasis on the salvation of human beings. Christianity also taught that the afterlife will involve our whole bodies, not just our souls, since Jesus was resurrected as a fully embodied person. Nonetheless, classical theism had difficulties in construing heaven as a physical place, so the resurrection of the body remained a riddle without any clear theological solution. The best classical theism could argue was that our heavenly forms will be stripped of all of the hardships, limitations, and distractions associated with our bodies. What physically is left, from the viewpoint of metaphysical immaterialism, is hard to say. Many theologians in the tradition of classical theism concluded that matter as we know it will be vanquished. Rather than being transformed, it will be replaced by a totally new substance. Christians affirmed the goodness of the world, then, but they remained deeply ambivalent about the stuff out of which the world is composed.

Christian theologians were also quick to agree with the profound but puzzling insight of ancient philosophy that matter itself, as a substance that makes up everything we know, is unknowable. That sounds paradoxical, but it is actually a fundamental proposition for any school of philosophy or theology influenced by Plato and

Aristotle. What we know about any object has to do with its properties, not its underlying substance, and those properties are immaterial. When we say that something is round or red, we are referring
to concepts or ideas that are in our head, not the external, physical
world. What we know are universals, not particulars. It follows that
knowledge is the union of immaterial minds with immaterial ideas.
This approach to knowledge is called idealism, and many modern philosophers, like the empiricists, reject it, but even those who insist
that we can really know the world as it is are often forced to admit
that the actual nature of material substance is hidden to us. No matter how far we go in breaking up matter into its smallest component
parts, we are still required to understand it in terms that describe
how it appears to us and not what it is in itself.

Modern science concurs. Revolutions in physics have taught us
that matter is not what we see, nor is it anything we can imagine or
depict. Waves are not really waves, and particles are not really particles. Scientists speak in terms of mathematical formulas rather
than the metaphysical language of substance and attributes or the
everyday language of things and stuff. When physicists name subatomic particles, they deliberately choose terms like *quark*, which
was taken from James Joyce's *Finnegans Wake*, to indicate just how
strange their findings are. Moreover, one of the truly astounding
discoveries of modern physics is that we can never be certain of
our knowledge about elementary particles. When we intervene in
the atom to locate an electron, we interfere with its motion, so
we cannot know its location and momentum at the same time.
Metaphysicians argue that what we know about matter is its shape
or form, and scientists now tell us that the form matter takes is the
product of what we have done to it. Matter is a mirror of our own
minds, it seems, and thus its nature is ultimately elusive. I point
out these perplexities not to deny that we are much more confident
than the ancients that we can understand the laws that govern the
universe and thus become masters of our environment but, rather,
to affirm that the fundamental identity of matter is actually still an
abiding mystery.

Mormonism renders matter radically knowable because it denies that there is any kind of supernatural reality that we can hold up as a contrast or opposite to the physical world. Matter is all there is, so if we know anything at all, we know material existence. Ideas, numbers, and other abstractions certainly exist, of course, but their reality is completely derivative, not original. Later in this book I will complicate that statement by discussing the importance of Joseph Smith's various declarations about the eternity of intelligence. For example, in his famous address known as "The King Follett Sermon" (1844), given at a funeral for a friend just a few months before his own death, Smith stated, "Intelligence is eternal and exists upon a self-existent principle." Mormon theologians have long debated whether these intelligences were originally many or one, plural or singular. Smith taught that our (material) souls preexisted our births so that our personal identities were taking shape long before our earthly sojourn, but just how far back our individual, conscious identities go is an open question in Mormon theology. There is a good reason why Mormonism does not define intelligence more precisely, and that is because it thoroughly rejects any dualism between mind and matter (or soul and body). The interpretation of intelligence that is most consistent with Mormon metaphysics, then, is that intelligence is an eternal spiritual-material reality that God drew from in order to organize our spirit bodies (which is roughly equivalent to what classical theists call the soul). Our spirit bodies were subsequently joined with a physical body when we were born on earth. Eternal intelligence is thus best thought of as the highest (next to God) form of matter. Neither the substance of the soul nor the matter of the body is prior to the other. Both are equally primordial because they originate in a spirit–matter unity that is the furthest our thought can reach into the beginnings of matter. All of this will be discussed in more depth in the following chapters.

So what is the essence of Mormon metaphysics? Let me contextualize it by making an observation. Everyone has felt the mood of resignation or even despair over the apparent insignificance of human life in the face of the unpredictable forces of nature and the inevitability of disease and death. Ecclesiastes, the book of the Bible that tries to salvage some wisdom from the arrogance and vanity of human striving, captures this mood in a memorable image: "There is no new thing under the sun" (1:9). Ecclesiastes is wisdom literature, not metaphysics, but it can be read as concurring with Greek metaphysics. Things under the sun change and thus are not dependable. Things above the sun do not change and thus are perfect. There is nothing new under the sun due to the cycles of life that bring all things to an end, but in the heavens above we will experience unending peace and unshakable happiness for the first time. The unchanging realm of the divine, populated by immaterial angels and the souls of the righteous awaiting the final judgment, is our true home and our only hope for untainted joy.

Contrary to this worldview (which is not necessarily the worldview of the Bible as a whole or even, when read closely, the book of Ecclesiastes), I propose that the most basic principle of Mormon metaphysics states that all of reality "under the sun" (the natural world) is of the same basic nature as all of reality "above the sun" (the supernatural world). Mormons believe that God has a body, as I pointed out in the introduction, but the warrant for that theological belief lies in the assumption that everything that exists is a body of one sort or another. Most traditional metaphysics divide the cosmos into spiritual and material realities, but Mormons believe that spirit is matter of a higher order or reality rather than a substance void of matter altogether. The sacred is not another world altogether, invisible and immaterial. The sacred exists in continuity with the physical world. Even God is one of the objects of the world, not an unimaginably perfect entity that exists in a totally unique fashion. Moreover, since God is composed of matter, God too is absolutely knowable, just like anything else we might experience in this world. True, God is often hidden to us, and God's form is unfathomably greater than anything we can fully experience in this lifetime. Nonetheless, God is not radically different from everything else that exists. Everything that exists has or is a body, so God too has or is a body. This does not mean that matter is easy to understand. It is not, even for Mormon metaphysics. Indeed, there is a case to be made that Mormonism makes matter even more mysterious than the traditional metaphysics of immaterialism. That is because the Mormon worldview implies that not all matter is homogeneous. Mormon metaphysics teaches that everything is a body but the substance of those bodies is not exactly the same. Matter is all there is, but there are gradations of matter, and matter at its lowest form has the potential to become more than "mere matter."

The Mormon view of matter is thus radically different from the materialism that has gotten a deservedly bad name among Christians. Materialism is typically an offshoot of secular atheism or militant humanism, because the denial of God's existence leaves us with only matter as the substance of all reality. Mormons, by contrast, defend a Christian version of materialism. To many readers that will sound like an oxymoron. Isn't the very essence of Christianity a belief in an immaterial reality? What is the supernatural, after all, if it is not the opposite of all that is natural? Aren't our souls separable from our bodies? Mormonism is unique in modern Christianity in the answers it gives to those questions. For Mormons, God is embodied, the supernatural is as natural as nature, and the human soul is not composed of an immaterial substance called "spirit." Most fundamentally speaking, spirit and matter are not opposites at all. Spirit and matter complement each other and are not ultimately different in substance. It is not always clear what Mormons mean by conflating the two (that is, putting spirit and matter on a continuum), but it is not always clear what Plato, Aristotle, and Aquinas mean by separating them either. To make sense of the materiality of spiritual entities such as angels and souls (or to make sense of the spiritual dimension of material objects) is not easy, which means that Mormon thinkers have a lot of work cut out for them in the field of metaphysics, but in recent years several Mormon thinkers have stepped up to the plate and have begun expounding the nuances and consequences of their rejection of immaterialism.

Earlier I said that metaphysics is born out of a sense of wonder at the fact that there is a universe rather than nothing at all. Mormon metaphysics is also born out of a sense of wonder, more specifically, the wonder that Joseph Smith experienced in his visions of God. So far, one might be tempted to conclude that Smith, the founder of Mormonism, was an amateur philosopher who sought to overthrow all of Western philosophy by claiming that matter and spirit are variations of the same basic stuff. That actually would not be too far from the truth, as I will demonstrate in the rest of this book. Smith, however, was an untrained Christian visionary, not a philosopher (or even a systematic theologian). His experience of God, not speculations about nature or analyses of matter, led him to his ideas about spirit and matter. Smith had a vision of God in 1820 that was later called the First Vision. In it, he saw "two personages, whose brightness and glory defy all description, standing above me in the air." Many people have visions of the divine, of course, and Smith's emphasis on the indescribable beauty of God's glory is consistent with most Christian descriptions of God. Smith, however, used the term *indescribable* to suggest that God's glory is beyond our abilities to adequately describe it, not that God's nature is inherently unknowable given our physical existence. Indeed, Smith treated the object of his vision as a literal fact, not a symbolic truth. He had the audacity to think that he had really seen the Father and the Son, not just representations of them. And if he really did see the Father and the Son, then their appearance, which was not unlike our own, is what they really were. Smith's logic was simple. What anyone sees, no matter what object it is, is a body, and if he really saw God, then God has a body. That insight led Joseph Smith on his quest to overturn traditional, Platonic metaphysics with an entirely new understanding of the nature of the spiritual world.

Smith had a worldview that was deeply committed to the material nature of all existing things, including God. What is important to realize is that this worldview originated in experiences he had that can be rightly called supernatural. He did not reject the supernatural; he just saw it in a new way. The earliest Greek metaphysicians were inspired by wonder. They marveled at the sheer existence of the world and wondered why there is something rather than nothing.

Smith was also inspired by an original experience of wonder, but it was a wonder of a very different kind than the wonder that there is something rather than nothing. Smith's wonder was that God is the greatest thing in the world without being absolutely set apart from everything else in the world. He was overwhelmed not by existence itself but by the fact that the existence of all things includes God. He thus did not think of God primarily as the cause of the world, hidden behind natural phenomena. That is, he did not begin with the existence of the world and then contemplate where the world came from and how God could have caused it to come into being. Instead, he began with the amazing idea that God exists just like anything else exists. God is in fact more real (not real in an absolutely unique way) than the reality of the objects that we touch and feel every day of our lives. God is not a mysterious force or power removed from the world of objective things. God is the most physically real of all physical beings.

Smith's First Vision was hardly ordinary. It was supernatural in the sense that it was above and beyond the ordinary workings of nature, but in order to make sense of it, he gradually adopted the metaphysical assumption that God is a material being (and its corollary that no being is purely immaterial). Smith's vision also had epistemological implications that set Mormons apart from other Christians. Epistemology is the study of how we can justify that what we think we know is really true. From the perspective of classical theism, it is not clear at all that we can claim that we know God, because God is not knowable according to the ways knowledge usually works. Traditionally, metaphysics separates all that is to be known into the material and the immaterial, with God, the soul, and spiritual beings such as angels on the immaterial side of the divide. Consequently, metaphysical immaterialism is constantly struggling to explain how humans can know what is essentially unknowable, given that we experience everything through our physical senses. Smith helps us to see that metaphysical materialism leads to a more firm foundation for the epistemology of the divine. Simply put, Smith thought that we can know God through our senses.

Put differently, God is one of us, or, more precisely, we can trust our visual or auditory experiences of God because we are like him. There is no unbridgeable gulf between God and us. God is mysterious but not indescribable, glorious but not unknowable, perfect but not infinite and unlimited. Knowing God is not a matter of turning our backs on the sensory information we receive in the act of perception. Knowing God is the ultimate perceptual experience, but it is not an experience of something so ultimate that our sensory system breaks down. Smith came to this conviction based on his vision of God, but countless non-Mormons throughout history and across the globe have had experiences of their own that would lead them to agree with him. A variety of social scientific studies, beginning in the 1890s with the Society for Psychical Research under the direction of the Cambridge Professor of Philosophy Henry Sidgwick and continuing to our own day with the U.S. National Institute of Mental Health, have concluded that seeing or hearing someone who is not physically present is a fairly common experience. That is the conclusion of a mental health expert who has studied this research: "Over at least the past one hundred years surveys of fully awake, healthy, 'normal' adults have consistently revealed that very many people have heard one or more disembodied voices speaking to them at some time during their lives. Indeed, it appears that a *majority* of ordinary, well-adjusted people have had such experiences at least once, and a significant number of others have had them more often."

Whether people trust what their senses tell them about these experiences depends on a variety of cultural factors. Many people who have a visual or auditory experience of God recognize that such moments are special, rare, and usually unrepeatable, but they think that they have really experienced something objectively real and that their sense perceptions were trustworthy during the experience. If such experiences are the subject of stigma and associated with mental illness or spiritual immaturity, however, then people will not be inclined to share them with others or give them any theological significance. It is not just religious skeptics who call these experiences into question. It is no exaggeration to say that the great majority of religious leaders in the West since the Enlightenment have worked hard to convince their own congregants that hearing voices is not something that should be associated with religious revelation. Respectable people just do not take such things seriously.

Even those who accept that auditory or visual glimpses of the divine can in principle occur have ways of downplaying their importance. Classical theism has a well-developed theory for what happens when the natural world is pervaded by concrete instances of God's appearance. Guided by the metaphysics of immaterialism, classical theists argue that God makes himself known to us by accommodating himself to our physical limitations. God assumes a shape or adopts a voice in order to let us think we have had an encounter of him. If this is true, then what we know in experiencing the divine is not really God. We experience instead an image or representation of God that God creates for the purpose of communicating with us in this life.

Smith thought that he really saw God with his own eyes and heard God with his own ears. As a result, he was a revelatory, not scriptural, literalist. He stood with all the countless ordinary people who thought that they had actually seen God with their own eyes or heard God with their own ears. Indeed, early Mormons valued the Book of Mormon more as a sign of renewed prophecy and revelation than for any of its doctrinal content or historical claims. Terryl Givens, one of America's foremost students of religion and literature and the most eloquent Mormon scholar writing about Mormonism today, makes exactly this point: "That may well be the Book of Mormon's most significant and revolutionary—as well as controversial—contribution to religious thinking. The particularity and specificity, the vividness, the concreteness, and the accessibility of revelatory experience—those realities both underlie and overshadow the narrated history and doctrine that constitute the record." People in Smith's day were looking for evidence that God was working in their midst and that God was still speaking to humankind. Ears were clamoring for the divine voice. Givens points out that Alexander Campbell, Smith's great competitor in the pursuit of the restoration of Christianity to its original purity, understood Mormonism all too clearly on this point. In a newspaper article entitled "Mormon Delusions," he wrote, "I would ask [Book of Mormon witnesses Oliver Cowdery, David Whitmer, and Martin Harris] how they knew that it was God's voice which they heard—but they would tell me to ask God in faith. *That is, I must believe it first, and then ask God if it be true!*" For Campbell, reason had to guide the restoration of the church, just as it should trump the preliminary evidence of the senses. Reason, not experience or testimony, should tell us what to believe. Smith, by contrast, was as wide-eyed as he was open-eared when it came to revelation. He believed first and then set about taking his beliefs as far as they could go, which led directly to the dismantling of the immaterial metaphysics of classical theism.

Mormon metaphysics can and should be subjected to logical analysis and serious scrutiny, but it does give Mormons the advantage of having a worldview that is spatially all-encompassing (by covering every kind of entity) and temporally comprehensive (by covering all of time, including eternity). In the introduction I suggested that Mormons have big ideas, and in this chapter I have argued that Mormon beliefs are elastic. Now I want to suggest that it would be better to talk about a Mormon ethos of expansiveness rather than elasticity. Elasticity and expansiveness are just metaphors, of course, but if they are helpful images, they can illustrate important differences in how religious ideas are constructed and employed in different traditions. Ideas need to be stretched if they are not formulated to meet new situations, and stretching them too far can ruin their original shape. Ideas are expansive if they are designed to grow as they assimilate new information. Mormon metaphysics is inherently expansive because it is all-encompassing and comprehensive in a way that the traditional metaphysics of the Plato/Aristotle/Aquinas sort is not. For Mormons, there are no gaps in our knowledge that we have to leap over in order to penetrate the unknown. There are no absolute limits to our experience that turn ordinary religious experience into the lofty flights of the mystical elite. There is no room for the suggestion that God can be known only in the dark night of the soul or that we must negate everything we know in order to step into the light. Mormon theology begins with who we are and what we know and then expands that to include the deepest mysteries of the divine. God is still mysterious, but his mystery is a matter of just how great, not how distant, he is.

Just as there is no metaphysical gap between God's nature and human nature, there is also no moral gap between God's perfection and human striving. The church of my youth inculcated a sense of permanent guilt in me that was not relieved even by several responses to altar calls and many nights on bent knees. We were taught, in accordance with good old-fashioned Protestant doctrine, that we were mired in original sin, which goes so deep that there is nothing we can do to get out of it. Our depravity was so total that we were guilty of sins that we did not even know we committed. There was little hope for moral reform if our sins were not repeatedly washed away by heartfelt appeals for Christ's mercy. These demands put me on an emotional roller coaster that still steers much of my inner life in unhealthy ways. In fact, numerous psychological studies have demonstrated a strong correlation between feelings of guilt, whatever their source, and clinical diagnoses of depression.

Mormons have no tradition of original sin. The very substance of our existence—our material being—is the same type of stuff that makes up God, so there is no inherent reason why we cannot be on the path toward God's holiness in this earthly life. William James, one of America's greatest philosophers, founder of the school called pragmatism, and the first American to write a textbook about psychology, made a famous distinction that is relevant for this discussion in a book called *The Varieties of Religious Experience*. He distinguished between two religious personality types that he called the "sick soul" and the "healthy minded." The person with a sick soul is always close to despair, because he or she feels unable to do anything to rectify his or her situation. A sick soul needs a doctor, and fast. In theological terms, the sick soul is mired in original sin, which acts like quicksand: the harder you try to get out, the deeper you sink. Healthy-minded people feel basically good about themselves even when they know that they need help from others as well as from God. A healthy mind knows its limits, but it is also confident that it can reach out for help when it reaches those limits. Sick souls need to be revitalized and reborn again and again, while the healthy minded tend to follow a more gradual path toward spiritual maturity. Needless to say, evangelicalism, at least the kind I grew up in, created a lot of sick souls, while Mormonism is a religion for the healthy minded.

Humans and the divine exist on a continuous scale, we could say, and this is nowhere more evident than in the Mormon view of salvation. Salvation for all Christians means ultimate unity or oneness with God in heaven, but for Mormons, this oneness takes on a new dramatic form given their metaphysical presuppositions. Since the physical world, right down to its atomic structure, is imbued with the divine, salvation begins here and now, and heaven will be a continuance, not a substitution, of life as we know it. Salvation is thus a process not a state. Heaven too is transformed by Mormon metaphysics. Heaven is a real place that exists in space and time, not an ethereal idea, for Mormons, and the ultimate destiny for the faithful is to become like God. This is perhaps the most controversial aspect of Mormon doctrine, but it follows quite neatly from its metaphysics. The saved will not share an immaterial unity in heaven. Instead, they will maintain their own very distinct identities, given that the body we have now will continue, in some mysterious way, in the afterlife. The saved will thus share in the power and privileges of the divine, rather than become submerged in an immaterial divine substance. Mormons even speak of the faithful "becoming gods." Admittedly, this language can be quite startling and even offensive to those who are not used to it, but when it is placed in the Mormon metaphysical framework, it makes much more sense (although it is certainly not above being critically examined).

Mormonism might not be for everyone, but I think that anyone can benefit from learning about its metaphysics. Its metaphysics is big, but size, of course, is not everything, and I certainly do not think that Mormon metaphysics, or my interpretation of it, is beyond criticism. Indeed, there are three questions to ask about my proposal. First, does it make sense of Mormonism? That is, does a metaphysical materialism form the foundation for all (or at least most) Mormon theological beliefs? Second, does it make sense period? Regardless of the theological beliefs it grounds, is metaphysical materialism internally consistent and structurally coherent? Third, is metaphysical materialism consistent with most (if not all) of the theological claims of traditional Christianity? I pointed out in the introduction that much of traditional Christianity is in debt to classical theism, which is equivalent to what I would call a metaphysics of immaterialism. Can metaphysical materialism be substituted for metaphysical immaterialism without radically altering traditional Christian beliefs? If so, what does that say about the promise of Mormonism for ecumenical dialogue and Christian unity?

Now I can hear the skepticism of many of my readers. Haven't I painted a rather rosy picture of Mormonism? There are plenty of books written by angry or disenchanted ex-Mormons who feel liberated by their departure from the Church of Latter-day Saints. Their stories are informative and often very moving, ranging from the bitter to the nostalgic. I have learned from them that leaving a healthy-minded community with incredibly strong communal ties can be just as hard as leaving a religious culture that immerses its members in guilt. Apparently it can be much, much harder, because Mormons believe that the ties that bind us together on this earth will continue in the next life. Consequently, they put an enormous emphasis on family life as the focus of religious education and practice. As a result, young people who depart from the Saints can be treated as though they are betraying the love and devotion of their parents as well as their church. Any defender or supporter of Mormonism should show great sympathy for those who, for whatever reason, have felt obligated to leave their childhood faith.

I found the largeness of thought and practice that I needed in Roman Catholicism, not Mormonism, but upon close examination of Mormonism and friendship with many individual Mormons, I have come to the conclusion that I could have found much of that largeness in Mormonism as well. Yet I am not trying to convert anyone to Mormonism or Roman Catholicism. I gladly admit that I do think Christianity is true and that I think all nonbelievers would be better

off (in this life and the next) were they to find their way to a form
of Christianity that inspires them and fulfills their most basic spiritual needs. I should also note that I am grateful for my childhood
church, which my parents still attend and which taught me the love
of Jesus and the reliability of the Bible. It has not stood still while
I was changing. An urban church, it has adapted to the poverty of
the near eastside of Indianapolis in amasing and inspiring ways.
The people there are passionate, engaged, and very active in their
neighborhood. The minister, Mike Bowling, is one of the best practical theologians I know, and his sermons, which I have heard on my
various trips back, are challenging in all the right ways. This church
demonstrates how far evangelicals have come in reaching out to the
world in innovative and healing ways.

Nonetheless, evangelicalism remains a subculture within the
dominant popular culture in America. Mormonism is too, of course,
as are most Christian churches today, given how secular our culture
has become, but Mormonism aspires to be a culture in itself, not a
subculture. The Mormon Church is ambitious in that it wants to be
the foundation for a way of life, not just a set of beliefs or a moral outlook. Being a Mormon should reach right into your gut—and it does,
given that Mormonism regulates what you eat (no alcohol or coffee).
That is one reason why Mormonism is sometimes considered a cult.
For those used to churches that give their members complete freedom over what to believe and do, Mormonism can appearing controlling, but what is a religion worth if it does not exert some formative
pressure on individual behavior? Many conservative churches used to
prohibit members from playing cards, drinking, dancing, and joining
Masonic lodges. The fact that even many fundamentalist churches do
not enforce such restrictions any more is surely one reason why so
many outsiders are prone to think that Mormon Church discipline
is cultish. The rest of us have forgotten that being a Christian should
require a high price in terms of outward signs of personal commitment. Mormons give more lax Christians a bad conscience, I suspect.

The word *cult* comes from the Latin *cultus*, which means worship. The word has come to refer to modes of religious belonging that

are socially disruptive and psychologically disabling. Such concerns about religion are valid and legitimate; as Jesus said, "Where your treasure is, there your heart will be also" (Matt. 6:21). In other words, we are what we worship. The simplest definition of a cult is that it is a religious group that worships its all-too-human leader rather than God. Mormons believe that revelation and prophecy did not end with the death of the twelve apostles or the closing of the New Testament canon. They believe that Joseph Smith was a Prophet and that his successors, the presidents of The Church of Jesus Christ of Latter-day Saints, are also Prophets. But they do not worship Smith or any other human being. It is true, however, that the God they worship is very much like us, which means that we humans are, by our very nature, very much like him. Mormons do not worship a human being (other than Jesus Christ), but they do believe that all human beings have the potential, beginning now but culminating in the next life, to share in the properties that make God divine. One could say, then, that Mormons honor and revere (but do not worship) the principle of the divine that resides in every human being.

Another reason Mormons are sometimes thought to possess some of the attributes of a cult is related, I think, to their healthy mindedness. The young men and women on their missions, for example, are so uniformly and nicely dressed, and they wear name tags no less! They look like young recruits at a Fortune 500 corporation, and they are so inevitably polite and respectful that their old-fashioned virtues can make them appear almost robotic. The Mormons I know smile a lot and seem very happy, which some people mistake for shallowness or mindless obedience to their church. What is strange is not how well adjusted most Mormons are but how cynical most Americans can be about them. I have come to realize that the main reason Mormons are suspected of being cultish is that they do not manifest any trace of the religious guilt and self-reproach that are still inculcated in many traditional Christian churches. They seem too happy to be Christian!

If one were to be cynical about it, one could say that Mormons have all the benefits of a cult—the closeness of community and the

certainty of convictions—without any of the psychological distur-
bances. One might even say that the charge of being a cult arises
from some level of envy on the part of non-Mormons. Mormons
display the fruits of Christian faith with a freshness and abundance that are often lacking in mainstream Christianity. That makes
Mormonism very attractive, even if some of its beliefs are not all
that tempting to traditional Christians. I have titled this chapter
"Mormon Envy," and by now it should be clear why I do envy many
aspects of Mormonism. Nonetheless, Christians should not envy
anybody, so I hope that my thoughts here reveal instead nothing
more than a healthy form of admiration.

Chapter 2

The Magic of Being Mormon

Several years ago my wife and I were having dinner with an old friend and her new boyfriend when my friend suddenly asked me, during the dessert course, if I believed in magic. "I don't know," I replied, trying to think of something gracious to say, "but this tiramisu is certainly magical." For the couple who had invited us, this topic was no joking matter. In fact, they were firmly divided on the issue. The woman said that life was not worth living if it was not magical. The man forcefully rejected what he called magical thinking. They had just started dating, and their invitation to us was one of their first public acts as a couple. They split up not much later.

Most people probably think of flashy tricks when they hear the word *magic*, whether they are performed by a professional at a Broadway show or a kid at a birthday party. Outside the world of entertainment, magic is not taken seriously by the great majority of people in the western hemisphere. Indeed, even in the entertainment industry, magic acts do not get much respect these days. Illusions that once amazed have lost their aura due to the many books, websites, and television shows that have revealed their secrets. The art of magic has been reduced to the technology of misdirection and the psychology of deception. As a result, magicians must stage increasingly spectacular stunts to hold the attention of bored and jaded audiences.

Throughout Western history, however, magic has meant much more than cards and rabbits. Magic in its broadest sense can include activities such as astrology, alchemy, faith healing, sorcery, spells, and incantations. With such a long list, however, it is hard to know what all of these things have in common. Moreover, there has been a renewed interest in pagan practices in recent years, led by groups like Wicca, which has rehabilitated the image of witches and their attempts to beguile and charm. The association between magic and paganism has a long history, of course, which is why many Christians can react with contempt to anyone who takes magic seriously. Nevertheless, Christians can also use the label of magic to criticize each other. To a Protestant, crossing oneself in the sign of the cross might be an example of magic, while mainline Christians might think that charismatic faith-healing services are magical tricks dressed up in religious veneer.

The magic label can also be applied to Christianity itself, since calling something magical is tantamount to ridiculing it. To an athe-ist, praying for people who are ill is hardly any different from casting a spell for them. If you do not believe in God, then the ban on taking the Lord's name in vain looks like nothing more than a silly super-stition. For hardened skeptics, all of religion is nothing more than magic that is taken seriously by large numbers of people. From this perspective, magic includes any attempt to cross over into an imagi-nary world of supernatural beings with the goal of gaining some ben-efit from it. Those who are committed to a purely naturalistic view of the world can thus solidify their identity by standing in opposition to anyone who "believes in magic." Magic takes them back to the Dark Ages, when ignorance and cruelty reigned supreme. For these hyper-rationalists, magic is just another name for gullibility and naiveté.

One thing magic-deniers miss is just how closely magic comes to science. Magic in times past was used both to explain and to con-trol forces of nature. During times of plague and starvation, magic provided a set of ideas to help people try to make sense of why bad things happen to good people—your child is sick because evil spir-its are in the air or your neighbor is jealous of your worldly goods. Magic also gave people tools for trying to fight back against those evil spirits or jealous neighbors. The forces it battled might have been mysterious, but its own practical use was not. Magic operated accord-ing to two causal theories: the law of similarity, which uses symbolic objects to effect change in their corresponding realities, and the law of contagion, which uses the physical contact between two objects to maintain and alter their relationship long after they are separated. Magic was thus a supplement, not an alternative to or competitor of, scientific thinking. Even Isaac Newton, as is well known, spent years working on alchemical equations that he thought were perfectly compatible with his scientific work.

Magic-deniers also miss the way in which magical practices originated in a struggle that is as old as humankind itself: the struggle between good and evil. Helplessness in the face of excessive suffering led people to imagine that evil is a vital force that can take both animate and inanimate forms. Magic was thus deeply entangled in Christian assumptions about the physical effects of the supernatural drama of Satan's rebellion against God. While some people tried to fight evil as directly as possible, whether through prayer or magic, others decided to flatter those forces in the hope of bending them toward their own wills. That is why magic in the West was always divided into two basic kinds, one that worked for the good and thus was socially acceptable and one that traded on evil and was shunned and persecuted. White magic tried to ward off evil spirits when all other forms of social protection failed. Black magic took the lethal risk of trading on evil's power to gain illicit goods or take revenge on one's enemies.

The great majority of people throughout Western history denounced black magic, but what about white magic? Church leaders and theologians condemned it too. They had three reasons. First, white magic brought people too close to the devil they were trying to cast out. It was, in other words, an example of playing with fire. Second, it clashed with the belief that God is absolutely sovereign and thus in complete control of all events. Even when it appealed to good spirits to drive out the bad, it tended to treat the divine as one side of a dramatic battle, the outcome of which was far from certain. Third, white magic presumed that God could be called upon (or Satan rebuked) by actions or words that did not originate in the liturgy of the church. These words had secret origins in pagan practices and obscure meanings that were passed down from masters to initiates. Christianity had its own institutional procedures for healing and exorcism and did not tolerate deviations from them. White magic competed with the church's monopoly over words and actions that try to tap into the divine power.

While it was once the topic of much debate and controversy, all that is left of magic for most people today is the hope that there might be more to life than the dull monotony of the daily routine. The dinner party I attended is a case in point. The hostess used the word *magic* as a synonym for anything romantic. Something is magical if it transcends the ordinary and every day by being unexpected or surprising. Magic in this sense is the secular equivalent to the religious category of miracles. That is what the hostess meant when she asked me if I believed in magic, and that is what her soon-to-be ex-boyfriend denied. Given their fundamental differences, it would have been truly magical if their relationship had worked.

The man at the dinner party rejected his date's dreamy idealism as a form of "magical thinking," a phrase that has become popular in recent years. Magical thinking happens when someone tries to influence an event or secure an outcome by doing something that has no direct causal bearing on that event or outcome. Magical thinking is more than just wishful thinking. It is a wish combined with an action that supposedly makes the wish more likely to come true. It can be as simple as the rabbit's foot I carried in my pocket as a young boy for good luck or as complicated as the private ceremonies a ballplayer performs before stepping up to the plate. Magical thinking can take a dark turn, as with compulsive behavior or phobias that are intended to prevent something bad from happening. An atheist is likely to think that prayer is a form of magical thinking, especially if the believer thinks that prayer can change the outcome of a future event. The early Christians thought that pagan animal sacrifices were a form of magical thinking, since they were convinced that God was not influenced by them and, furthermore, the sacrifice of Christ on the cross was sufficient to repair our relationship to the divine.

Philosophers committed to a purely scientific view of the world put all such thinking in the category of a causal fallacy. From the perspective of scientism, causality is a strictly physical phenomenon that can be established only by the careful application of rules for collecting and weighing evidence. Defining causality this narrowly rules out not only magical but also positive thinking, where people feel as though something is more likely to come true if they keep a good attitude about it. Scientism might work for practicing scientists, but it is a hard philosophy for everyday life. A narrow conception of causation makes it futile to seek meaningful relations among a group of events or objects that are not immediately connected with each other. It is hard to imagine anyone living up to these standards of interpretation. The human condition requires us to make patterns out of our worlds even when we do not have enough evidence to demonstrate the connections we need to make. Christians, for example, make sense of the world by relying on the doctrine of providence, which claims that all of history is under God's guidance and direction and that the Bible provides the pattern according to which every human life can be understood. Scientism renders the doctrine of providence little more than a sophisticated version of magic. Providence, however, has many secular forms, as when we use stories to make our lives appear more coherent than they really are. If giving one's life a narrative coherence violates the laws of causality, then magical thinking is just another name for being human.

I hope to have shown that magic, for all of its power to disturb and provoke, is more complex and harder to define than many people suspect. That is an important claim for this book because Mormonism came of age during a time when magic was still very much a part of Christianity. The earliest critics of Mormonism delighted in pointing out that Joseph Smith was a "money-digger" as a young man, using a seer stone that he found in a well. The implication is that anybody who would have been involved in money-digging surely could not be trusted to have found golden plates written in an ancient script. Even today, many people treat Smith's early adventures in trying to locate lost objects and buried treasure as sufficient information to stop them from taking Mormonism seriously. That is a shame because it obscures the events, like the First Vision I discussed in chapter 1, that truly do make Smith stand out among his contemporaries.

The focus on a couple of money-digging episodes also obscures the way in which Smith was part of a society that was saturated with physical manifestations of the supernatural. The great majority of Americans in the nineteenth century drew no hard and fast line between religion and magic. Scholars often give the label of "folk customs" or "folk magic" to practices like treasure seeking in order to distinguish them from magical rituals that have their origin in ancient written documents. Folk magic is not a part of the official theological and liturgical life of Christianity, but that does not mean that it is always practiced in opposition to the church. The Roman Catholic Church, for example, often either tolerated or assimilated European folk customs in order to facilitate the spread of the Gospel. What the category "folk magic" helpfully highlights is the absurdity of imagining that our Christian ancestors, when they laid their hands on the sick, used medicinal herbs, or chanted and danced to drive away evil spirits, were clandestine pagans trying to overthrow the purity of Christian faith.

The charge of magic is often made to try to associate Mormonism with non-Christian traditions, which is one reason why Mormons are so sensitive to it. They have every right to be defensive, since the charge is often overstated and abused, akin to saying that the fact that Catholics cross themselves shows that they are still mired in an ancient pagan mindset. The charge has also been used to try to exploit and embarrass the LDS Church. Mark Hofmann is a counterfeiter, forger, and convicted murderer. In the 1980s, he forged a number of documents with the intent of damaging the reputation of Joseph Smith. He then sold them to the LDS Church. The most notorious of these documents was called the Salamander Letter. Supposedly written by one of the witnesses of the original plates that Joseph found, it says that Smith was deep in the occult and that he had originally claimed that a white salamander, rather than an angel, had appeared to him. The media had a field day with these documents before they were proven beyond doubt to be forgeries.

Another reason why Mormons are sensitive to the charge of magic is that it is so alien to their liberal and humanistic assumptions about reason, human nature, and social progress. In fact, it is hard to imagine a more optimistic version of Christianity. Mormons reject the doctrine of original sin, which says that every person is born into sin and consequentially, even our best efforts to do good in the world are stuck in greed, lust, and pride. For Mormons, by contrast, progress, not regress, is built into nature; it is the destiny of all matter to become more spiritual. The entire cosmos has a history, and if it were plotted on a graph, the line would doubtless have its dips, but its main direction would be up. Mormons are optimists about the power of reason because they reject the division of reality into a supernatural realm that is mysterious and unknowable and a natural realm that is organized and orderly. All of reality is material and thus in principle knowable. That is why Mormons reject the idea of a miracle when it is defined as a supernatural intervention into an otherwise closed physical system. Like other Christians, Mormons pray for miracles and talk about miracles, but they see them as entirely natural events. Miracles are rare and surprising, but they are mysterious only due to the current (and not inherent) limits of our knowledge. How ironic, then, that a religious tradition that rejects a supernatural understanding of miracles is accused of believing in magic!

To better explain the confusions and paradoxes of Mormonism and magic, we need to return to the topic of metaphysics. As I pointed out in chapter 1, the word *metaphysics* is often associated in popular culture with the occult. It might seem like a big leap from the study by ancient Greeks of the most basic features of reality to the art of conjuring spirits and casting spells, but the occult was born in ancient philosophy just as science was once part of religion. The reason this connection is not better known is that professional philosophers have a vested interest in keeping the history of their discipline disentangled from a word that implies unmitigated speculation.

Philosophers are generally restrained about their speculations, preferring to focus on clarifying what we can know rather than expanding our knowledge to include the unknown. Professional metaphysicians reflect on data drawn from universal human experience, and they limit their tools to the rules of logic and rational analysis. Outside of the technical world of philosophy, however, many thinkers are far less circumspect Metaphysics in the form of the occult is more exuberant about its sources and methods. To occultists, studying the most basic features of this world naturally leads to an inquiry into the existence of other worlds, just as taking immaterial ideas seriously leads to the study of immaterial agents who are the source of those ideas. Moreover, the keepers of the occult are not content just to study the divine. They want their studies to be practical as well as theoretical. The point of metaphysics for the occultist is not just to understand God but to discover the key to God's power.

Professional philosophers thus treat the occult as a manipulative, exaggerated, and superstitious form of metaphysics—if they think about the occult at all. The relationship between metaphysics and the occult is actually much more complex than this. For historians of philosophy, what the occult is and how it is related to metaphysics are much contested topics. There are three stories that historians tell to try to answer these questions.

The first is the standard story that philosophers tell about themselves. The standard story emphasizes philosophy's rational purity and portrays the occult as the absolute opposite of everything philosophy represents. This story has to deal with the fact that Plato himself was a lover of stories and many of the stories he told were about heavenly realities and mystical visions. In the *Phaedrus*, for example, Plato presented an allegory about the immortality of the soul, likening it to a charioteer ascending to divine heights. There is little doubt that Plato believed in the preexistence of the soul, which is how he accounted for various features of human nature, such as being born with a longing for the divine and a capacity to intuitively understand abstract ideas. The standard story of philosophy, however, treats the charioteer allegory as a myth that Plato used for rational, not religious, purposes. The standard story denies that Plato took any of the details of the myth literally (or even seriously). Plato was trying to persuade his audience to free themselves from worldly concerns in order to take flight not to the gods but to the highest realms of abstract thought. By treating Plato as a lover of stories that he did not believe, the standard story of philosophy is as hard to believe as any of the stories that Plato told.

Something else makes the standard story hard to accept. Although it is premised on the separation of reason and faith, it actually has its roots in Christian theology. Theologians in the early church adopted Plato with the same zeal that they condemned the religious culture that was so much a part of his thought. Christian thinkers were thus the first to try to strip Plato of his religious associations and mythic sensibilities. Even today, theologians committed to classical theism with its transcendent and unapproachable deity are hesitant to acknowledge the mythical basis of Plato's worldview.

The second story, which is really just a modification of the first, admits that philosophy is a search for wisdom, but it insists that the philosophical way of life was in direct competition with the official forms of religion in Greece and Rome. That later philosophers became interested in the occult is evidence that philosophy eventually degenerated in the West after the rise of Christianity. This story admits that Plato had religious beliefs. After all, Plato said, "We should make all speed to take flight from this world to the other, and that means becoming like the divine so far as we can." Advocates of this second story argue, however, that imitation of the divine for Plato takes the form of moral effort, not mystical ascent or magical practices. The path to spiritual maturity is lit by the lofty goal of righteousness, not the tedious business of ritual. God is perfectly free of the world, and thus we should be free of all worldly desires. Some theologians like this story even more than the first one because it portrays Plato as a pagan on his way toward the ethical rigor of monotheism. From this perspective, Plato is like the Israelite prophets, who criticized animal sacrifices, and the Apostle Paul, who downplayed the importance of religious law. Augustine, for example, interpreted Plato as paving the way for Christianity's triumph over paganism by criticizing the sensuality and mutability of the Greek gods.

The third story says that metaphysics and the occult were always two sides of the same coin. The occult is just another name for the mystical and magical aspects of metaphysics that were passed down primarily by oral tradition and practiced by the educated elite of the ancient world. Proponents of the third story like to point out that Plato himself did not develop a coherent and systematic set of doctrines, at least as far as the dialogues go. Nobody knows how the dialogues functioned in the Academy that Plato founded or even why they were written. It is thus just as likely that we will find the views of Plato in the later Platonic tradition as we will in the dialogues themselves. In fact, the strong separation of Plato from later forms of Platonism began in the nineteenth century and had no parallel in the ancient world. Nineteenth-century scholars wanted to treat the dialogues as sacred scripture in the same way that restorationist Protestants wanted to strip Christianity of everything accrued after the writing of the New Testament. This third story points out that the *Timaeus* was Plato's most influential dialogue down through the Middle Ages, and it is full of speculations about the divine, the world soul, and the relationship between the supreme principle of the one (identified with the demiurge, Plato's term for the god who fashioned the world) and the plurality of individual entities in the world. If Plato did not come to any settled judgments about these matters, then the claim of his followers, even centuries after his death, to be developing his ideas needs to be taken seriously. Very few Christian theologians accept this story, because it entangles theology's favorite philosopher in religious speculations that Christians decidedly (and sometimes violently) rejected centuries ago. Nonetheless, this story is becoming more accepted in scholarship on the history of philosophy, to the point where it is almost becoming the new standard for how to read the relationship between metaphysics and the occult.

All three stories undoubtedly contain elements of truth. I am most convinced by the third story, which is also the one most helpful in situating Joseph Smith's relation to metaphysics and magic.

Not surprisingly, then, the first two stories are most compatible with classical theism. Classical theists focus on the famous and thorny topic of Plato's theory of forms. Plato can be said to have invented the idea of immaterialism by equating ideas with immaterial entities. For Plato, eternal forms or ideas provide the foundation for the world as we know it, and thus they are not a part of the physical world. They are real, but they exist in an ideal realm accessible to the intellect, not the senses. Indeed, the forms are more real than worldly things precisely because they do not exist in space and time. Not being limited by space, they are universally true, and not being limited by time, they are eternally true. Philosophers after Plato argued passionately about the relationship of the forms to the particulars that embody them, whether the forms are located in the mind of God, and how the human mind comes to know them. Plato's theory of matter as the eternal stuff that God united to the forms was a particularly difficult topic of debate. Nonetheless, the great majority of metaphysicians accepted the basic Platonic claim that reality and immateriality are perfectly commensurate.

Christian theologians gradually came to accept most of the Platonic philosophical framework, although they revised it in significant ways. Christians decided that Plato's ideas, for example, must exist in the mind of God, not in an ideal realm that is as timeless as the divine. God used these ideas to create the world, but the world is not the product of God shaping matter according to the patterns of the forms. Instead, God created the world out of nothing, by which theologians meant that God created the world out of nothing *material*. The ideas God used to create the world were God's thoughts and thus did not exist prior to or independently of God himself.

While theologians revised some aspects of Plato's metaphysics, they accepted his view of reality and immateriality. If the Platonic forms exist outside of space and time, then so does God, who, after all, is the one who thought up the ideas in the first place. Christians agreed with Plato that God is perfect and that God exists at the highest level of reality, so they also agreed with Plato that God must be immaterial. If God were material, then God would be subjected to all the vagaries of time and all the limitations of space. A material God could not be perfect because objects in time change from one moment to the next and thus have the potential to improve as well as deteriorate. If God has the potential to change, then God would have unfulfilled or incomplete aspects of his being. That cannot be true since God is not limited in any way. Being immaterial, God is eternal in relation to time and infinite in relation to space. A corollary of this position is that God has no needs or wants. Being outside of time and space, God is not dependent on anything for God's existence. Whatever emotions or desires God has must be directed inward, at himself, rather than outward toward any other being.

Whatever the occult is, it definitely does not treat God as a purely immaterial being. On the contrary, the occult treats the divine as a kind of pervasive energy that can be tapped into and employed with the right words and actions, and that is how the occult gets its bad reputation. Even Christians who are not Protestant have been influenced by the Reformation's insistence that salvation is a gift that comes through faith alone. This is often taken to mean—especially in theological circles influenced by John Calvin—that all of our interactions with the divine should be passive and thus any attempt to influence God is an insult to God's freedom and authority. According to Calvinism, God chooses those who will be the recipients of grace, and there is nothing we can do to alter the divine plan. In fact, God is impervious to our pleas and petitions because God is not affected by any of our actions. God needs nothing outside of himself, so there is nothing we can give God that he does not already have. It goes without saying, then, that God cannot be manipulated, cajoled, threatened, or bribed. From this perspective, the stories of characters in the Bible doing their best to please God or begging for special treatment are for our benefit and are not to be taken literally as indications of God's nature. We should act, perhaps, as if our actions could harm or benefit the divine, because that will be beneficial for us, but in reality nothing we can do will add to or subtract from God's eternal life.

From the perspective of classical theism, those who practice the occult are guilty of acting like bulls in a china shop. Impatient and imprudent, occultists do not approach God with the right kind of reverence and circumspection. They want action when they should seek knowledge instead. They want to connect with the divine within themselves when they should be content to worship the God who is totally above and beyond them. In sum, occultists are not just philosophically wrong. They are also spiritually ignorant and morally debased.

Standard philosophical prejudices against the occult go a long way toward explaining why Mormon metaphysics seems so radical. I am not saying that Mormon metaphysics is a direct heir of the occult tradition. Indeed, it does not fit very easily into any of the usual categories that scholars use to describe the history of Western metaphysics. Mormon metaphysics is not like the traditional kind because it is not the study of immaterial ideas or agents. It is not like the occult because Mormons do not believe that the divine is all that mysterious. Mormons seek neither to understand that which is unfathomable (a perfectly simple immaterial being) nor to harness divine energy in order to influence others or control natural events. Instead, Mormon metaphysics is a new thing altogether.

Nonetheless, Mormon metaphysics resembles the occult version of ancient metaphysics much more than it does the immaterialism of classical theism. Mormons believe that there is an essential continuity between this world and the other world, so that there are no gaps or gulfs between matter and spirit. God is not a unique entity who stands outside of the world and requires us to do likewise if we are to know anything about him. God is very much a part of the cosmos (or the cosmos is a part of him), which means that the way we come to know God is not different from the way we come to know anything else in the world.

That might suggest that Mormons have no need for metaphysics altogether, but Mormonism is actually inclined to a metaphysical scheme that is simultaneously speculative and practical. Because God is a material being like us, God is subjected to the same laws that govern the movement of all matter. God plays a special role in this metaphysics, since he exists in the highest state of material development, but God still has a material form. Matter, according to Mormonism, exists according to gradations of spiritual refinement, so that even spiritual entities like God, angels, and the soul are composed of some kind of matter. Ordinary matter is regulated by the laws of science, but even the lowest kind of matter is not absolutely dead and lifeless. For Mormons, science and metaphysics are partners in trying to fathom how all of matter aspires to the highest, spiritual state of exis tence. The ultimate law that governs the cosmos, then, is the law that explains the way in which ordinary matter can become even more glorified matter (which is to say, spirit). Mormonism does not claim to know the precise nature of this law. How matter and spirit coexist on a continuum is not a relationship that can be reduced to a mathematical formula (at least yet). Nonetheless, the purpose of nature is to elevate material beings into a fuller and richer (yet still physical) life. As Jesus said, "I have come that you may have life, and have it more abundantly" (John 10:10). The transformation of matter into a godly and perfect state, no matter how mysterious it appears to be, is not haphazard or random. The regularity of that process is what Orson Pratt, whose work I will discuss in the next chapter, called "the law of increase." It could also be called the "law of becoming," since all of matter is in the process of becoming more than what it already is.

Becoming is an important concept for Mormon metaphysics. Traditional metaphysics, and this is especially true of Plato, is the study of the universal principles that explain how things are, which is why traditional metaphysicians talk about *being* so much, sometimes even capitalizing it as *Being*. *Being* is a static word that connotes sameness and immutability. Plato thought that change is a sign of weakness and decay, while the standards of truth, goodness, and beauty are beyond all change. Mormon metaphysics depicts reality as *becoming*, not being. Reality is fluid, connected, changing, and moving. Even God is in the process of becoming (God is ever becoming more Godlike!), rather than being the one entity that is beyond every kind of being. Becoming does not mean that reality is in a state of random fluctuation. It means that everything is always moving toward a goal, but the goal is not peace and restfulness. Instead, the goal is the perfectly dynamic creativity that God has already achieved—and even God is capable of surpassing himself with new experiences and new knowledge.

Joseph Smith rejects Plato's understanding of Being, but there was more to Plato than that. In chapter 1, I discussed how Smith tried to overturn Platonism, even though he was not a student of philosophy and never, as far as I know, mentions Plato. I now want to qualify that claim by offering a reading of the relationship between metaphysics and the occult along the lines of the third story I discussed above. True, Plato invented the immaterial realm (the realm of Being, where first principles and perfect entities are eternal and unchanging), and Smith was a thoroughgoing materialist, but both of them wanted to bridge the gulf between spirit and matter in their own way. Plato was a lover of wisdom who drank deeply from a longing for oneness with the divine. He sought a transcendental unity behind reality that most people today would recognize as God. Unfortunately, many philosophers now treat Plato as if he were a professional academician like themselves, who never let pagan religious practices or mythical beliefs interfere with his logical arguments and rational analysis. Indeed, in most philosophy classes students are taught that religion is nothing more than magic and that philosophy and religion are so separate from one another that they should be taught in different departments with different teachers. Any sign of their mingling is a form of intellectual pollution that must be cleaned up by logical analysis.

In fact, it was Plato who said that "wonder is the feeling of a philosopher, and philosophy begins in wonder." All philosophers, until the discipline became confined to universities, thought that only those who live a good life can have any hope of discovering life's deepest mysteries. Prior to the modern world's separation of every activity into separate spheres of specialization, philosophy was a way of life, not a topic of study bound by the canons of objectivity and detachment. Plato, however, would only have half-agreed with the second story I described above—that the moral prerequisite of being a philosopher was simply doing good works. Like all ancient and nearly all medieval philosophers, he thought that the attainment of wisdom requires an inner transformation that goes well beyond doing good deeds. To attain unity with the one, the philosopher has to undergo what Christians would later call a conversion. This makes philosophy not a substitute for religion but a complementary path to the same goal. The purpose of ancient rituals and myths was to purify supplicants of everything that kept them from achieving unity with the gods. The goal of philosophy was to teach students how to put away the distractions of the world in order to become one with truth, goodness, and beauty. What religion did outwardly, with great drama and spectacle, philosophy did inwardly, through contemplation and reflection. Logic and analysis were merely preliminary skills that prepared the student for a life of spiritual equilibrium and pious rumination.

What was true for Plato was even truer for his heirs. The philosophers who came after him are called Middle Platonists and Neo-Platonists, and most of them, especially the Neo-Platonists, were even more explicit about the connection of religion and reason than Plato was. For that very reason, modern philosophers often show little interest in them, and the many thinkers who populate the Platonic tradition (other than Aristotle, Plato's greatest student) are rarely taught in undergraduate philosophy courses. Plotinus (A.D. 204–270), the greatest of the Neo-Platonists, is a case in point. He directed all of his thoughts toward what he called the One, which was his name for God. The One is indivisible, incorruptible, and indescribable. It is the first principle of everything, but rather than the One creating the world or causing it to come into being, everything flows out of the One like water overflowing a fountain. The One for Plotinus is basically indifferent to this process. It is also so far beyond everything that it is impossible to know in any ordinary way. Mystical experience, not logical argument, is the best way to approach the One. Nonetheless, Plotinus thought that philosophy was still the best path for souls striving to return to their origin in the immaterial realm of unchanging absolutes precisely because philosophers are trained to be indifferent to the material realm. Plotinus's last words were, "Try to bring back the god in you to the divine in the All."

Plotinus did not think highly of Christianity, but he and his theological contemporaries shared a common enemy in the Gnostics. "Gnosticism" is a label scholars give to a variety of heretical groups that were associated with Christianity in the second and third centuries. Plotinus saw the cosmos as a series of emanations from the perfection of the One that results finally in the lowest level of reality, which is matter itself. Gnostics put personal faces on those emanations by telling stories about heavenly battles between the gods, and they were also more pessimistic than Plotinus about the lowest level of reality. For Gnostics, an evil god, with less power than the true God, created the material world in order to punish souls by trapping them in flesh and bones. Salvation is possible only if souls can be freed from this world in order to escape the wrath of this evil god. Some Gnostics identified themselves as Christians because they taught that Jesus Christ was a perfect soul who sneaked into the world to do battle with the evil god and lead some elect souls back to heaven. The journey back, however, was not going to be easy. Souls had to be armed with proper information, including secret passwords and signals, to pass through the various levels of the cosmos and return to the good God, who is above all of these messy conflicts and clashes. The Gnostics mixed fantasy, mythology, magic, philosophy, and theology into a religious stew that managed to annoy and offend both Platonists and Christians. Nevertheless, they are further evidence of how hard the ancients struggled to understand God's nature and thus the proper worship that is due the divine.

Some of Plotinus's successors were more enthusiastic than he was about religious ritual as a means of achieving the mystical goal of the philosophical life. Neo-Platonists like Iamblichus (240–325) increasingly sought out the help of intermediaries between God and humankind to facilitate spiritual growth. They called these intermediaries *daimons*, which they treated as helpful, not evil, spirits. Christians were quick to associate these demons with the work of Satan and thus denounced the Neo-Platonists even as they embraced Plato. Plotinus taught that life begins with the One and involves a descent into the material world, where the oneness of reality is soon forgotten. Significantly, for Plotinus, some part of our soul remains with the One (it is undescended) even after we are born in human form, so that we only need to be reawakened to our divine origin. For Iamblichus, the soul is thoroughly damaged during its descent into the material world, which means that it cannot depend solely on its rational faculties for the return trip to the divine. Unlike Plotinus, who depicted the ascent as a journey into one's innermost self, stripped of bodily distractions, Iamblichus emphasized the importance of external aid in the form of rituals and mythology. This journey for Iamblichus is a physical one, since it involves not just our immortal (and immaterial) souls but also our astral forms, which are composed of a subtle matter similar to the luminous substance that gives the stars their eternal light. (The idea of an astral substance or subtle matter worked its way through history to eventually influence Orson Pratt's understanding of spiritual matter, as we will see in the next chapter.) Everyone has an astral form that connects the finite body to the immortal soul and thus provides a bridge from this degenerate world to the unchanging (but still material, although Iamblichus could be ambiguous about this) unity of divine perfection.

It is worth thinking about Iamblichus's view of matter more carefully. Matter for Plotinus was off the charts when it came to the outpouring of the world from the divine, while Iamblichus emphasized the continuity between the gods and the physical stuff that makes up the world. Far from being nothing (having no ontological status) or being evil (impeding the return to the one), matter for Iamblichus is an index of divine presence. More specifically, matter functions as a mirror that reflects the moral condition of the soul. The closer the seeker of wisdom comes to God, the more authority the philosopher will be able to exercise over matter's recalcitrant ways. This does not mean that the philosopher will become a magician in the crass sense of that term. Instead, the philosopher will be able to overcome all physical impediments to spiritual harmony. In the words of one scholar, the philosopher will "become his own demiurge" (Plato's term for the creator god). For Plato, the form of the beautiful could be made accessible to us through material objects of the right sort, but no other form is given over to our sensory perception. Iamblichus's view of matter led him to a profoundly different position. For Iamblichus, rituals reveal the fundamental forms that hold the cosmos together. The gods give us rituals so that we can participate with our bodies in the divine nature. Moreover, the religious symbols used in rituals give us a direct glimpse into the divine mind. Rituals are knowledge-in-action, shaping us in quite literal ways in preparation for the soul's ascent to the beyond by initiating the transformation of matter into spirit. It follows that rational reflection alone is insufficient in the search for truth if it is separated from what Christians called grace.

The name for sacred rituals that move the soul toward the divine is *theurgy*. Neo-Platonists like Iamblichus borrowed their rites from Oriental and Egyptian sources as well as the practices passed down by the followers of the Greek philosopher Pythagoras. They also drew from the volume of literature known as the *Hermetica*. A collection of these texts was translated by Marsilio Ficino into Latin and published as the *Corpus Hermeticum* in the sixteenth century. This volume, which influenced some of the more radical Protestant Reformers, was widely read during the Renaissance and entered into the European mix of alchemy, witchcraft, astrology, the Jewish mystical system known as Kabbalah, and other forms of esotericism. Because of his connection to the *Hermetica*, Iamblichus acquired the reputation of being an advocate for magical practices, not unlike Joseph Smith's standing with some of his harshest critics. (Iamblichus was also poorly received in the West because his work was used by the Emperor Julian [r. 361–363], who apostatized from Christianity and tried to rejuvenate pagan temple rituals, especially animal sacrifices.)

The accusation of magic against both Iamblichus and Smith is understandable but ultimately unjust, but that has not stopped scholars from trying to indict Smith for being guilty for associating with the wrong crowd. Indeed, Smith is sometimes placed at the very end of the narrative I have just told, as if he was a modern Neo-Platonic occultist. There is actually some truth to this charge, but it is not the truth that Smith's critics think they have found. John

Brooke, for example, wrote a book called *The Refiner's Fire* that tries to make the case that Joseph Smith was a hermetic magi. (*Magi* is a word that roughly means someone who practices the ancient rites of magic. It is used in the second chapter of the Gospel of Matthew to refer to the three wise men who visited Jesus after his birth.) Brooke admits that there is no hard proof for this connection, but he thinks that the circumstantial evidence should raise our suspicions. Smith's ideas, he claims, are drawn from the world of ancient and medieval magic even if he was completely unaware of this debt. Brooke defines hermetics as it was filtered through Renaissance Christianity as the attempt to recover all the perfections Adam had before the fall. He traces hermetic thought more to the ancient Gnostics than to the Neo-Platonists. He also emphasizes the role of alchemy in this tradition. By the time of the Renaissance, practitioners of the occult wanted to master nature by turning the lower orders of matter into higher forms. Hermeticism taught them that material creation is living and eternal and thus has the potential to be refined and purified. Alchemists sought what philosophers called prime matter—or, more colorfully, the philosopher's stone—which was part of the original creation and is still imbued with divinity. Through various elaborate experiments, alchemists tried to isolate prime matter in order to transform metals, as well as human beings, into a godly state. This is the closest connection Brooke actually makes between Smith and hermeticism, since Smith was known as a young man to have used precious stones to aid him in seeking buried treasure.

There are two major problems with Brooke's thesis. First, it is a lot simpler to find the precedents for some of Smith's beliefs and activities in the Bible, rather than going back to the ancient hermetic tradition. Sorcerers and magicians are condemned throughout the Bible, presumably because they claim to draw power from false gods and use that power against the faithful, but acts that look a lot like magic, when commanded by God, are acceptable and even celebrated. Some of Jesus' miracles look a lot like magic, as when he spit on the ground, made mud, and used it to heal a man's blindness (John 9:6) or when he tells Peter to catch a fish, open its mouth, and find a coin in it (Matt. 17:27). Peter had the power to chastise Ananias and Sapphira, and through his words they immediately died. Was that a form of magic?

The Old Testament is especially full of stories about magic, and it was the Old Testament that most inspired Smith's theological imagination. Moses transformed a rod into a serpent in order to scare the pharaoh into letting the Israelites leave Egypt, and examples like that could be multiplied. When Jacob was bargaining with Laban for his wages, he offered to take only the speckled and spotted sheep. Laban took them first, so Jacob peeled some sticks to make them look both white and dark and put them in front of the flocks. When they mated, they produced the speckled and spotted offspring that Jacob could call his own. This was clearly a magical practice that followed one of the basic principles of magical thinking, the law of similarity, which states that causal relations can be established by means of symbolic imitation. Another example of magic in the Old Testament is the use of seer stones, like the Urim and Thummim mentioned without any condemnation in Numbers 27:21 and 1 Samuel 28:6. Smith used stones to translate and called them by these same names.

The second problem with Brooke's thesis is that he traces Smith's metaphysics to the wrong source. Smith was hardly a Gnostic, since the Gnostics believed that the material world is evil, having been created by an evil deity. Although one might expect that Gnostics would disdain dealing with the material world in any way, they were actually deeply immersed in a magical worldview. Plotinus criticized them for being dependent on magical spells and formulas rather than rational reflection. For the Gnostics, navigation back to the one through myriad levels of angels and demons required a litany of secret names, sounds, and gestures. They promoted themselves as experts in knowing how to pacify and disrupt the hostile powers that pervade the universe. Gnostics had such a low regard for the material world—including their own bodies—that they thought these hostile powers were deeply embedded in matter itself. Treating matter with disdain was not incompatible with using magic for material gain. On the contrary, precisely because the physical world was so loathsome,

Gnostics were not reluctant to use spells to harm their enemies and profit themselves. Smith does not fit into this magical scheme at all.

Nonetheless, there is much to be learned by comparing Smith's worldview with Neo-Platonism. By positing a law that connects all matter to spirit in a process of divine evolution, Mormon metaphysics can look a lot like Neo-Platonism, which envisioned the entire structure of emanations from the one and the return of all things to their original source as a highly rational system. It is with Iamblichus, however, who took a turn to ritual that was not as prominent in other Neo-Platonists, where the comparison is most pertinent. Just as Protestants have long accused Smith of advocating a works-righteousness wherein believers have to earn salvation, Iamblichus was accused of defending rituals as a way of gaining the favor of the gods. Again, both accusations are unfair. For Iamblichus, the gods have to take the initiative, not humans. He thus had a notion of grace that was not totally dissimilar to that of the Christians of his day. Theurgic rituals, he believed, are a gift from the gods to help us draw closer to them. When we perform rituals, we are inviting the gods to act on our behalf, but we cannot compel them to do anything they do not want to do. As Iamblichus wrote in *On the Mysteries*,

For it is much more true that god is all, and has power over all, and all things have been filled by his own self, and he alone is worthy of highest esteem and blessed honor. But the human being is shameful, and is as nothing, and a toy compared with the divine. And I even laugh hearing this: that the god is spontaneously present to some whether by reason of the cycle of creation or through some other causes. For the superior being will no longer be unbegotten if it is the cycle of generation that brings it, nor will it be the primordial cause of everything if itself be co-ordinated with some things by reason of other causes.

On the Mysteries was written to his fellow Platonist Porphyry, who was proud of his philosophical efforts and thought that he could attain salvation through rational reflection alone. Iamblichus firmly believed that the gods are in control and that our destiny is in their hands.

For Iamblichus, the gods are free and thus can freely choose to be approachable and accessible. The whole point of rituals is to create fellowship between gods and humans. Rituals give participants a vision of the divine that permits them to participate in the power and knowledge of the gods. That might sound perilously close to magic, since the whole point of magic is to use divine power to accomplish specific tasks on earth. For Iamblichus, however, the more we know about the gods, the more we will be like them. Sharing in their power will result in a moral transformation of our souls. Being able to understand the world in the way that the gods do, we will be able to overcome our passions, desires, and self-interests. The pursuit of divine power, then, strives for the same goal that Porphyry sought: a contemplative life full of wisdom. Smith's notion of what it is like to become like God is much more active than that. He had a dynamic view of heaven and even went so far as to imagine that the saved will imitate God's creative activity by themselves becoming creators of new worlds. Nonetheless, he shares in Iamblichus's emphasis on the gifted character of rituals and the correlation between closeness to God and moral transformation.

Theologians are quick and eager to identify with Plato by honoring his memory and borrowing his arguments, but the later Platonists are looked upon with suspicion and condescension. Smith never read any Neo-Platonist, let alone one as neglected as Iamblichus, but if the history of philosophy was told differently, then Smith's reception among theologians would also be very different indeed. The idea that magic and religion are opposites has as one of its primary sources the judgment that Plato has nothing to do with the later Platonists. Plato is the West's greatest thinker, and to associate him with someone like Iamblichus is to impugn his reputation. Christians especially have a vested interest in protecting Plato from Neo-Platonic influences because the alleged purity of his immaterialism is so important for classical theism. Opening the door of Platonist studies to Iamblichus would have the same effect on philosophy that opening the door to

Joseph Smith would have on theology. It would expand the philo-sophical imagination by restoring all things material to the desire to become one with God.

Even so, all of this talk about Smith's roots in magic really has little to do with his mature theology. When he received his revela-tions from the Angel Moroni about the Golden Plates, he became passionate about the texts on the plates, not the gold. He left behind the pursuit of hidden treasure to become a translator of a new scrip-ture. There is no evidence that he ever again practiced anything like the money-digging activities of his youth. After his discovery of the plates was widely reported, some people sought him out and asked him to make predictions about the future, but he declined their pro-posals. He did not deny that he had spiritual gifts and powers, but thereafter he used them for sacred purposes, not secular gain.

As the Mormon Church grew, Smith's dabbling in folk magic was long forgotten, to the point where many Mormons doubted that it ever happened. Today, however, Mormons have learned to put Smith's early magical thinking into a providential context. If God really did send an angel to someone to guide him or her to find buried plates, whom would God choose? If God wanted a revival in America with new signs and wonders, would God speak to impoverished and mar-ginalized people who associate with folk magic or highly educated members of the established churches? From a providential perspec-tive, Smith's early experiences, far from discrediting him, prepared him for his prophetic vocation.

Still, the idea that matter and spirit are inextricably connected to the point where neither can be conceived in absolute isolation from the other, which is at the heart of Mormon metaphysics, will always carry an echo of the occult for many people in the West. Some critics think that Mormon temple practices are where Mormons cross the line into magic, and I will discuss those practices in chapter 7. Others point to their temple garments, more popularly known as "sacred underwear," as an example of magic. The garments are received at a temple endowment ceremony, and they are supposed to be worn at all times, with obvious exceptions. On the Internet you can find countless curious people wondering if Mormon couples wear these garments during sexual intercourse, and the answer is no. They do not wear them when they are swimming or bathing either. The garments are simple in design, and they have evolved over the years from one piece that extended to the ankles and wrists to two pieces with shorter sleeves and legs. The purpose of the garments is to remind Mormons of the temple ceremonies and thereby strengthen their resolve to resist temptations of the flesh. There are plenty of stories in Mormon folklore that tell of the garments protecting Latter-day Saints from physical harm, but Christians of all traditions have told similar stories about sacred objects providing physical comfort and safety. How many soldiers in America's various wars have claimed that their pocket Bible stopped a deadly bullet from taking their lives? What is really disappointing is the shortsightedness of the critics who obsess about these garments as an example of how anti-Christian Mormonism is, while the real problem with clothing in America is that so many Christians waste money on fashions and luxuries that they do not need. Contemporary styles are designed to show as much of the body as possible, while Mormon garments are designed to remind the wearers that their bodies are holy and belong first to God before they give themselves to someone in marriage.

All religious traditions change and grow, but Mormonism, with its affirmation of ongoing prophetic authority, is a branch of Christianity that had evolution built into it from its very beginning. If I am right that magic and religion are close relatives, then it simply makes sense that a new and exuberant religious tradition like Mormonism would mix the two together, but it also makes sense that Mormonism can show the rest of Christianity how to retrieve a truly magical (in the sense of wonder and awe at the works of God and the beauty of Christ) way of being in the world. The history of Christianity is full of attempts to establish, adjust, police, and enforce the line between magic and religion. As much as theologians have insisted through the centuries that God's gifts to us are the result of a free choice on God's part called grace, most Christians think that God can be influenced through prayer, ritual, and other religious actions. Religion has always been one of humankind's means of exercising control over the harsh realities of scarce resources and unpredictable diseases, and Christianity is no exception. Christianity was able to conquer and eradicate paganism in part because the Church claimed to have more supernatural power than heathen spells and charms. Saints replaced daimons as intermediaries who could be persuaded to intervene in worldly affairs. Devils were cast out by the prayers and invocations of exorcism. Benedictions of salt and water guaranteed good health, and holy water was sprinkled on humans, animals, and fields to promote healing, growth, and fertility. In all of these activities, proper words had to be used and the same procedures had to be followed to make the rituals effective. This was true of the greatest miracle of them all, the transformation of bread and wine into the body and blood of Jesus Christ, called transubstantiation. Medieval Catholics attributed incredible power to the bread (the wine was reserved for the priests alone). Some would take it home on their tongue and use it to cure fevers or ward off bad omens.

One could venture the hypothesis that the magical worldview in the West did not begin its slow decline until the Protestant Reformers challenged the doctrine of transubstantiation. Transubstantiation involves more than just the transformation of bread and wine into the body and blood of Jesus. Transubstantiation is the ritualistic foundation of Catholic Christianity because it reveals the fundamental relationship between matter and spirit. Jesus Christ united divinity and humanity in his own incarnate form, but that unity, Catholics believe, is made visible and accessible to his followers in the Eucharist. It is no exaggeration to say that the entire edifice of the Catholic Church rests on the presupposition that the simple material of grain and grapes can become a conduit of God's real presence in the world. In this ritual, the incarnation becomes a reality that pervades everything Christians do and believe. The Eucharist is where Catholics experience the potential of matter to become spirit by consuming the life-giving properties of Christ's perfect flesh. The battle between matter and spirit is reconciled in these basic elements, unveiling an ultimate unity rather than an absolute division.

During the Reformation, Protestants began interpreting many medieval Christian practices as forms of magic, but their biggest target was transubstantiation. After all, a priest had to say the correct words and make all of the right gestures to ensure that the ritual worked, and the resulting transformation was invisible to the naked eye (or even a microscope). For many Protestants, every problem plaguing medieval Catholicism, from corrupt hierarchies to uneducated priests and repugnant superstitions, could be traced to transubstantiation. The word, after all, appears nowhere in the Bible and even worse, it was term straight from the handbooks of medieval philosophy. Transubstantiation was the perfect target for Christians who did not understand and had no patience for the logical and speculative achievements of the Middle Ages. The modern conviction that metaphysics is nothing but superfluous speculation began with the Protestant critique of transubstantiation as an onerous and unbiblical concept.

The sixteenth century experienced a crisis in the meaning of communion. The term *hocus-pocus*, in fact, originated as a way of ridiculing the sacramental words "This is my body" (*Hoc est corpus meum*). Some Reformers tried to retain the idea that God is really present in the bread and wine without the elements undergoing any change, while other Reformers took their critique to the logical conclusion that the bread and wine have only symbolic value. The Eucharist became the Lord's Supper, a memorial meal enacted to recall Christ's promises to his disciples. When this central ritual of Christian faith was reduced to an occasion for personal reflection and silent meditation, the metaphysical consequences were enormous. Matter and spirit were definitively split apart, with nothing left between them to fill the gap. Only God's grace could overcome their newly imposed segregation, which is why Protestant theologians worked so hard to make grace, not Christ's body, the center of their theologies. Not only did grace have to do the work of the incarnation and Eucharist. It also could not replicate what Protestants found so distasteful in the Catholic understanding of transubstantiation. That is, grace was conceived as God's decision about the state of our soul and thus could not be imagined as changing human beings in any physical way. With the Eucharist stripped of any of its altering power, Protestant theologians began talking about justification (how we are justified before God) in terms of a forensic act, by which they meant that God decrees our salvation by a legal judgment that leaves us exactly in the same condition. We are pardoned, but we are not changed—saved from sin but still the same sinners. Protestant theologians have been backing off the forensic view of justification in recent years, and some have even begun appreciating the doctrine of *theosis*, which emphasizes the power of grace to initiate our journey toward becoming like God. It is hard, however, to reconceptualize salvation without getting to the heart of the nature of matter, and the fact remains that the Protestant Reformation evacuated the physical universe in all of its material density of any direct participation in the life of God. Matter became inert, dead, and meaningless. Matter became the province of scientific mastery, and any attempt to connect the divine to our material condition became nothing more than magic.

One way of understanding Mormon metaphysics is to see it as an attempt to reunite the magical and rational worldview that once was so central to Catholicism. It does so by claiming that the world can be transformed in ways that seem magical by comparison with the assumptions and methods of the modern natural sciences. Indeed, Mormonism and Catholicism have a lot in common, in spite of the fact that Joseph Smith had little contact with Roman Catholics during his formative years. These two traditions share a love of ritual, an affirmation of the holiness of space (the desire to worship in holy places), robustly conservative moral traditions (especially a commitment to traditional views of marriage and gender), a respect for authority (especially in its role as an ongoing, institutionalized, and living voice), and a strong sense of a community of believers that transcends the limits of time to include the dead (Mormons baptize the dead, while Catholics pray for them and ask for their prayers).

With so much in common, how can Catholics and Mormons have such different understandings of the Eucharist? For Catholics, the entire story of matter—its origin, purpose, and destiny—is concentrated in the singular ritual of the Eucharist. Mormons, by contrast, have a very Protestant, indeed, a very rationalistic, understanding of communion. The Saints treat the Eucharist as a common, ordinary, and token meal, hardly more than a symbolic and visible lesson of invisible truths. To the Catholic mind, this suggests that Mormons have imbibed a bit too deeply from the Protestant cup of anti-ritualism, which turns communion into an inward, subjective, and immaterial experience.

Mormon communion confused me when I first began studying Mormonism. Mormons, for example, substitute water for the wine, which can be quite surprising to Catholics visiting a Mormon church for the first time, since it almost seems as though they are indifferent to the actual material used in the sacrament. Sometimes the substitution of water for grape juice or wine is explained by reference to the health code known as the Word of Wisdom, which forbids Mormons from consuming "wine or strong drink." (This can be found in section 89 in the *Doctrine and Convenants* [D&C], a collection of revelations received by Smith.) I have also heard it said that water is the purest possible liquid and thus the best representation of the purity of Jesus. Smith received a revelation in 1830 (recorded in *D&C* 27) that it did not matter what the Saints ate and drank when they took the sacrament and that the Saints should not purchase wine from outsiders (evidently there was some concern that enemies of the Mormons might try to sell them poisoned wine). In any case, how could Mormons have such a creative view of the divinization of matter and at the same time have such a low, pragmatic, and somewhat informal view of the Eucharist?

The answer to that question only came to me when I began to realize that both Mormons and Catholics believe in transubstantiation. They just locate transubstantiation in different theological places. Both Catholics and Mormons believe that Jesus Christ initiates, instantiates, and consummates the process of redeeming material creation, so that our hopes and dreams for eternal fulfillment in God include our bodies, not just our souls. For Catholics, transubstantiation is dramatized in a quite literal way in the Eucharist, where the bread and wine become the first fruits of the eschatological economy of Christ's abundantly capacious body. That drama for Mormons is not localized in such a specific way. Arguably, transubstantiation is such a pervasive feature of the Mormon worldview that it can easily be overlooked.

Mormons can appear to treat the Lord's Supper as a purely mental event because the Saints actually locate transubstantiation in the potential for every event, no matter how mundane, to convey the physically uplifting power of God's grace. Matter itself is bursting with transubstantiating power. As Elder Jeffrey Holland has written,

> A sacrament could be any one of a number of gestures or acts or ordinances that unite us with God and his limitless powers. We are imperfect and mortal; he is perfect and immortal. But from time to time—indeed, as often as is appropriate—we find ways and go to places and create circumstances where we can unite symbolically with him, and in so doing gain access to his power. Those special moments of union with God are sacramental moments.... These are moments when we quite literally unite our will and God's will, our spirit with his spirit, where communion through the veil becomes very real. At such moments we not only acknowledge his divinity, but we quite literally take something of that divinity to ourselves. Such are holy sacraments.

For the Saints, everything we do should rise to the occasion of the Lord's Supper.

Where Mormons focus their imagination of transubstantiation the most is on the afterlife. No Christian tradition has ever had such a concrete, specific, and creative view of heaven. Every good thing we do in this life, the Saints believe, will be done in the next, only with purer pleasure and greater results. No other Christian tradition has taken with such heartfelt trust these words of Jesus: "Very truly, I tell you, the one who believes in me will also do the works that I do and, in fact, will do greater works than these, because I am going to the Father" (John 14:12). What greater works could these be if they are not to be done in a future glorified state? In the next life, as Mormons picture it, the saved will exercise God's own power over matter sufficient to create and rule new worlds. The true limits of matter will be discerned as the necessary conditions for matter's rehabilitation from every evil, and all false limits will be vanquished. The cosmos, which Mormons believe is already infinite, will multiply exponentially. Transubstantiation will become the law of the cosmos, not just a Sunday morning ritual.

Arguably, Catholicism and Mormonism need each other to renew and reshape the Christian hope for Christ's return in all his bodily beauty. How does Mormonism need Catholicism? Mormon speculations about heaven can look too presumptuous to those who like to keep the mysteries of the afterlife vague and imprecise. Even for those who have a more graphic theological imagination, Mormon eschatology (beliefs regarding the end times and the afterlife) can appear to depend upon an unwieldy cosmological model of worlds beyond worlds. It can also look too much like a self-interested way of hoping that all that we have here and now will continue in the same form after we die. Mormon eschatology thus lacks, at times, sufficient attention to the role of sacrifice in the spiritual life. Precisely because it is so expansive, Mormon metaphysics can float free from the centrality of Jesus Christ (just as the metaphysics of classical theism can, by the way). That is why Mormonism needs Catholicism, with its insistence that transubstantiation is all about Christ.

And how does Roman Catholicism need Mormonism? The Catholic version of transubstantiation can easily lead to an arid and formal ritualism when it is not connected to our deepest passions about this life and our highest hopes for the next. Catholicism, which used to provide the cultural resources for the West's greatest artistic and literary works about heaven and the divine, needs Mormonism's exuberantly unrestrained imagination. Classical theism, in the hands of St. Thomas Aquinas, once inspired some of the greatest intellectual achievements the world has ever seen. Perhaps one of the providentially ordained purposes of Joseph Smith's life and teachings is to put a little of the magic back into non-Mormon Christianity.

Chapter 3

What's Up with Mormons
and Matter?

When the scientific community celebrated the discovery of the Higgs
boson in July 2012, the rest of us had to trust them that something
very important was going on. Atoms, after all, are not what they used
to be. Those of us who remember our high school physics classes have a
rough idea of a nucleus containing protons and neutrons surrounded
by a cloud of electrons, but we also know that the atom keeps getting
divided into smaller and smaller pieces, like quarks, which come, like
a brand of cereal, in six "flavors": up, down, strange, charm, bottom,
and top. I know that only because I just Googled it. I also searched
for the Higgs boson, which the media likes to call "the God particle."
A boson is a particle so small and weird that it typically lacks mass,
and thus two of them can occupy the same space at the same time.
The Higgs boson is a special kind of boson that was predicted to exist
if the Higgs field could be pounded hard enough to make a piece of
it break off. The Higgs field permeates all of space, and thus space is
not really empty, although the Higgs field represents the lowest state
of energy in the universe, and thus space is as empty as you can get.
The Higgs boson, by the way, does have mass, although most bosons
do not. Now, here is the thing about the Higgs field: it explains why
other particles have mass, because they slow down as they travel
through it, just like a traffic jam makes you more aware of the law of
gravity. Calling the Higgs boson the God particle can be misleading
because it suggests that tiny bits of stuff called particles are at the
heart of reality. The Higgs field, which is really a form of quantum

energy, is more basic than the Higgs boson, so perhaps it should be called "God's field," since the image of a divinely saturated matrix more accurately conveys the way in which everything that exists does so because of its relationship to something else.

You might want at this point to step back and ask a simpe question: What is matter? The whole purpose of this chapter is to persuade you that nobody, from the brightest scientist to the smartest philosopher, knows what matter is. I do not mean to suggest that scientists do not know a lot about matter. On the contrary, they know so much about matter that they disagree among themselves about what it is. The most common definition of matter is any object that takes up space and has mass. As we have seen, however, some bosons do not have mass, and space is as hard to define as matter. It is tempting to imagine that matter occupies empty space, but quantum mechanics suggests that space plays a role in creating matter. Is space more real than matter, and if so, what is its material constitution? It is also tempting to drop the idea of particles altogether and simply talk about energy instead, but given that matter can be converted into energy, isn't energy just another form of matter? Perhaps it is helpful to imagine matter as the concentration, conservation, or coalescence of energy—particles, then, would be energy vibrating very slowly—but energy is still something rather than nothing. Energy is the work, force, or action a physical system performs. It would seem to be a quality matter has, not the essence of what matter is. Then there is the fact that most of the matter in the universe consists of dark matter and dark energy, and nobody knows what those substances are. And what do you do with antimatter, which destroys regular matter if the two come into contact? Is antimatter another form of matter or something beyond matter altogether?

Scientists will no doubt continue to make incredible progress in solving the puzzle of matter, but the case can be made that they will never get much beyond the conceptual parameters first established by ancient philosophy. Democritus, who lived from roughly 460 to 370 B.C., was a strict materialist who wanted to explain the world without recourse to God or a first cause of any kind. He was the first to propose that the world consists of an infinite number of atoms moving through empty space. That seems prophetic in some ways, but Aristotle faulted him for not explaining what made these atoms move, and he could never successfully explain what held them together. Plato's theory of matter was more influential and, arguably, has more relevance today. Indeed, the great majority of philosophers throughout Western history have followed Plato's insistence that matter is more of a name than a thing. For Plato, matter is essentially mysterious because we can know only its form (or properties) and not what it is in itself. Matter is always the matter of something, and that something is a combination of form and matter. We know matter only when we perceive an object, and what we perceive are qualities like size, color, number, taste, smell, hardness, and so on. When you take away those qualities, what do you have left? If you strip away all the properties from an object, you have nothing left that can be known, since we know things only by how they appear to us.

Take, for example, a ball that is hard and blue. You can let the air out and paint it another color, and it will be soft and red. It is the same ball, but its properties have changed, which suggests that the properties of an object do not belong to it in an essential or fundamental manner. Color, for example, is a result of how our brains interact with the electromagnetic waves emitted by objects. Colors occur in us. Wavelengths have no color in themselves. The world is colorless, and the same goes for the other properties we attribute to the various objects around us. We think of objects as hard or soft, but any object is mostly empty space. So what is the ball itself, stripped of its hardness and color? We could say that a ball is any round object, by which we mean that every point on its surface is equidistant from its center. No ball, however, is perfectly round. Perfect roundness exists only in our minds as a concept or definition. That does not mean that balls do not exist. It just means that when we think about a ball, we are thinking about our idea of a ball, not any particular ball. The same goes for matter in general. When we think of matter, we can think about a specific material object, but if we try to grasp the substance that pervades or constitutes all objects, we will always latch onto a set of attributes, not the thing in itself. Even if we try to think about every object in the universe combined together in one huge lump, that object will possess some set of properties, and when you strip away those properties, what do you have left? You have matter in itself, but without some form, even of a most general kind, we will never be able to comprehend it.

A scientist might respond to Plato and his heirs by saying that matter takes all kinds of forms but the most essential forms are entities like electrons, protons, and quarks. Isn't that what matter is? The answer is no, because you still have to ask what all of these particles have in common. If you remove the properties that distinguish an electron from a proton and a quark, what do they have in common? Nobody knows, because the further we look into matter, the more we find a multiplicity rather than a simple unity. We find, in fact, a web of relationships amid fields of energy regulated by various laws that do not cohere into a single picture of the universe.

Someone else might respond that matter always takes the forms of liquid, solid, gas, and plasma, but scientists now think that matter can take other forms as well. Be that as it may, what is the material stuff that takes these different forms? For Plato, all we know about matter is its forms. We can keep breaking up matter to discover new and smaller forms that it takes, but matter is form all the way down. We will never discover formless matter, because by definition, something that is formless is impossible to know or understand.

In fact, formlessness was Plato's definition of matter. He thought that matter is much more like nothing than it is like something. Matter always takes some kind of form, so even if you could strip an object of all of its properties, you would not find anything when your work was done. You would end up with nothing—or at least nothing that you could put your finger on. Aristotle basically agreed with Plato and clarified his teacher's point by calling matter in general "pure potentiality." Objects exist because they have actualized matter's potential to exist in various specific ways. In other words, matter is only the potential for an object to exist, since matter never exists on its own.

These statements might seem obscure or baffling, but they are important precisely because nearly all Christian theologians have accepted them as the proper way to think about matter. For theologians in the tradition of classical theism, matter exists only because God initially created it and continues to keep it going. Without God, matter would be literally nothing. Even with God, matter does not amount to much of anything, because what is most real in the world is our minds and souls, and they are not made of matter at all. If you put everything in the cosmos on a scale of value, you would put bare matter in its most elementary form (whatever that is) at the very bottom and God, who is not material at all, at the top—and the values would go up the closer you came to the divine. From this perspective, matter is dead weight, lifeless and inert. Only an immaterial God can bring it into being, and only our immaterial souls can make it come alive.

Mormons are the only significant Christian denomination or movement to demur from this line of analysis about matter. Mormons claim to know what matter is, and they claim that matter is absolutely good in every way. Far from being nothing, matter, for the Saints, is the very stuff of the divine. Mormon theology defends this position because, as I pointed out in chapter 1, Joseph Smith rejected the philosophical move, stretching all the way back to Plato, of dividing the world into immaterial and material substances. Even today, Platonic dualism (often in its modern, Cartesian form, named after Descartes, who went even further than Plato in dividing the world into mental and material phenomena) lives on as the only serious mainstream alternative to the increasing prestige of materialism, a worldview that reduces everything mental and spiritual to the complex interactions of chemistry and biology. Could it be that Smith, who was dismissed by many of his contemporaries as "the ploughboy of Palmyra" (he was living in Palmyra, New York when he had his First Vision and discovered the plates that contained the Book of Mormon), foresaw a middle ground between Plato's immaterialism and the secular, atheistic ideology of materialism?

That designation, "the ploughboy of Palmyra," is ironic because it alludes to a reply that the great Reformer William Tyndale, one of the first to translate the Bible into English, made to a fellow priest who questioned his work. Tyndale said that he "would make a boy who driveth the plough know more of scripture than the priest himself." During his life Tyndale was just as controversial as Smith was during his. Tyndale wanted to get the Bible into the hands of everyday believers, while Smith wanted to open the ears of ordinary people to divine revelation. Reformers like Tyndale broke the Catholic Church's political and religious power in Europe and let loose a host of social changes that they could not have anticipated and were not able to control. Could it be that Smith, who had virtually no formal education, put in motion ideas that will overthrow the consensus of Western theological immaterialism?

That claim sounds incredible, but it is actually very plausible. The world of ideas today seems to be stuck between a rock and an empty place—that is, between the hard, reductive, yet scientifically successful explanation of all things by reference to material causation, and the insistence that our minds, as well as all that we most value in life, are not the product of random forces that operate on us in controlling ways. The mechanical view of matter treats nature as a machine that follows the law of strict causal determinism, which leaves no room for freedom. Immaterialists respond to reductionists by declaring that our minds are not identical to our brains. Our thoughts and ideas are real, but they do not occupy physical space. Reductionists scoff at the possibility that anything can exist without being located somewhere, while immaterialists bemoan the picture of a world bereft of all the qualities that make human life meaningful and unique. The debate between the two camps seems interminable and unceasing. Is there a solution?

Mormon metaphysics opens the possibility of a third way between these stark alternatives. Plato invented the idea of immaterial substances when he argued that our knowledge of something is really knowledge of an idea. Recall the ball example. When we see a ball, we are identifying an object as belonging to a certain class of objects. We recognize immediately that the big blue ball in front of us is a ball. For Plato, we are able to do that because we have some intuitive understanding of the concept of what it means for anything to be a ball. We have not gone out and found a bunch of balls and compared them with each other in order to determine if they all deserve that label. Instead, we experience an instantaneous connect between an idea and an object. Ideas are more real than objects, for Plato, because they are not limited by matter. An idea is a purely mental construct that does not change. A big blue ball can always become a small red ball, but the idea of a ball remains the same, forever.

And that is precisely why early Christian theologians liked Plato so much. Christians believed that their God, contrary to the pagan deities, with their all-too-human flaws and inconstant desires, never changes. God, for Christians, must be as immaterial as Plato's forms. Plato assumed that God (or the gods; he speaks of the gods and god as well as the divine) is perfect and thus not subjected to any of the indignities of the material world. Aristotle was more explicit than Plato about what this means. For Aristotle, God is an unmoved mover (so are the stars in their own way) because he never changes. Rather than doing nothing, however, he thinks his own unchanging thoughts for all of eternity. He is pure existence, and the closest mere humans can come to that kind of life is in the act of contemplating ideas, since ideas are also unchanging.

Christians differed from Plato, of course, by insisting that God does much more than contemplate ideas, since they believed that charity, not rationality, is the highest form of life. God for Christians creates the world and becomes incarnate in it in order to demonstrate his love for us. Plato's metaphysics has no conceptual room to even consider the possibility that the highest god would ever want to become material. Much of the dynamic development and creative ingenuity of Western thought is born out of this clash between Plato and the incarnation. Theologians turned this tense and uneasy alliance into a productive and creative relationship that continues to this day.

Smith challenged that uneasy alliance when he claimed the following revelation, which was collected in the volume known as *Doctrine and Covenants* (*D&C*), a book that functions for Mormons as sacred scripture: "There is no such thing as immaterial matter. All spirit is matter, but it is more fine or pure, and can only be discerned by purer eyes; we cannot see it; but when our bodies are purified we shall see that it is all matter" (131:7–8). Mormonism is a very complex branch of Christianity, but if all of its beliefs can be traced back to a single philosophical root, this would be it. This philosophical principle in turn is grounded in Smith's First Vision, which I discussed in chapter 1. Smith thought that he saw God the Father and God the Son as two individual and fully embodied persons, and he drew the conclusion that God really does look like us. When he reflected on his vision, he realized that what we see with our physical eyes on earth is only a glimpse of what we will see with the eyes of our perfect bodies in heaven, but he surmised that what we will see in heaven will still be made of the same (or similar) kind of stuff that we see on earth.

His conclusion might seem obvious, but it was actually quite radical. He could have denied the reality of what he saw by treating his vision as an example of how God, infinite and mysterious, accommodates himself to our finite state by momentarily pretending to be a finite creature himself. Or he could have treated what he saw as an empirical fact. That is, he could have treated his vision as no different from seeing a couple of farmers walking down the road. He did neither. Instead, he accepted the reality of what he saw while at the same time affirming the even greater reality of what all Christians will see in heaven. In other words, he inferred from his vision that the world consists of levels or layers of matter, rather than two kinds of substance, one material and the other not material at all. These layers can be graded on a scale from the most material to the most spiritual. Even at the bottom of the scale, however, no bit of matter, however miniscule, is completely isolated from God's sweeping majesty, just as at the very top of the scale, from souls to angels and God himself, no spiritual being is void of material form. Indeed, the very criterion of becoming spiritual entails the perfection, not the evacuation, of material existence.

There is biblical precedent for the idea that we can see God with our physical eyes in this life, if we are granted that blessing, and its corollary, that seeing God even more clearly in the next life with our spiritual eyes will complete, not replace, our physical sight. Our spiritual eyes will be perfected matter, not an immaterial substance. The Old Testament is full of stories about people seeing God. The Psalms, for example, often cry out for God to show the psalmist his face. "Do not hide your face from your servant" is a regular refrain (Ps. 69:17). Many readers today immediately think that the word *face* is being used metaphorically, but evidence abounds that God revealed his physical form (classical theists would say that he appeared *in* physical form) to many people. The list of these witnesses includes Abraham (Gen. 18:1–15), Jacob (Gen. 32:23–33), Moses (Exod. 33:11), David (2 Chron. 3:1), Solomon (1 Kings 3:15), Isaiah (Isa. 6), Jeremiah (Jer. 31:2), and all of Israel at Mount Sinai (Exod. 19–20). I would go into these examples in some detail except that many people will contend that I am reading too much into them already.

Christians often show a bias against the Old Testament by dismissing these visions as indications of the primitive state of Israel's religious development. A fancy word explains it all: *anthropomorphism*, which means the projection of human form onto nonhuman entities, such as treating a pet as a member of the family or seeing faces in clouds. When it comes to religion, anthropomorphites have the understandable but unfortunate habit of projecting human features onto God's featureless form. Anthropomorphism is the very first metaphysical mistake that any beginning student in any theology class will learn not to make.

Yet, if the Old Testament is primitive, then so is the New. Jesus himself said, "Blessed are the pure in heart, for they will see God" (Matt. 5:8). Platonism, however, is so powerful in the West that even biblical literalists do not take these descriptions of God's revelations literally. Indeed, the very danger of lapsing into crude anthropomorphisms is exactly what Platonism is designed to guard against. That God is not really like us is evidence that even the least theologically astute Christians have appropriated Plato, whether they know it or not. Take away Plato from Christianity, and you will get . . . well, you will end up with something very much like the Mormon conception of the divine.

You will also end up with a little-known heresy from the ancient world associated with a group known as the Messalians. The Messalian movement originated in Mesopotamia in the middle of the fourth century. Messalians were religious enthusiasts who thought that constant prayer could enable them to see the Trinity. They claimed to see demons and even argued that all people have demons within them until those demons are replaced by the Holy Spirit. Their opponents accused them of laziness, since they apparently did not work for fear of reducing their prayer time. They were also ridiculed for sleeping more than praying, although all such criticisms should be taken lightly given the polemical intensity of theological factions at the time. Messalians were condemned by several synods (meetings of bishops) and at the general council that took place at Ephesus in 431, after which they were subjected to intense persecution. What makes them especially fascinating for my purposes is that many scholars now think that their real mistake was not being sufficiently Platonic in their theology.

The main gist of most of the criticisms against the Messalians comes down to the allegation that they were anti-intellectual. This was a serious charge because it carried moral implications. From a Platonic perspective, concepts are the true object of knowledge, which suggests that only the crude and crass are unable to rise above the material world and grasp the immaterial ideas that tell us what things really are. To picture God as a physical body is a sign of a mental failing so great that it must have physical repercussions. The problem is not just that Messalians were not smart enough to realize that God is beyond our understanding. The problem is that they were stubbornly mired in all things worldly and thus were not sufficiently spiritual to advance in religious wisdom.

Not content to criticize Messalians, Platonic theologians developed very sophisticated theories to account for visions of God. They had to, given that Plato left them with the quandary of explaining how we can perceive through our bodily senses a being who is absolutely immaterial. They came up with three possible strategies to solve that problem.

First, some Platonic theologians simply bit the bullet and admitted that we cannot see God in this life or the next. God is beyond our human capabilities, and the best we can hope for is that our souls, stripped of their bodies, will be able to unite with God in a way that we presently cannot comprehend. It follows that divine revelation is a very peculiar form of knowledge. God can reveal himself to us, this position agrees, but the content of such revelations tells us nothing about God's nature. The truths of revelation have to be taken on faith alone. They carry an authority that cannot be questioned since there is an absolute gulf between what we perceive in revelation and what those revelations mean.

Second, other Platonists argued that we can think about God even if we cannot see God, because our minds are as immaterial as God is. This position seems to suggest that only those who overcome their bodily limitations and purify their minds can know God. We can know God by negating everything that we know (and thus this position is called negative theology). Those who resist moving from everyday knowledge to abstract reflection will never fully understand the divine. Negative theology smacks of cultural elitism, which was the case in the orthodox persecution of the Messalians.

Third, the most sophisticated Platonists speculated that we have a special spiritual sense (*spiritus sensus* in the Latin) that operates in a way that is analogous to our five physical senses. Think of the spiritual sense as a mode of intuition, only stronger than that. It is an organ of the soul, so to speak, that can be sharpened and developed like any of our corporeal senses.

The problem with a spiritual sense is not just that there is no evidence for it. The main problem is that Platonist theologians never explained how it works. The spiritual sense seems to be midway between a physical and an immaterial organ, but is that possible? If it is physical in some way, then we should be able to pinpoint it with reliable descriptions. If it is immaterial, then how is it a faculty of sense perception? Defenders of the spiritual sense use mixed metaphors like "the ears of the heart" or "the mind's eye" to describe it. If those metaphors really point to our ability to perceive God in some way, then the gulf between the spiritual and the material must not be unbridgeable. In other words, if the spiritual sense really lies midway between bodily perception and intellectual conceptions, then it must share in both the physical and the spiritual. It follows that the spiritual and material must overlap and interpenetrate, rather than oppose and contradict, each other.

Smith did not know the history of arguments about a spiritual sense, and he did not use that terminology, but he grasped the basics of what was at stake in these debates. He lived in a time when there was great hunger in America for religious visions and concrete knowledge of God. He personally sought out God with his own ears and eyes, but he also knew that all of our senses are weak when it comes to the divine, and thus they need to be transformed and uplifted by revelation itself if we are to have any hope of divine knowledge. Evidence for his sensitivity to the basic human desire to have physical contact with the divine can be found in the Book of Moses, which Smith produced in 1830 and 1831 as part of his quest to present a new translation of the Bible. Smith thought that much of the Bible had been poorly translated, riddling it with errors and confusion, and he felt inspired to set the scriptures straight. In doing so, he plumbed the depths of spiritual perception. Take these two verses about Moses: "And he saw God face to face, and he talked with him, and the glory of God was upon Moses; therefore Moses could endure his presence" (Moses 1:2); "But now mine own eyes have beheld God; but not my natural, but my spiritual eyes, for my natural eyes could not have beheld; for I should have withered and died in his presence; but his glory was upon me; and I beheld his face, for I was transfigured before him" (Moses 1:11). In the first verse, Moses actually and literally sees the face of God. In the second verse, Smith makes it clear that Moses did not see God with his natural vision. Our natural eyes have to die, metaphorically speaking, for new vision to arise. It is the death of our old eyesight that is metaphorical, not the birth of new vision. That death is metaphorical because Smith contends that spiritual vision is a refinement or purification of our physical eyes, not their replacement. God's grace transforms rather than obliterates our natural bodies. We need both physical and spiritual sight, then, and the two can work together when God grants us our deepest desire to see his face.

Smith's reflections on spiritual perception culminated in his teaching about spirit and matter (in *D&C* 131) that I quoted above. That climatic doctrine was recorded in 1843, about a year before Smith was murdered by a mob at the Carthage, Illinois, jail. He did not live long enough to develop his convictions about matter into a full-fledged theological worldview. Brigham Young inherited Smith's political leadership of the Mormons, but Orson Pratt did the most to adopt and refine Smith's ideas. We need to turn to Pratt to find the true revolutionary potential of Smith's metaphysics.

Orson Pratt was an early convert, but there was nothing in his background to suggest that he would end up being Mormonism's first systematic thinker. He was born in 1811 to itinerant farmers who idealized the early church found in the New Testament and resented the way denominations competed against each other for members. He worked as a common laborer during his teenage years, and like many of his peers, he had virtually no formal education. In 1830, Orson heard about Smith from his brother, Parley, and spent a month with the Mormon Prophet. Smith trusted him enough to send him on a mission, and Pratt spent the rest of his life evangelizing for his faith. He was the first Mormon missionary to visit Scotland, where he absorbed the heated debates about science and religion that were sweeping through Edinburgh. His travels brought him into contact with a wide range of ideas, and he took to writing pamphlets, almanacs, and books in defense of Smith's revelations. He was not just an apologist, however. He was a creative and quirky thinker of a kind that was common in the nineteenth century but increasingly rare in the twentieth, when higher education became professionalized and the various fields of knowledge specialized. During Pratt's lifetime there was no hard and fast line drawn between amateurs and scholars. Someone with enough ambition, energy, and intelligence could master the basics of scientific thought regardless of a lack of the proper credentials and formal training, and individuals outside the mainstream could contribute to the sciences by the sheer boldness of their imaginations.

Amateur is from the French and means "a lover of" something. Today it is used to refer to someone who pursues an activity as a hobby rather than a career, but Pratt was an amateur in the original sense of the term. He had a deep love for knowledge. Indeed, I am convinced that he was one of the most inventive, fascinating, and bold thinkers in nineteenth-century America. I am also completely aware that he was absolutely wrong about most of the scientific ideas he persistently proposed. He was an intellectual adventurer, which to some people means that he was a crank or oddball not worth taking seriously. It is true that he had too much confidence and too little self-criticism, but his mind was endlessly active, and his conjectures were always original.

The one topic he would not contradict was Smith's revelations, though he was not afraid to disagree with Smith on matters of church policy. When it came to metaphysical speculation, however, Smith was the forerunner and Pratt was the real thing. Smith postulated the continuity of spirit and matter, but Pratt took that hypothesis and built a coherent conceptual world out of its many implications. Pratt put Smith's vision to work by showing how it could be used to dismantle much of Western philosophy and point the way toward a totally new theological foundation for Christian faith.

Pratt approached theology as a scientific inquiry, and he wrote about God in terms that were no different from how he wrote about gravity and astronomy. He accepted experiential evidence as the final court of any rational appeal. Even Smith's revelations were a set of facts that needed to be explained just like any other data. Pratt was an empiricist who believed that knowledge begins and ends with the senses, but he was also a romantic who thought that nature was alive with the divine. He died in 1881, before he had a chance to absorb Darwin's new ideas, which is a shame, because his own view of evolution was organic, not mechanistic. Matter is alive, not dead, for Pratt, and purpose, not randomness, is built into its very fabric.

If the spiritual is material, then science has no limits, and theology, far from being the queen of the sciences, is simply science in its most applied form. Pratt thought that the restoration of Christianity also inaugurated a new era of learning. A truly grand and unified theory of the cosmos was within human reach, but only if science and theology learned to cooperate with each other. Smith commenced this cooperation by demonstrating that prophetic authority and scientific authority were complementary, since both the scientist and the prophet, no matter how different their focus, are ahead of their time in imagining new depths of the same world. Nevertheless, when Pratt wrote about science, he kept his theological ambitions in check, although his religious motivations are obvious to the modern reader. His interest in science was mostly directed to astronomical topics, and the source of his fascination is not hard to find. Pratt, like all Mormons, believed that the afterlife was out there, somewhere among distant galaxies, and not totally beyond us in a different reality altogether.

He devoted most of his scientific efforts to two projects that came to fruition in publications and books but had virtually no impact on the scientific community. The first project was a law for planetary rotation. Pratt proposed a mathematical theory that would predict the rotation (or axial spin) of the planets in our solar system. The second project was about the movement of heavenly bodies, which Pratt called celestial mechanics. This project entailed two postulations. First, he theorized that the universal ether, which was a staple of scientific accounts of the rarefied element that fills space, consists of atoms. Second, he argued that gravity is not instantaneous but, rather, has the velocity of light. Ether was a commonplace of his day, but his description of its constitution and function was creative. His ideas about gravity were even more original, since nineteenth-century scientists universally thought that gravity was instantaneous. Combining these postulates, Pratt argued that the ether slows down planetary motion while gravity propels planets forward. Planets follow their orbits because the resisting and propelling forces are perfectly balanced.

Neither of these theories was taken seriously by scientists of his day. Pratt did not take into account alternative explanations of the phenomena he studied or the most current sets of data. What these theories demonstrate, however, is a mind thriving on new ways of thinking about the world. Pratt's ideas were original, but his method was thoroughly old-fashioned. In all of his work, he began with a firm set of first principles. This combination of an audacious imagination and deductive logic meant that Pratt was systematic in his creativity. Everything had to flow from a specific set of starting points, and all of his starting points, whether scientific or theological, flowed from one basic principle: that anything immaterial simply does not exist.

Some of Pratt's most pointed arguments against immaterialism came in an essay written as a response to a British theologian named T. W. P. Taylder. Taylder wrote a pamphlet criticizing Pratt from the perspective of traditional, Platonic philosophy. Pratt responded with a treatise entitled *Absurdities of Immaterialism*, which was the first Mormon essay dedicated to this topic. Taylder defined an immaterial substance as one that is entirely different from a material object. Pratt went after that rather loose definition. He argued that an immaterial substance must share either none or some of the properties of material substance. If it shares none of the properties of matter, then it is hard to avoid the conclusion that we cannot talk about the immaterial realm other than to say that it is the equivalent of what we mean, when we are talking about material things, by nothingness. But what if an immaterial substance shares some of matter's properties? If that is so, then why call it immaterial? Indeed, no material object, Pratt argues, shares all of the properties of any other material object. So if an immaterial substance shares even just a very few properties with material objects, why not just call it material? It does not matter if immaterial entities only share properties with certain kinds of material objects. "The superiority of some qualities has nothing to do with the immateriality of the substance," he writes. Oxygen is lighter than any metal, but it is still material. Besides, scientists agree that light is made of matter even though they cannot say what light is.

Spiritual entities are superior to material ones, Pratt confesses, but if we can know and experience them, what else can they be but objects of a more refined kind of matter?

Pratt liked to argue from the definition of terms, and much of his debate with Taylder stemmed from differences in first principles. Pratt thought that the very idea of an immaterial substance was absurd because he assumed that for something to exist, it must have location and duration. Without having read any Kant, he agreed with the greatest of Enlightenment philosophers that time and space are conditions for anything's existence. "Conceive if you can, of a locality outside the bounds of boundless space," he mockingly challenged immaterialists in his treatise: "Do not your judgments, and every power of your minds revolt at the absolute absurdities and palpable contradictions?" We know spirit and matter only by their properties, so if we cannot advance beyond the properties of matter to determine what it precisely is (and here Kant, who says that we cannot know things in themselves, agrees with Plato), then why do we think that we can advance beyond the properties of spirit to determine that its substance is immaterial? That very question is the reason theologians have long argued that all of God's attributes are exactly the same. That is, if God's omnipotence is different from his omniscience or his immutability, then those attributes must describe different aspects of God's nature. And if God has a nature that expresses itself in different ways, then the divine nature must be a kind of substance that is different from its properties, just like matter is different from the forms it takes. It follows that there must be something like a prime divinity analogous to prime matter. It also follows that prime divinity must be divisible, since it has parts (that manifest themselves in different ways), but divisibility is one of the fundamental definitions of matter. So if all of God's attributes are not redundant statements of God's nature, then God must be material. In order to avoid that conclusion, classical theists claimed that all of God's attributes are identical with each other. That claim, however, simply underscores how unknowable God is, since to the human mind, attributes are meaningful only if they are different from each other (by describing different aspects or parts of an object). Classical theists end up redefining the divine attributes to the point of making them meaningless.

Pratt admits that solidity is the one property of matter that most gets in the way of thinking of spirit as material. Are God, angels, and the soul solid? Pratt agrees that they do not appear to be, but he solves this problem by denying that solidity is in fact a property of matter. Instead, solidity is matter's essence. This is another example of his predilection for arguments by definition, but it is a very creative move. "Solidity is the essence to which all qualities belong—taste, smell, color, weight, etc. are the affections of solids," he wrote in *Absurdities of Immaterialism*. So God, angels, and the soul are solid, but only in the sense that they really exist. Pratt did not explain in any detail what he meant, but I think that we can infer the following points. The experience of solidity, such as touching an object that presses back against us, is merely nature's way of telling us that something is there. What confuses most people is that they equate solidity with hardness. The hardness of an object can vary while its solidity remains the same. Indeed, all of the attributes of any entity can vary without regard to its basic solidity. Thus, God can appear to be beyond hardness (God is not affected by material constraints in the same way that we are, for example) while still remaining essentially solid. That, at least, is the best spin I can put on Pratt's reduction of matter to solidity.

His speculations about solidity notwithstanding, Pratt was at his best in *Absurdities of Immaterialism* when dealing with the much more mundane matter of distinguishing between Mormon and atheistic forms of materialism. Nearly all of his contemporaries would have immediately assumed that materialism is nothing more than atheism. Pratt turns the tables by arguing that immaterialism is the chief cause of atheism in the modern world: "A being without parts must be entirely powerless, and can perform no miracles. Nothing can be communicated from such a being; for, if nothing gives nothing, nothing will be received. If, at death, his followers are to be made like him, they will enjoy, with some of the modern Pagans, all

the beauties of annihilation." An immaterial God is deified nothingness, he proclaims. The idea of immaterialism so lessened the reality
of God and challenged our ability to experience God that it left the
modern world with little to believe in and thus is the primary cause
of atheism.

In later works Pratt extended his thesis on solidity by developing
an uncompromising atomism. He defined matter as "every substance
in space, whether visible or invisible," and he thought that material
substance consists of "inconceivably minute, solid, hard, impenetra-
ble, moveable, immutable atoms." That these atoms must be eternal always struck Pratt as obvious. Perhaps the best way to imagine
what Pratt meant by atoms is to compare them with seeds, since
the potential for intelligence is inscribed in each and every material
particle. Pratt often directly attributes intelligence to atoms, which
can sound absurd and off-putting to most readers, but he means
that atoms have the capacity to apprehend each other, no matter
how rudimentary this capacity is. This capacity, which is neither
emotional nor self-conscious on an atomic level but nevertheless
is quite real, is how intelligence comes into the world. Intelligence
begins with a very basic kind of awareness and grows from there.
Intelligence and matter are thus coequal in eternity, and God, who is
the supreme intelligence, is also supremely material. How these three
entities, God, intelligence, and atoms, fit together is not very clear
in Pratt's thought, since he wavered between the traditional mono-
theistic language of God's exclusive uniqueness and the more radical
rhetoric of multiple origins of the universe, each of which is equally
primordial. With reference to God's relationship to intelligence, Pratt
argued for God's relative uniqueness (if uniqueness can be qualified
in that way). Everything operates according to what Pratt called "the
law of increase," but not everything increases at the same rate. God's
capacity to improve his intelligence is not unique, but what he has
done with that capacity does set him apart from everything else. He
is supremely self-surpassing even if his capacity for growth and progress is built into the nature of the cosmos. God exemplifies, we could
say, the upper limit of the law of increase.

Pratt's universe, including the divine, is busy with change. Matter, which cannot be destroyed, is always in motion, and the goal of every object, for Pratt, is not unity with God but, rather, realization of the attributes that God most splendidly exemplifies. This is an utterly crucial point. Most accounts of heaven portray a unity between individuals and God's nature. Since God's nature, according to classical theism, is unchanging, infinite, and immaterial, this unity is always depicted as essentially mysterious and beyond description. For the Saints, the faithful in heaven will unite with God's attributes, not God himself. Everyone will retain his or her individuality even as the saved begin participating in the power, love, freedom, and beauty of God. Our lives in heaven will thus be just as active, indeed more so, as our lives on earth.

Although he had a general definition of matter, Pratt did not treat all matter alike. He distinguished between spiritual and gross matter mainly in terms of gradations of intelligence. Gross matter exists on the lowest level of the universe, yet it is still receptive to intelligence in the sense that it is not completely bound to causal laws. Spiritual matter is actively and dynamically intelligent. It is basically equivalent to the mind. The difference between the two is one of degree, not kind, since even spiritual matter cannot occupy the exact same space that is already occupied by another entity. Spiritual matter can influence gross matter because all matter is porous, which permits the two to join in incredible intimacy without violating every entity's essential impenetrability. Spiritual matter is less bound to the earth and has more capacity for development and purification than gross matter. Nevertheless, even the crudest forms of matter possess some kind of incipient intelligence, and all of matter also has an inherent capacity for free movement. How else, Pratt asked, could gravity, which Newton understood to be action that takes place at a distance, work? For Pratt, Newton left gravity an immaterial mystery. Every force, he argued, must be composed of some kind of matter. The solution he proposed is that even the smallest of particles freely chooses to follow the basic laws of the universe. Atoms are free, but they are not wild and reckless.

They exist in an interconnected community organized by their own choices for the good, and the sum of their mass behavior is what we call scientific laws. For Pratt, there are no mysterious forces that pull particles toward each other. Every single particle, more than any Higgs boson, is a "God particle."

That the mind is made of matter seemed obvious to Pratt by the way that our thoughts accompany our bodies as we move from place to place. Moreover, the mind perceives its own existence, Pratt observes, which suggests that the mind exists as something material. The relation of the mind to the body is an old problem in philosophy, beginning with Plato's argument that the mind (or soul) is immaterial. How can something immaterial act on something material, given that all causation takes place on the material plane? Descartes sharpened this problem by accepting the full consequences of two kinds of substance that do not interact. His position is called mind–body dualism. Pratt went in the opposite direction by positing a material mind that exists along with or in the body. If mind is material, Pratt thinks, there is no mystery behind its interaction with the body. This can sound as though Pratt is solving the mind–body problem simply by defining it away. Moreover, he is left with the burden of explaining how we can be free (in our thoughts and actions) if our minds, now construed as material, are the product of causal factors.

Pratt's solution to that problem—how a material entity can be free—was to envision freedom (or intelligence; he treated these two words as synonymous) as an aspect of matter even in its most basic state. Freedom of thought is not the product of complex chemical interactions in the brain. Rather, freedom of thought is an original property of matter, regardless of the degree of its organizational complexity. Pratt did not have the conceptual or scientific resources to explain how the smallest particles of matter can exhibit the property of intelligence. With quantum physics, however, scientists are much more open to the idea that small particles like electrons show some of the characteristics of free action since their location is unpredictable. Some scientists and philosophers think that quantum mechanics simply demonstrates the limits of our ability to understand the laws that govern the motion of the smallest levels of reality, while others conclude that there is nothing in nature that determines the course of these movements. Even if quantum mechanics is interpreted as evidence against causal determinism, it is a big step from the unpredictable behavior of electrons to the conclusion that elementary particles are free and an even bigger step to the hypothesis that they are motivated or prompted by something like a free will. Indeed, the fact that everything is not caused, strictly speaking, by anything happening before it does not mean that everything acts in a purposeful manner, but it does open the door to the possibility that things might in some way cause themselves. That is, particles might act in a way that anticipates what we call freedom when people act based on their own will and not external compulsion. In any case, we can probably all agree that matter is a lot more mysterious than anyone could have imagined even just a few decades ago, even if atoms might not be as similar to human beings as Pratt sometimes imagined.

Pratt's most creative application of his theory of matter to theology concerns the Holy Spirit. The third member of the Trinity has always been a somewhat overlooked and neglected aspect of the divine. Augustine defined the Holy Spirit as the mutual love of the Father and the Son, but that does not give it much independence as a divine person in its own right. The Greek word for spirit, *pneuma*, means wind or life, which is an apt image for a force that seems to be personal and unpredictable. The New Testament also calls the Spirit our advocate and comforter. The Spirit inspires us to keep following Jesus after his ascension to heaven. Clearly, the Holy Spirit has tasks that make it distinct from the Father and Son, yet traditional theology hesitates to affirm any constitutive differences among the three, due to the conviction that God is immaterial. If God is immaterial, then God cannot be divided. Even the work that God does in the world has to reflect the unity of God. The ancient rule of the church is that all the members of the Trinity act in absolute concert and harmony with each other. We cannot think of one divine person doing something that the others do not also accomplish. What one does the others do as well.

By affirming a material God, Mormons have a more robust understanding of the individuality of each member of the Trinity. They do
not have to presume that a description of what one member of the
Trinity does has to apply equally to the others as well. For Pratt, the
most significant difference among the divine persons concerns their
material status. Simply put, the Father and Son are embodied beings
in a way that the Holy Spirit is not. This means that the Spirit can do
things that the Father and the Son cannot. The Holy Spirit is a kind
of supermaterial substance that is in a class of its own (it is thus a
third kind of matter, beyond both the gross and the refined). Pratt
was inspired in his views by Joseph Smith, who set the Holy Spirit
apart from the Father and the Son by teaching that it does not have
"a body of flesh and bones" like the Father and the Son "but is a personage of Spirit" (D&C 130:22). Smith's statement, however, could
be interpreted in different ways. By the twentieth century, this was
taken to mean that the Holy Spirit has a body of human form distinct from the material composition of the Father and Son but, like
them, is still unable to be omnipresent. Rather than literally dwelling
in the believer's heart, the Holy Spirit's influence is mediated by the
light of Christ. In Pratt's day, the nature of the Holy Spirit was still
an open question, with some Mormons following their Protestant
contemporaries in thinking of the Spirit as the power of God or (in
Augustinian fashion) an emanation flowing between the Father and
the Son. Pratt interpreted Smith to be saying that the Spirit is made
of a material substance that is not a body of flesh and bone. The Holy
Spirit, he argued, like every other entity in the universe, is composed
of particles, but every one of those particles has a capacity for infinite
intelligence. Because each particle is supremely alive, the Holy Spirit
is all-knowing (omniscient), and because each particle is potentially
infinite, the Holy Spirit can be present everywhere (omnipresent).
The Holy Spirit can take the form of a person, but it does not have to.
As an infinite material substance, it is capable of assuming any shape,
but as the most diffuse matter of the universe, it is not limited by any
shape. It is, in fact, something like space itself. Perhaps the best we
can say is that Pratt seems to indicate that the Holy Spirit has pure

extensionality without being located in any specific dimension of space. In any case, due to the peculiarities of its material substance, the Holy Spirit (and it alone) is omniscient and omnipresent, which makes it the very model of divine perfection.

Pratt's position on matter (or the Holy Spirit) did not become Mormon doctrine. Brigham Young, Joseph Smith's successor, never understood it very well (not that anyone could blame him), and what he did understand he impatiently rejected. Nonetheless, there is much to learn from Pratt's speculations. His inquiries into the Holy Spirit show just how convinced he was that nature is as mysterious as God is intelligible, and thus the study of reality must involve both theology and science. The Holy Spirit provided the key to the cosmos for Pratt. His descriptions of it make it sound a lot like the ether that was a standard scientific postulate at the time. He often called it the Holy Fluid, because its substance was uniquely available and universally distributed, even though it was, Pratt admitted, undetectable. Pratt sometimes describes this fluid as a glue holding the universe together, but at other times he attributes cosmic structure to atoms by themselves, since they move of their own volition. The Spirit does seem to sustain physical reality, because it is a structure within and not outside of the cosmos, enabling interconnections throughout the galaxy that would not otherwise be made. For example, it permits minds to communicate with each other across great distances, which is how the Father and the Son communicate with us and how people, dead or alive, can communicate with each other from afar. The Holy Fluid is even faster than light in its ability to pass through opaque bodies and convey its message across vast expanses of space. The communicative power of the Holy Spirit explains why Pratt flirted with various forms of spiritualism that were popular in his day. (*Spiritualism* in this case refers to an assortment of theologies that promoted various means, like séances and mediums, for communicating with the dead.) The Holy Spirit is a kind of gravitational force that, rather than moving physical objects toward each other, lifts the spiritual substance of every object toward higher levels of perfection. It is, in fact, very close to what the ancients called the *world soul*.

The Holy Fluid also provides a metaphysical framework for making sense of the phenomenon of spiritual sight that has been an important but neglected part of Christian tradition. Pratt interpreted Smith's prophetic office in terms of spiritual sight, and he was eager to give spiritual knowledge an empirical foundation. For Pratt, the more our physical vision is saturated with the Holy Spirit, the better we will be able to see objects made of refined matter. "The spirit of man has eyes, as well as his body," Pratt wrote in a book, *Spiritual Gifts*, published in 1856: "The eyes of the spirit are in conjunction with the eyes of the body. When things are seen naturally, the eyes of the spirit behold through the instrumentality of the bodily eyes. When things are beheld spiritually, the spiritual eyes discern without the aid of the natural eyes." That explains why the blind can see spiritually and how unbelievers with great eyesight can be spiritually blind. It also means that we can sharpen our spiritual sight even in our present physical state. Those who are more open to the Holy Spirit can see spiritual phenomena through their physical eyes, such as God's presence at work in the world. They can also see, at special times, God's very form. In the next life, the perfection of this capacity will result in our physical eyes becoming the portal of our celestial shape, and this visionary power will reveal to us all that we want to know. Indeed, we will eventually know everything there is to know as we partake of the Spirit's infinite capacity for understanding.

For all of his speculations about what the Holy Spirit is, it must be admitted that Pratt left open the question of a causal mechanism for how the Holy Spirit guides and influences physical processes. He is honest in admitting that this is a major problem in his theology, but he does not offer much hope for a detailed solution. The best that he can do is to probe human anatomy in order to suggest that there might be more to the body than most scientists ever dreamed. For Pratt, all sensory knowledge is a kind of feeling that parallels the ways atoms themselves apprehend each other. Sensory input becomes spiritual knowledge not by a process of abstraction or contemplation but by intermediary links that must themselves be material in graded ways. Light, for example, must be the source of inner illumination in a way that deepends on its physical properties. "Does the optic nerve act directly upon thy spirit, or are there still further channels of conveyance, intervening between the optic nerve and spirit?" Pratt couched his ruminations about the material effects of religious forces in the form of questions to indicate how reluctant he was to dig any deeper. It is the job of theology, he thought, to push scientists to keep looking closer for the means by which matter gives rise to thought.

The problem with all of these speculations is that Pratt never fully escaped the framework of mind–body dualism. He got rid of it in theory, but in practice, he still had to explain how his two kinds of matter, spiritual and gross, interrelate. Indeed, his two kinds of matter look a lot like what other philosophers call mind and body. True, Pratt argues that there is a continuum between them, but he typically describes that continuum in metaphorical terms, calling it a gradation or refinement. These terms are not sufficiently precise to carry his argument. Besides, his primary metaphorical framework does not refer to *levels* of reality but, rather, to *mixtures* of different kinds of atoms. Because all substances are porous, the atoms of spiritual and physical bodies can be contiguous with each in the most intimate ways. Physical atoms can be compressed and their dimensions can be reduced to make even more room for spiritual atoms to cohabitate in the same space. Every human being, for example, has a spiritual body (an expression Pratt preferred to "the soul") of the exact same shape as his or her physical body. Pratt does not come right out and say this, but at times it seems as if he thinks that spiritual atoms can be best pictured as a liquid that can be poured into bodies made of gross matter to create a new set of sensory possibilities. Spiritual atoms are more fluid than regular atoms, it seems, because they are infinitely smaller. When the spirit saturates a physical body, gross material atoms are surrounded by a sea of spiritual atoms. Their interaction, however, does not result in a new chemical compound, since each form of matter retains its own integrity. Spiritual bodies, for example, are not subject to physical death. Cohabitation seems like a better way to describe this process than a continuum. In fact, Pratt in the end seems to give up on the possibility that these two basic kinds of matter can actually become united. They have a mechanical, not organic, relationship. The Holy Spirit can force physical atoms to make room for an overwhelming spiritual presence, but that does not leave much hope that spirit and matter are continuous and convertible. Pratt thus leaves them looking like two substances that, for all practical purposes, are as far apart as the material and the immaterial in traditional metaphysics.

Pratt's theology of the Holy Spirit is stunningly original, but it has logical problems that make it very precarious—so precarious that it was not even accepted, in full, by his own church. Perhaps most disturbing from a Trinitarian point of view, Pratt appears to elevate the Holy Spirit above the Father and Son in terms of importance and power. Mormons have a dynamic concept of divinity. God does not exist in a static state. Even God the Father is capable of becoming more divine over time. Pratt, however, attributes to the Holy Spirit the pinnacle of eternal perfection. Only the Holy Spirit, not the Father or Son, is omnipotent and omnipresent. Augustine defined the Holy Spirit as the love shared by the Father and Son, but Pratt defines the Holy Spirit as the summation of all perfections that the Father and Son do not fully possess. He also at times attributes the ordering of matter to the Holy Spirit, since, as it is the universal glue of the cosmos, every physical law is a byproduct of its infinite expanse: "What are called the laws of nature are nothing more nor less than the fixed method by which this spiritual matter operates." The Father and Son speak a word of instruction, but the Holy Spirit does all the hard work of governing the cosmos. Gone is the New Testament teaching that Jesus Christ is the Word of God who was with the Father from the very beginning and that "all things came into being through him" (John 1:3). In terms of creation and compassion, the Holy Spirit takes the place of Jesus Christ. The worst heresy in the early church was the subordination of the Son to the Father. Pratt has invented an utterly new form of this heresy by subordinating the Son to the Spirit.

The idea that the Holy Spirit is perfect matter that can take any form also calls into question the uniqueness of the incarnation. In traditional Christian teaching, it is the Son who becomes material in human form, and that relationship (of the divine Son of God to his human body during his earthly life as Jesus) is marked by the most intense intimacy and unity. God identifies with the body of Jesus in such a pronounced way that worshiping Jesus Christ is totally appropriate. The first chapter of Genesis reinforces this point by telling us that humans are created in the image of God (Gen. 1:26–27). According to Genesis, there is something unique about human nature. According to the New Testament, that uniqueness is confirmed by the Son's decision to become embodied as a human being. For Pratt, the Son is already humanlike before the creation, but the Holy Spirit, and not Jesus Christ, tells us what matter really is. The Holy Spirit is perfect matter, yet it is so completely fluid that there is no intrinsic connection between its malleable structure and human nature. Matter, when all is said and done, has very little relationship to the human body.

Nevertheless, Pratt's view of the Holy Spirit is as philosophically prescient as it is theologically deficient. In many ways he anticipates one of the most important philosophical movements of the twentieth century, Process philosophy, which was born out of a frustration with the way philosophy lagged behind the sciences in thinking about matter. Founded by Alfred North Whitehead, an English mathematician and philosopher of science, Process philosophy begins with the premise that the features of the most complex organisms can be found, in some form, in the least complex. Rather than hypothesizing that matter consists of tiny, solid particles or reducing all matter to something nebulous called energy, Process philosophy contends that nature is composed of events, each of which is intimately related to every other event. There is no ongoing substance called matter in Process thought. Nature is always in flux, changing and developing with each new occasion reconfiguring the relationships established by prior events. Nature is just another name for a fluid field of becoming. In nature, the past flows into the future in a process that is every bit as mental as it is physical.

Whitehead wanted to bring together religion, art, and science in a single conception of the physical world, and the result was a holistic cosmology that attributed consciousness and feeling to every level of reality. Every event is an occasion of experience, and even the simplest event exhibits some of the features that we associate with freedom and intelligence. This position, that every single object in the universe has consciousness to some degree, is known as Panpsychism. Whitehead was not the only thinker to defend it, but he was the most systematic. He did not think that mind could emerge from matter unless matter was already in some sense mental. And he did not think that God could be described in terms that radically differ from the vocabulary we use about the physical world. God, for Whitehead, is not an omnipotent and omniscient being. God is no more immaterial than any other event in the cosmos. Rather, God is the one entity who is most intimately related to every other entity. The nature of that relationship, however, is not causal in any controlling way. God is involved in every event in the universe without dictating the outcomes of any of them. He has a persuasive, not a causal, influence on the world. God is like an ongoing event that happens again and again, holding the world together and moving it forward. Whitehead's God, in fact, looks not a little like Pratt's Holy Fluid.

Whitehead was only one of many metaphysicians throughout the last hundred years who have sought to overthrow the traditional view of matter as lifeless and inert. Pratt was a homespun and somewhat naive thinker, so he cannot stand in their company, shoulder to shoulder, but he definitely was working toward the same goal. Although he liked to think about matter in terms of liquid imagery, which was in conflict with his atomism, he would not have been surprised, given his emphasis on motion, to find that vibration is now the preferred model. Physicists who defend what is known as string theory argue that matter is nothing more than vibrations in hyperspace (superstrings vibrate in and out of different dimensions, which some scientists think results in the production of matter). In fact, *vibration* and *fluidity* are often used interchangeably to describe the unpredictable and unsystematic way that matter flows through space.

String theory has also given rise to speculation about the multiverse, rather than universe, and some of Pratt's writings also point in this direction. If there are dimensions of the universe that we cannot ordinarily experience, then it is possible that there are other worlds right here with us, rather than up above and far away. When Pratt describes what he calls our spirit bodies, he seems at times to be thinking in these terms. He also embraces the idea that many worlds were made before our world came into existence and more worlds are yet to come: "We can come to no other conclusion but that worlds, and systems of worlds, and universes of worlds existed in the boundless heights and depths of immensity before the foundations of our earth were laid." He does not refer to dimensions in this and similar quotations, because he was more impressed by the immense expanses of outer space that astronomy was discovering in his day, while dimensionality has to do with the immense expanse of inner space that physicists have discovered within the atom. Nonetheless, Pratt was confident that this universe is not the only one that has ever existed. His theology, in fact, demanded multiple universes in order to provide enough time for matter to achieve its destiny. For Pratt, the length of time it took for matter to evolve into all the organisms that populate planet earth is but an instant compared with the time it must have taken for matter to evolve into the God who shaped and guided the organization of our world, and there must be other worlds that we cannot see in this life that will give us the time and space to become like God ourselves.

Pratt would also be unsurprised by the finding of quantum mechanics that subatomic events are not only inherently uncertain but also immune to the usual barriers put up by long distances. Particles exhibit what physicists call entanglement, which means that what happens to one particle happens immediately to its entangled partner, no matter how far apart they are. Another name for this phenomenon is "nonlocality," since the actions and effects of particles in some situations do not seem to be limited to their location in space. For Pratt, remember, the Holy Fluid makes connections faster than the speed of light. Atoms are connected together in ways that defy the laws of physical nature but not the laws of spiritual nature. Pratt would be quite happy with the thought that scientific breakthroughs are making the physical world look more and more spiritual all the time.

Another trend that Pratt anticipates is the return of cosmological studies in theology and philosophy and especially the reconsideration of the ancient idea, with roots in Plato, that the world has a soul. Many ancient philosophers thought that the world was a living being, with all of its parts connected and held together by an immaterial substance or soul. Christian theologians rejected this idea due to its pantheistic implications (pantheism is the notion that God is identical with all things and thus the world is divine). The idea of a world soul has become popular again in ecological circles that seek to portray the world as an interconnected web whose whole is much greater than the sum of its parts. Some ecologists call the earth Gaia after the ancient Greek goddess as a way of suggesting that nature nurtures us like a mother and deserves our utmost respect. Others talk about the world as God's body, with the implication that God personally feels any violence we inflict on nature. The point to all of these theological innovations is to motivate people to treat the earth as sacred and to reverse practices that push ecological systems out of balance. Pratt imbibed the western pioneer spirit of self-reliance and rugged individualism, but he also provided a rationale for the world having a substantial unity and unique identity long before it became popular in the age of environmentalism.

The world soul is connected to another new idea in physics: the zero-point field. In quantum theory, there are no absolutely empty states of space. Even a vacuum state, which is defined as the lowest possible level of energy, is not completely empty. Physicists call the vacuum state the zero point of energy, but according to quantum mechanics, it will still have fluctuations occurring. Matter at its most basic level seems to be something like a vibrating field of wavelike impulses of energy. In this field, particles pop into and out of existence in unpredictable ways, which has led some scientists to treat the zero-point field as the origin and sustainer of the material universe. Matter comes from vibrations in a wavy field of energy, but where the vibrations come from nobody knows. Some of the most adventurous scientists even think that one day we will be able to tap this field for its energy potential, harnessing its resources for the creation of perpetual energy machines. The controversial biologist Rupert Sheldrake has proposed that the forms of all living organisms are shaped by resonating fields that store and transmit the information necessary for the building of life. Popular books like *The Field: The Quest for the Secret Force of the Universe* by Lynne McTaggart treat this field as the source of human creativity and the means by which everyone is connected to everyone else. Telepathy, spiritual healing, prayer, clairvoyance, the transcendence of mind over matter, and even the resurrection of the dead have all been attributed to the bizarre properties of this field. Needless to say, the zero-point field provides a field day for skeptics looking to police the boundaries between science and pseudoscience. Nonetheless, scientists are agreed that matter is stranger than anyone ever expected it to be. When matter was thought to be hard, dead, dull stuff, it was easy to assume that God and matter were as far apart as they could possibly be. It will not be easy to rethink God's relationship to us by taking into account new views of the material world, but if we want to do that, Pratt's work might end up helping to lead the way.

Speculating about what Pratt right now, in his reconstituted body slipping through the spatial gaps in time, would think about theories of matter today is fun, but it is also completely serious. Matter is up for grabs, and Christian theologians should be bold and creative in rethinking the spiritual realm in the light of new thinking about the nature of matter. Pratt's position is not the only possible one on this issue, but it is audacious, and it should be inspiring to anyone who wants to honor the material world as the basis and foundation of the spiritual.

If contemporary theologians follow the spirit but not the details of Pratt's work, they will treat matter as good, knowable, and a perfection of the divine. Those three attributes of matter need further explication. First, few thinkers have ever emphasized matter's basic goodness as much as Pratt. For Pratt, goodness is built into the very being of every single atom in the universe. Many Christian traditions argue not only that humanity fell away from an original perfection in Adam and Eve but also that the very fabric of nature was torn apart by the fall. For Pratt (and Mormons generally), nothing in nature is inherently ruined because everything has the potential for intelligence and consciousness. Matter is wounded, but wounds are meant to be healed. Matter is motion, and becoming closer to the divine is its goal. The whole universe is involved in a game of catch-up with God, who is matter's leading edge and guiding spirit.

Second, matter is knowable for Pratt in a way that breaks with the Western philosophical tradition from Plato to the present day. True, Pratt's own view of the Holy Fluid indicates that matter is also extremely mysterious. Yet, even in its most spiritual form, matter is wholly identifiable and intelligible. Beginning with Plato, philosophers have treated the essence of matter as lying beyond the furthest reaches of human intelligence, and even modern physics, with all of its spectacular successes, opens up a Pandora's box of mystery with every new hole scientists poke into the atom. For Pratt, science is to be celebrated because nature is truly God's dwelling place and God wants us to know everything about him. Indeed, the closer we come to understanding matter, the more we become like God, and vice versa. In the next life, matter will be revealed in all of its splendid glory. Matter will no longer weigh us down with death and disease but will be the means for our continual transformation and elevation into eternal happiness.

Third, and finally, Pratt insisted that matter is one of the perfections of the divine. God's perfections or attributes are usually divided into positive and negative lists. Positive attributes include truth, goodness, beauty, omnipotence, omnipresence, justice, and intellect. Negative attributes define what God is not rather than what God is, and they usually include simplicity, infinity, and immutability. *Simplicity* means that God is not divisible, *infinity* means that God is not finite, and *immutability* means that God does not change, though theologians admit that how something can be indivisible, infinite, and unchanging is impossible for us to say. By attributing matter to the divine, Mormons, including Pratt, require significant revisions of this list. For one thing, the negative attributes are gone. A material God is divisible, finite, and changeable and thereby not simple, infinite, and immutable. Indeed, it is hard to imagine, from the perspective of Pratt's metaphysics, anything that God cannot be (besides immaterial, that is). A material God also calls into question one of the positive attributes, God's omnipresence, but Pratt solves that by assigning it to the Holy Spirit. Bodies cannot be omnipresent, but the Holy Spirit is not a body. In any case, making matter a perfection of God not only changes how we think about matter but also, and even more importantly, changes how we think about God.

When most believers hear about the idea that God is material or that God has a body, they think that Christian materialism takes the mystery out of the divine. A God who looks like us is not God enough for them, so to speak. Perhaps the most important legacy of Pratt's voluminous writings is to make the case that a material God just might be even more mysterious than an immaterial one. Above all, Pratt's God is able to identify with us just as we are able to relate to him as members of a single community of physical beings. A material God might be even more difficult to describe, given that any such description of the divine must reflect on the essence and potential of matter, yet a material God might be even more surprising, more beautiful, and more loving than an immaterial God. It is probably true that few theologians today will be persuaded by Pratt to explore a material conception of divinity, but at least Pratt demonstrates that metaphysical questions about God's nature are not permanently closed by the long reign of classical theism and that thinking about God can be the source of endless fascination as well as spiritual renewal.

Chapter 4

Branches on the Family Tree: Relatives or Impersonators?

Most people have distant relatives that they hardly know, and some people have relatives that they wish they did not know. My dad was one of eleven children but the only one to leave Kokomo, Indiana, where he grew up, for work in Indianapolis, where I was born. When I was a young boy, we visited Kokomo almost every Sunday afternoon, after church, going from grandma's house to this uncle and that aunt and cousins galore. I had over forty first cousins alone, and since my dad was one of the youngest in his family, many of my cousins had children and even grandchildren when I was just a kid, which gave me more second and third cousins than I could count. I loved all of those Webbs, but I did not know most of them very well, and some of them I did not know at all. And that is not even counting people related to me by marriage and relatives who had friends that were just like brothers or sisters to them. I accepted them all, of course, because my family was a jumble of relations that I did not get myself into. I was born a Webb, no matter how hard it was for me to figure out which Webbs belonged to what branch of the family tree.

What helped when we got together every year for the Webb family reunion was that most of the families brought the same dishes. So I knew them as the Webbs who bring the banana pudding, the aunt who makes the great apple pie, or the family that always contributes carry-out fried chicken. Still, things could get confusing, especially when different branches of the family would tell stories about Grandma and Grandpa Webb that I had never heard. Some of the stories were so surprising that I was often unsure whether they were talking about my grandparents or my great-grandparents—or some line of Webbs entirely unknown to me.

Family trees can be so complicated that they come to resemble scrubby bushes more than elegant oaks or maples. When you look back into the past from the perspective of your own immediate family, the world gets bigger and wider pretty quickly. If you double the number of ancestors in each generation, then ten generations back gives you 1,024 ancestors! If you were to keep going back to a thousand years ago, you would find that you have more ancestors than the total population at that time, which is why genealogists assume that most of the marriages of our distant ancestors were between second cousins. That the human family truly is interrelated, even if it is not one big happy household, is one of the great truths that both history and biology should teach us. Nevertheless, most human families are not perfect, and many people have a side to their family that they do not want to totally claim as their own.

When I was growing up I could still hear older folks at my church call each other brother and sister (as in "Hello, Brother Bob"), but even though that custom has declined in most churches today, Christianity remains a family affair. In fact, one of the reasons Christianity grew so rapidly while it was being persecuted in the Roman Empire is that it gave people family ties that were not dependent on clan, village, or bloodline. Mormons do a better job than any church I know in not only retaining the language of family (everyone is a brother, sister, or elder) but actually putting those family bonds into practice. Mormons are well known for taking care of their own, a practice that has deep roots in their history. During their years in Missouri, Smith came up with the idea of what he called consecration. People were asked to deed their property to the church, which would then distribute resources on the basis of need as well as talent. The goal was efficiency as well as generosity, with the year-end excess made available to the less fortunate. This practice was briefly and unsuccessfully revived by Brigham Young in Utah, and some commentators have called it an experiment in socialism. Like all radical redistribution schemes, this one failed. The intention behind consecration later morphed into the obligation of all Mormons to tithe 10 percent of their income to the church. Much of this money is used to support a Mormon welfare system that has been lauded as a model of charitable activity. Indeed, studies have shown that Mormons are much more likely to give a full 10 percent of their income to the church than evangelicals, their closest competitors in church donations.

Mormons try to be a family to each other, which can bother outsiders put off by their tight-knit connections. They can seem like an elite club, a closed clique, or a secret society. It is not easy for any group that sets itself apart from the world to have good public relations. Nevertheless, levels of suspicion and mistrust between Mormon Christians and non-Mormon Christians that are completely understandable are often taken way too far. Many Christians treat Mormons as members of an exotic religious species that has nothing in common with the Christian genome. It pains me to say it, but conservative Christians are some of the loudest and meanest voices when it comes to deriding and mocking Mormonism. Social trends have contributed to this situation. The powers of political correctness exercise a kind of vigilante control over much public discourse, especially in schools, and as a result, some groups earn an unofficial privilege by being designated "off limits" to criticism, especially of the impolite kind. People who do not belong to these groups resent their favorable status, of course, which builds up pressure to find new scapegoats to take their place. Mormons are no longer subjected to physical persecution, but they are still subjected to thoughtless and frequent verbal abuse. To make matters worse, Mormons do not fit any of the criteria for claiming a protected minority status. Being a subset of the dominant Christian culture, they cannot claim to be powerless, and being primarily white (in America, at least, though not in the many churches they have planted abroad), they are not the victims of racism. Furthermore, they are traditionalists when it comes to gender and sexuality issues, so they uphold unpopular patriarchal values in very public ways. Besides, they have a lot of political power in Utah, so what could be so wrong in ganging up on them every so often?

What really makes them a target, however, is the fact that people who find their beliefs repugnant come from *both* the Christian and the secularist camps. I can think of no other group that brings together Christians and atheists in such a unifying manner—and not just any kind of Christian or secularist but the most fervent and hard core. Fervent Christians see in Mormonism a mirror distorting their own faith, reflecting an image strangely recognizable yet recognizably strange. Hard-core secularists think that Mormonism is the best example of the strangeness inherent in all religious belief. Some agnostics are open to the possibility that there is an ethereal spiritual being working behind the scenes in some vague way, but the idea that God has a body not unlike our own can be a scandal to the materialistic mindset. Deriding Mormonism thus pulls off the neat trick of making the devout and the godless feel as if they are on the same side, and with both Christians and anti-Christians eager to denounce Mormons, such mockery does not often get censured and denounced.

Non-Mormon Christians need to think long and hard about why they do not at least acknowledge, let alone embrace, Mormons as their brothers and sisters in the faith. I am not throwing any stones here, because I too used to think of Mormonism as little more than an exotic abnormality on the Christian tree—a blight that a spray of orthodox pesticide could go a long way toward eradicating. I was not overtly hostile. When I taught Mormon history to college students, I congratulated myself on my high-minded tolerance in emphasizing its remarkable spirit of endurance, its organizational savvy, and the sheer scope of its religious imagination. Yet I regret to say that I did not try to hide my condescension. With a nod and a wink I conveyed to my students the impression that my more orthodox faith was so far above Mormonism that I could not even be bothered to criticize their doctrines in any detail.

I have come to repent this view, and not just because I came to my senses about how wrong it is to be rude toward somebody else's faith.

I changed my mind because I came to realize just how deeply Christ-centered Mormonism is. Mormonism is more than Christianity, of course—most obviously, by adding the Book of Mormon to the Bible as a "third testament"—and for many Christians, that makes it much less than Christianity as well. Nevertheless, the fact that Mormonism adds to the traditional Christian story does not necessarily mean that it detracts from Christianity to the point of denying it altogether. After all, what gives Christianity its identity is its commitment to the divinity of Jesus Christ. And on that ground Mormons are more Christian than the many Christians who, under the spell of skeptical historians and demythologizing theologians, do not take seriously the astounding claim that Jesus is the Son of God.

The leading theologians of many mainline Protestant churches have backed away from strong claims about the divinity of Jesus Christ. These theologians typically self identify as liberal, but I want to point out that liberalism means something very specific in theology, whatever it might (or might not) mean in politics. In theology, *liberalism* refers to a very particular intellectual movement, and scholars are in agreement about how to define it (unlike in politics, where the meaning of the word *liberal* is the subject of much debate). In its original form, liberal theology promoted the fatherhood of God, the brotherhood of man, the infinite value of the human soul, the moral example of Jesus, and the church as a means to establishing a moral kingdom on earth. That is a long list, and some of these tenets have been revised over the years, but the moral example of Jesus is probably still the most important item on the liberal agenda. Liberal theology rejects or minimizes the supernatural as a distraction from the task of making this world a better place. Christians are called to love their neighbors and side with the poor in the struggle for justice, and the church, liberals believe, should be on the vanguard of any movement that is working toward those goals. Liberals look to the life of Jesus for reassurance and guidance in their dedication to serve others. There is no need, then, to think of Jesus as a divine human being. Consequently, much liberal theology assigns the idea that he came down from heaven, was born of the Virgin Mary, and became man to the dustbins of discredited mythology.

Liberal theology, which was founded in Germany in the nineteenth century and took off in the United States in the early twentieth, is alive and well in many churches today, and to be fair, it has developed and grown over the years. In fact, one of its main undertakings is to ensure that Christianity keeps up with progressive social trends by changing with the times. Liberal theology, for example, no longer advocates the idea of the infinite value of the human soul. Humans are set apart by God, but they are a part of creation and are not absolutely unique. Nonhuman animals also have moral value. Moreover, the male language in the list I gave above would need to be changed if the list were to be updated to include feminist concerns today. The emphasis on the moral teachings, rather than the divine personage, of Jesus, however, has changed only in the sense that its defenders have become more strongly convinced of its truth. Liberal theology uses historical scholarship to argue that the four Gospels were written long after the life of Jesus and cannot possibly be taken as historically reliable records. All we know about the historical Jesus is how he inspired others to change their lives, and that is what we should learn from Jesus today. Any attempt to treat him as a uniquely divine human being who was the Son of God is nothing more than metaphysical speculation.

Whatever one thinks about Joseph Smith's claims regarding the origins of the Book of Mormon, it is impossible to deny that the book is full of a Jesus who is very divine. Smith's Jesus is as far from liberalism as it is possible to get. There is also no question, however, that the Book of Mormon adds to the Gospel portrait of Jesus. The Book of Mormon, that is, has stories about and sayings by Jesus that do not appear in the New Testament. The really crucial question, then, is the following: Does the Book of Mormon add to the Gospels in a way that is consistent with the New Testament, or does it damage or deface the Gospel portrait?

Keep in mind that the New Testament depiction of Jesus is already complex and multifaceted. There are four Gospels written from distinct points of view as well as letters from the Apostle Paul and others. I agree with those Christians who believe that the four Gospels can be harmonized to show how they fit together without any significant contradictions or major inconsistencies, yet I admit that this process of harmonization is not easy. Part of the richness of the New Testament is the unfinished quality of its depiction of Jesus. Jesus Christ was too great a figure to be captured by a single narrative, and even four Gospels do not do him justice. How do I know this? The Gospels themselves say so. The Gospel according to John ends with these words: "But there are also many other things Jesus did; if every one of them were written down, I suppose that the world itself could not contain the books that would be written" (John 21:25). Indeed, the claim that the disciples passed along teachings that are not recorded in the Bible is fundamental to Roman Catholicism. An ongoing tradition of oral teaching, preserved and promoted by the successors to the original apostles, is foundational to Catholic belief and practice. Catholics also insist that the Holy Spirit guided the early church in its theological development, drawing on verses like this one, also from John: "I still have many things to say to you but you cannot bear them now. When the Spirit of truth comes, he will guide you into all the truth; for he will not speak on his own, but will speak whatever he hears, and he will declare to you the things that are to come" (John 16:12–13). Clearly, the Bible itself authorizes the idea that the written texts passed down to us do not exhaust all that we can know about Jesus.

Let me be clear: I am not asking non-Mormons to consider the truthfulness of what is in the Book of Mormon, although that would not be a bad idea. All I am asking is whether traditional Christians can consider the possibility that the Book of Mormon adds to the plural but coherent portrait of Jesus that emerges from the four Gospels in a way that complements or expands on that account without marring it in any significant way. Of course, there are additions, and then there are additions! Adding too much sugar to a cake recipe might make some kids happy, but it can destroy the dessert for the adults. Adding certain chemicals together in a lab without proper supervision can

be explosive. Not all additions, however, have such a negative outcome. I can add more soy milk to my cereal in the morning, and it
will still be the same cereal. And I can add wheat germ to it, and it will
be even healthier cereal. It is important, then, to examine the Book
of Mormon and subsequent teachings by Joseph Smith to determine
just how expansive and supplementary his portrait of Jesus is.

I have already confessed that I used to join the crowd in making light of Mormon beliefs. Now I must confess that I only read the
Book of Mormon for the first time four or five years ago. I already
knew the basic outline of its narrative, and I had read a lot about it,
but there is no substitute for the real thing. The Book of Mormon
recounts the journey of a people God led from Jerusalem to the
Americas six hundred years before the birth of Christ. In America,
they split into two groups, the good guys (the Nephites) and the bad
guys (the Lamanites), and they battled each other until there were
no good guys left—except for Moroni (Mormon's son), who buried
the chronicles of their wars and then, in 1823, appeared in angelic
form to a farm boy from upstate New York and told him where to
find them.

That is the outline that I already knew. When I actually read this
book, however, I was utterly surprised by what I found. The Book of
Mormon, I found, is utterly obsessed with Jesus Christ, and I concluded that everything it teaches is meant to awaken, encourage, and
deepen faith in him. There are many characters in this book, and many
events, but Jesus stands out from beginning to end: "And we talk of
Christ, we rejoice in Christ, we preach of Christ, we prophesy of Christ,
and we write according to our prophecies, that our children may know
to what source they may look for a remission of their sins" (2 Nephi
25:26). And not just Jesus: the whole Gospel in all of its theological
details—right down to debates about baptism, the relationship of law
to grace, and the problem of divine foreknowledge—is taught to the
people of the New World centuries before Jesus was even born.

Christians have long interpreted the Old Testament in terms of
the New. When Ezekiel had a vision of "something that seemed like
a human form" (Ezek. 1:26) seated on a throne on top of a dome, it

was only natural that early Christians would claim that Ezekiel saw Jesus. Sophisticated theologians such as Origen and Augustine, however, put a stop to this kind of literalism because it suggested that Jesus had a body (or at least some kind of physical form) before the incarnation. They thought that Jesus in his identity as the Son of God before he became man was just as immaterial as God the Father, and so there was nothing to him that could be seen. Today, it is completely unfashionable to try to find Jesus in between the lines, so to speak, in texts written by and for the Jewish people. Smith is a throwback to the earliest years of Christian interpretation of the Old Testament. He was an unabashed enthusiast for multiple revelations of Jesus. Rather than finding hints or symbols of Jesus' presence in the ancient world, Smith thought that Jesus made himself completely accessible long before the incarnation. Smith replaced the figurative with the figure himself. The truth of Jesus is eternal, Smith thought, so it should not be surprising to learn that Christ was made known in times and places beyond our imagination.

Smith's Christocentric view of sacred history is made clear in the first chapter of the Book of Moses, a revision of the Bible based on a revelation he received in 1830. When Moses sees God face to face, God tells Moses about his only begotten Son, who will be the Savior of the world. Mormons believe that ancient Israel lost this saving knowledge, which resulted in distortions of the original Old Testament texts, necessitating Smith's revisions. The Book of Mormon set Smith on a path to discover the hidden depths of the Old Testament, and out of those depths emerged a historical perspective that is Christ-centered without remainder or reserve. Rather than being seen as an insult to the integrity of the Old Testament, then, the Book of Moses should be seen as the highest compliment that Smith can pay to the ancient Israelites: God did not withhold from them the full truth of divine revelation. The Old Testament is not merely a preparatory history that can be superseded by the New. Jesus is the face of God from the very beginning of creation.

Long before his birth in Bethlehem, Jesus was eager to appear to the chosen people in order to tell them the most specific details of his future life and ministry. Nephi, for example, who wrote the first two books of the Book of Mormon and was part of the migration from Jerusalem, already knew all about Jesus: "For according to the words of the prophets, the Messiah cometh in six hundred years from the time that my father left Jerusalem; and according to the words of the prophets, and also the word of the angel of God, his name shall be Jesus Christ, the Son of God" (2 Nephi 25:19). Likewise, a Nephite king named Benjamin declared around 124 B.C., "And lo, he shall suffer temptations, and pain of body, hunger, thirst, and fatigue, even more than man can suffer, except it be unto death; for behold, blood cometh from every pore, so great shall be his anguish for the wickedness and the abominations of his people. And he shall be called Jesus Christ" (Mosiah 3:7–8). King Benjamin is referring here to Christ's suffering in the Garden of Gethsemane.

The climax of the four Gospels is Jesus' resurrection. Likewise, every page of the Book of Mormon prepares the way for a stunning amplification of that climax, which is a post-resurrection appearance of Jesus to the ancient peoples of America. For Joseph Smith, Christ's appearance in the Americas is no more (and no less!) miraculous than Christ's appearance to so many people in and around Jerusalem after his resurrection. Non-Mormon Christians, of course, do not believe that Jesus visited the Americas, but why should they be troubled if the Saints tell stories about Jesus that seem far-fetched to them? To address this question, let me return to the language of family relations with which I began this chapter, and let me create a thought experiment to help clarify what is at stake in the attitude creedal Christians (Christians committed to the early creeds, especially the Trinitarianism of the Nicene Creed) have toward Mormon Christians.

Imagine the following scenario. Your family gathers at the funeral of your dearly beloved grandfather, a world traveler. Your relatives begin telling the familiar stories about his legendary adventures. Soon, however, you notice another group of mourners at the other end of the room. As you eavesdrop on them, you realize that they are talking about your grandfather as if they knew him well, yet you have never met these people or heard some of the stories they are telling.

These new stories are not insulting to his memory, though some ring more true than others. Indeed, this group seems to have as high an opinion of your grandfather as you do. What do you do?

Do you invite them over to meet your family? That is a tough call. Some of your relatives will dispute the credibility of these stories, and others might make a scene. Others will feel left out—Why didn't Grandfather tell us all of his stories?—if they think that the other family's stories are true. The funny thing is, though, that this other group of mourners knows all of the stories your family likes to tell about the deceased, even though your family does not know their stories. And their stories sound strangely familiar, more like exaggerations or embellishments than slander or deceit. Clearly, the two groups have a lot to talk about! However you decide to handle the situation, there is no need for you to change your love for your grandfather. There is also no need for you to react to this other group's love for your grandfather as if they are trying to threaten or harm you. Whether or not you decide to expand your family to include this group, you can still welcome them for their sincere efforts to honor and respect your grandfather's memory. And the more you love your grandfather, the more you will be drawn to discover for yourself whether these new stories are true.

Of course, Jesus Christ is not your grandfather, and the stories Christians tell about him are grounded in scripture, not legends and lore. Still, the Book of Mormon raises a very awkward question for Christians. Can you believe too much about Jesus? Can you go too far in conceiving his glory? Can you be too credulous about his work in sacred history? Let me answer those questions by posing several of my own. Isn't the whole point of affirming Jesus' divinity the idea that one can never say enough about him? Will we ever be done fathoming the vastness of his glory? Is the story of his eternal existence reducible to the three years of his earthly ministry, much of it spent along the shores of the Sea of Gaililee?

And here, perhaps, are the two most important questions of all. Shouldn't Smith's stories be judged by whether they draw people to the four Gospels in order to learn more about Christ? And if they do that, doesn't that weigh in favor of their plausibility, if not their truth?

I am not denying that the Mormon Jesus is different from the Jesus of traditional Christianity. Most of those differences, however, are theologically insignificant. Mormons, for example, stress that the atoning suffering of Jesus began in the Garden of Gethsemane and culminated on the cross. To some evangelicals, this downplays the soteriological function of the cross, but it is arguably an accurate reading of the Gospels (see Luke 22:44). Some critics who play the game of "gotcha" point out that the Book of Mormon places the birth of Jesus in Jerusalem, not Bethlehem. This is good news for biblical fundamentalists who use such discrepancies to score debating points. The Mormon response to this criticism, however, is a game ender. The Book of Mormon (and remember, the events in it take place among people several generations removed from their time in Jerusalem) places Jesus' birth "at Jerusalem which is the land of our forefathers" (Alma 7:10) in much the same way that I say I live in Indianapolis to non-Hoosiers rather than explaining that I actually live in Brownsburg, a suburb on Indianapolis's western border.

Of course, the one significant difference is that Mormons believe that Jesus Christ was never purely immaterial. Smith developed his materialistic interpretation of the spiritual realm mainly after the Book of Mormon, but it is anticipated in that book's most extraordinary scene. In an appearance to the unnamed brother of Jared, Jesus is so sensitive to the overwhelming impression made by the revelation of his corporeal form that he reveals only his little finger. Jared's brother says, "I saw the finger of the Lord, and I feared lest he should smite me; for I knew not that the Lord had flesh and blood" (Ether 3:8). Later Jesus shows Jared's brother his whole body, which, it turns out, is a premortal spirit body, composed of a finer material substance than anything known on earth. Is this revelation an insult to the incarnation? I do not think so, because the preexistent Jesus is not embodied in the exact same way that we are. His birth on earth is still a marvelous and wondrous miracle. In fact, I think that Smith expands the mystery of the incarnation without diminishing it in any significant way. Christianity traditionally limits the incarnation to a fixed number of years that can be dated on a calendar; Smith makes the incarnation a movable feast.

Christianity has always affirmed the goodness of matter and the integrity of the human body, but Mormonism takes that Christian virtue to an extreme. For Smith, Christ's preexistent form was already the model for what we were to become. The importance of Smith's claim resides, I think, in his vision that, although the incarnation happened in a particular place and time, the Son has always been Jesus. No other Christian has taken Hebrews 13:8 so literally: "Jesus Christ is the same yesterday and today and forever." The body of Jesus Christ is the eternal image of all bodies, spiritual and physical alike. Mormons do not use this exact same language, but I would say that they raise the possibility that the incarnation is a specification (or material intensification) of his premortal state, not the first (and only) time that God and matter unite.

The material view of divinity has metaphysical implications that are counterintuitive to anyone immersed in classical theism. For example, the Saints believe that souls cannot become perfect without becoming embodied, which is the exact reverse of Plato's assumption that perfection involves the soul's escape from embodiment. The Saints also believe that God the Father progressed into his bodily form, as did Jesus Christ in his premortal state. To traditional Christians, these are disturbing thoughts, but is it a compliment or an insult to propose that Christ's preexistent form is so perfect that it took countless billions of years to evolve? Mormons are committed to this dynamic view of divinity because they believe that there is no eternity outside of time. Everything is in time, and if so, then everything grows and changes, including God. From the perspective of traditional concepts of eternity, to say that Christ grew into his glorious identity is a slur. It implies that he was not fully divine. From the Mormon perspective, however, nothing exists without undergoing change. Indeed, the longer a being has been evolving, the more that being has changed and thus the more perfect it is. That is why

Mormons like the biblical passage where Paul calls Christ the first born of creation (Col. 1:15). Christ is the very definition of what being born means because he has grown into the fullness of divinity long before the world was made.

By treating the spiritual as a dimension of the material, Mormons overcome every trace of dualism between this world and the next. Matter is perfectible because it is one of the perfections of the divine. Even heaven is an aspect or dimension of this world, far away but not radically different from planet earth. For Mormons, our natural loyalties and loves have an eternal significance, which is why marriages will be preserved in heaven. Mormons take the lid off heaven when they interpret our participation in God to mean that we will share God's power and creativity. Our bodies are literally temples of the divine, which is why the Saints wear sacred garments underneath regular clothing.

It goes without saying that none of this should be taken lightly. Mormon metaphysics calls for the revision of nearly every Christian belief, which is why Smith—who was a reviver, not a revivalist—combed through the earliest Christian traditions looking for practices and beliefs that later theologians discarded on the assumption that the spiritual is immaterial. The result can look like a hodgepodge to an outsider.

Mormons are certainly nonconformists when it comes to many aspects of orthodox dogma, but creedal Christians should examine aberrations from Christian tradition from a Christological perspective. Many scholars believe that Islam, for example, was born out of heretical teachings about Christ that were common in Muhammad's day. Islam denies that Jesus died on the cross and rejects his divinity. Nonetheless, this has not stopped many leading theologians from claiming that Muslims and Christians worship the same God. Gnosticism also departs from traditional teachings about Jesus by portraying him as a playful and enigmatic cynic who reveled in ridiculing religious authority. Yet Gnostic forms of spirituality are making a comeback today precisely because they strip away from Jesus the stories of his miracles, his claims to divinity, and the evidence of his resurrection. Mormonism runs in the exact opposite direction of Muslim and New Age portraits of Jesus. Where they fall short, Mormons go overboard. Where Islam, Gnosticism, and much of liberal theology trivializes the divinity of Jesus, Mormons eternalize his body. If any follower of Christ had to choose between a Jesus who began his ministry long before he was born in Bethlehem and a Jesus whose ministry was hardly different from any other great moral teacher, I hope it would be a very easy decision.

Chapter 5

Mormon Overreach? Brigham Young and Parley Pratt

Mormons tend to treat their history as a sacred script, and who can blame them? The early years of Mormonism are so full of persecution and triumph, exile and sojourn, as well as incredible adventures at home and abroad that they have taken on sacramental significance in the Mormon mind. This history, which has only recently been discovered by secular, professional historians, who have rushed in to mine its incredible characters and unbelievable episodes, is a perfect complement to Mormon metaphysics. The stories of individuals such as Joseph Smith, Brigham Young, and the Pratt brothers (Orson and Parley) are as monumental as the ideas they suffered to defend. There is surely a correlation between the largeness of their lives and the largeness of their ideas. Anyone who reads about early Mormons, whether leaders or followers, quickly discovers, no matter what one might think about Mormonism as a branch of Christianity, that these men and women were unusually heroic in their fight for religious freedom. They faced enormous hardships with integrity, humor, and grace. They could do so because they were convinced that they had something new to tell the world. Their lives were as oversized as their message.

That does not mean that everything the early Mormons believed was true or that everything they did was morally upright and virtuous. Indeed, big ideas are risky because they can easily get out of hand, just as adventures are dangerous when people stray from well worn paths. Two ideas are often held up as particularly indicative of

the hazardous consequences of early Mormon enthusiasm and boldness. The first is theocracy, the idea that the only true government
is one that answers to God's authority and thus church and state
should be one and the same thing. The second is polygamy (or plural
marriage, as Mormons called it), which Latter-day Saints President
Wilford Woodruff terminated in a manifesto issued in 1890 (a prohibition that was effectively enforced by President Joseph F. Smith
beginning in 1904). Polygamy is ancient history to Mormons today,
and so is theocracy, although I will argue that the attempt of early
Latter-day Saints to meld theology and politics has been replaced by
a similar effort regarding religion and economics (broadly construed).
That is, the Saints gave up trying to exercise political power over their
beloved Utah, but they did not give up on the dream of building the
kingdom of God in this world and not just the next. Capitalism has
replaced politics as the social means by which the Saints advance
their mission.

   I want to examine these two ideas, theocracy and polygamy,
through the lens of two of Mormonism's greatest heroes, Brigham
Young and Parley Pratt. These two men led lives at a level of ambition and passion that is almost unimaginable today. They also left
their mark on Smith's revelations, developing his theology in significant and sometimes radical ways. Their stories are evidence of how
inspiring Smith's theology could be, but both men also took some
of Smith's ideas in extreme and controversial directions. Young
pushed hard to make Utah a theocracy, and after many successes, he
ultimately failed. Nonetheless, during his lifetime he also came to
realize that economics would have to supplant politics as the means
of building up the Saints' kingdom of God. Pratt, meanwhile, lost
his life to a conflict that arose from his plural marriages. His tragic
tale presages the end of the Saints' most distinctive and notorious
early practice. The story of these two men demonstrates that Smith's
ideas were not only ambitious and far-reaching but also ultimately
elastic, since the Latter-day Saints gave up polygamy altogether and
reinvented theocracy to meet the new challenges of the changing
political landscape.

BRIGHAM YOUNG

Photos of Brigham Young do not show him in the best light. His hair is long and unkempt, like a pageboy without the bangs, and his lips are pursed between a smirk and a smile. His eyes display a slight squint, as if he is daring the viewer to guess his state of mind. Joseph Smith's successor in the Mormon Church, Young was as tough looking and rough spoken as Smith was handsome and charismatic. He was a schemer, while Smith was a dreamer, which helps explain why Smith is immensely easier to love (or at least appreciate). Smith, for all of his charisma and revelations, was a modest man who went out of his way not to draw attention to himself. Young was pugnacious and seemed to delight in controversy. Both Smith and Young lacked a formal education, but Smith, who was not a particularly eloquent speaker, was at home in the world of books and ideas, while Young loved to take center stage, and his speeches, which must have been the only entertainment many of the early Mormon pioneers had, were theatrical performances. Young was, in the words of John G. Turner, the author of the magnificent biography *Brigham Young: Pioneer Prophet*, "blunt spoken, pugnacious, and sometimes profane." He was not a cautious speaker or a careful thinker, but he was a great leader. He was a man of action who was as good with his hands as he was loose with his words. He was sufficiently bold and strong, in fact, to begin implementing the audacious metaphysical system that he inherited from Joseph Smith.

Young's personality was as big as the Utah territory he spent thirty years defending from the U.S. government, non-Mormon emigrants, and its own native population. He was, in a word, a character, but he also had great character, in the sense of strength of will and depth of vision. Without Young, Mormons would not have had much of a history to tell or a church to spread. Young was thrust into the limelight with Smith's assassination, and he rose to the challenge. Smith imagined countless kingdoms in the heavens above, but Young built one in the Great Salt Lake basin that is still going strong. Young delighted in the comparison his followers made between him and

Moses—both were lawgivers as well as determined men of action who fought against impossible odds for religious freedom—except that Young made sure that he did not die before he entered (and ruled) his promised land.

Young compared himself with Moses because they both got things done, but in the early Christian world, it was a commonplace to treat Moses as a philosopher, not a city planner. Jewish thinkers and Christian theologians claimed that the Greeks borrowed their best ideas from Moses. Philo of Alexandria (20 B.C.–A.D. 50), whose synthesis of Greek and Jewish thought was a significant source of inspiration for Christian theology, suggested that the Greeks refused to acknowledge Moses's philosophical superiority out of envy. The ancients thought that anyone who could bridge the gulf between humans and God must have an abundance of wisdom, and Jews and Christians thought that nobody, prior to Jesus Christ, bridged that gulf better than Moses. Moses was not a philosopher in the modern sense of a professional who publishes in journals and gives papers at meetings or even in the ancient sense of valuing contemplation over action, but he did, after all, found the first religion based on a belief in a single God. Young too brought an entire people to knowledge of God and did so as a result of trying to bridge the gulf between the spiritual and the material. Young, in other words, was just as much a *practical* philosopher as Moses. According to Philo, Moses gave his people the perfect law, and thus he was a philosopher king. In that sense, Young too was a philosopher king, but since the law of his land was often in conflict with the federal law of the United States, he was more successful fusing the Mormon faith with the world of trade and commerce.

Young's accomplishments have to be put in the context of the battles he had to fight. He was full of verbal antics and theatrical inclinations, but he was also incredibly successful in transforming the American West. He led the Saints to Utah, where they staked their claim to approximately one-sixth of the western United States. Young was thus one of the greatest colonizers in American history. He also oversaw the settlement of thousands of emigrants to Utah.

He did all of this while marrying at least fifty-five women, making him one of the most-married men in American history. He could be intemperate in dealing with subordinates, but nobody who studies his life can be unmoved by the enormous responsibilities he faced and the ingenuity and industry of his undertakings.

Young's exemplary life gave voice to many of the cultural and theological tensions that Mormonism holds together. His pioneering spirit was evidence of his belief in good works over grace, yet his sermons emphasized just how much the faithful should depend upon and support one another. He was a man of enterprise who loved theological speculations; a defender of the right to divorce, especially for women, who sealed marriages in the Mormon temple for all of eternity; and a staunch believer in lay leadership who ruled over the Mormon Church like an autocrat. Perhaps most paradoxically, he was forced to build a city in the middle of the desert in order to have a place where Mormons could begin their audacious dream of collapsing the distance between heaven and earth.

None of this could have been predicted based on Young's early life. After he was born in Vermont, his family moved to rural New York looking for prosperity but found destitution and misery instead. His mother died when he was a teenager, and after that he was on his own, a situation that forced him to develop the independent streak he demonstrated throughout his life.

He was nearly thirty and dirt poor when he became acquainted with the Smith family. "When I saw Joseph Smith," Young later recalled, "he took heaven and brought it down to earth; and he took earth, and brought it up." Like Smith, Young was not comfortable with the plethora of competing Christian traditions clamoring for his attention. The audacity of Smith's Book of Mormon lit his imagination on fire: "I found it impossible to take hold of either end of it; I found it was from eternity, passed through time, and into eternity again." For the rest of his life Young never faltered in his confidence in the story Smith claimed to have translated from golden plates.

Smith sent him to England "without purse or scrip" to "preacht as opertunity presented" (Young was always embarrassed about his poor spelling and bad grammar). In London he took in the tourist sights and began showing his genius for organization. The mission was a great success, with hundreds sailing for America and thousands more to follow over the years.

Before Smith's death, Young's leadership style was collaborative and deferential, traits that would change dramatically when Young became Smith's successor. Young was outside of Boston when he heard about Smith's assassination. He had already assumed a prominent role in the church's ritual of proxy baptism for the dead, and he married more women in Nauvoo, Illinois, than anyone else, including Smith. What really helped him rise to the top of the Mormon hierarchy after his return to Nauvoo was his ability to divert the loyalty that Mormons had to the Smith family into new social bonds and religious practices.

Smith left behind a number of secret rituals, increasingly specu-lative theological ideas, and a worldly ambition that knew no bounds. Young was determined to carry on the full range of this legacy, and knowing his value to the Saints, he was also resolved to avoid becom-ing another martyr to his faith. After his succession was secured, his first order of business was leading the Mormons out of Nauvoo and into Utah, and this exodus brought out the best characteristics of his leadership style. He was steady and calm under fire, comfort-able with power, and exercised his authority without hesitation or compunction. His tremendous energy was always focused on mak-ing Mormonism both a religious and worldly success, and he was not above finding scapegoats in order to advance his agenda. When his authority was threatened, for example, he often resorted to sharp-ening his millennial rhetoric by denouncing the United States and predicting its imminent demise.

Like Smith, Young was constantly looking for rituals that would tie the Mormon community together. "Men will have to be sealed to men," he proclaimed in 1859, "until the chain is united from Father Adam down to the last Saint." He was also always coming up with quixotic schemes to make the Mormon Church more financially solvent. He even tried to create a unique phonetic alphabet for the Latter-day Saints.

Evidence that he tried to outspeculate Smith lies in his theological teachings on Adam, which were much maligned in his lifetime,
even within Mormon circles, and are fortuitously neglected today.
Young begins with the idea that if Christ is a second Adam, as Paul
claimed (1 Cor. 15:45, 47), then Adam must be a kind of first Christ
(Rom. 5:14), at least in his pre-fallen state. This view of Adam is certainly daring, but Young takes it beyond the realm of serious consid-
eration by arguing that Adam had a hand in organizing this world
before he became a member of it, which means that Adam can be
called "our Father, our God, and the only God we have to do with."
Needless to say, Young was not a systematic theologian, and he could
get carried away by the power of his own rhetoric. The same speaking
skills that enabled him to connect with every stratum of society led
him to overestimate his ability to splice church doctrine.

If Young had a preferred rhetorical trope, it would be hyperbole.
His expansive rhetoric was reflective of the wide-open spaces of the
West, and his ecclesial leadership depended on big gestures and dramatic performances. Young's public speech was often not intended
to be taken literally. Take, for example, his chilling advocacy of blood
atonement for capital crimes, which Young presented as "a form of
spiritual charity." While it is true that Young promoted this doctrine
off and on for several years, it is best understood as a product of his
theatrical flair rather than a serious judicial proposal.

Young ruled with a strong hand, and he welcomed hard times,
firmly believing that only fierce struggles with trials and tribulations
could turn individual Mormons into a people set apart by their own
enduring character. He praised hard work, fought hard to build up
the wealth of the church, and died a very wealthy man. He wanted
the Mormon people to be as prosperous as their beliefs were peculiar.
He also bestowed on future generations a tendency toward defen-
siveness and secrecy as a protection against outsiders and enemies.
Smith's metaphysical principles were as wild and radical as Young's
leadership was consistent and stable. Smith's philosophy sought to
unite the spiritual and the material, and that is exactly what Young
set out to accomplish in Utah. If this world already, even in its most

material form, anticipates the next world, then the sacred and the secular are one and the same thing. There can be no separation of church and state, reason and faith, or religion and politics. Of course, Mormons today accept and affirm the Constitution and all of its principles, but that is why Young is so important. When he established the Mormon kingdom in Utah, he brooked no division between the Mormon Church and every aspect of social and cultural life. Nonetheless, by the time of his death, he had compromised many of his goals in order to open the way for Utah to become part of the United States.

Young took Smith's emphasis on the eternal law and turned it into a guide for living: "Our religion is nothing more or less than the true order of heaven—the system of laws by which the gods and the angels are governed." The Mormon Church governs its members, he argued, by the same principles that govern the heavens and the cosmos, with the goal of beginning here and now the exaltation that is fulfilled in the afterlife: "We are in eternity, and all that we have to do is to take the road that leads into the eternal lives. Eternal life is an inherent quality of the creature, and nothing but sin can put a termination to it." Knowledge is thus completely unified: "There is one true system and science of life, all else tends to death." Mormonism is the quest to put the eternal law into practice. As a result, the differences between philosophy and theology collapse: "Natural philosophy is the plan of salvation, and the plan of salvation is natural philosophy." The comprehensiveness of the eternal law means that absolutely nothing is unknowable: "There is no mystery throughout the whole plan of salvation, only to those who do not understand." Putting religion to practical use is not a betrayal of a pure philosophy of religion, nor is it merely the application of the theory of theology: "A theoretical religion amounts to very little real good or advantage to any person. To possess an inheritance in Zion or in Jerusalem only in theory—only in imagination—would be the same as having no inheritance at all. It is necessary to get a deed of it, to make an inheritance practical, substantial and profitable." A practical religion is what Jesus preached: "The religion of Jesus Christ is a matter-of-fact religion, and taketh hold of the every-day." By trying to bring heaven to earth, Young thought that he had solved the very old battle between works and grace. Hard work and gratitude were two sides of the same profitable coin.

Two provocative implications follow. First, taking responsibility for yourself and your family is such a fundamental obligation that it should precede worrying about the afterlife: "If you have not attained ability to provide for your natural wants, and for a wife and a few children, what have you to do with heavenly things?" Even heaven will not relieve us of the duty to work to the fullest of our capacities: "Everything in heaven, on earth, and in hell is organized for the benefit, advantage and exaltation of intelligent beings." The possibility of prosperity is built into the fabric of material existence. We can be confident that God provides us with what we need to succeed, but we must do our part: "You know that it is one peculiarity of our faith and religion never to ask the Lord to do a thing without being willing to help him all that we are able, and then the Lord will do the rest."

Second, God wants our glory, not his own. Calvinists insist that the purpose of life is to glorify God. Young is as far from Calvinism on this point as it is possible to get: "We don't labor for God's glory but for our own benefit! The Lord is perfectly independent. He has received his glory, he reigns supreme and omnipotent. He is not dependent upon you and me." God does not need us but he does enjoy helping us to become more like him. Young's theology is anthropocentric, not theocentric, although it should be remembered that *theos* and *anthropos*, for Young, are overlapping categories.

Young also grasped the way that Mormonism overthrows the traditional Christian emphasis on death. Most Christian traditions emphasize the cross over the resurrection as the crucial moment in salvation history and, likewise, death over birth as the transitional moment for humans. Mormons do not focus on death in their theology: "Tradition has taught us that the great purpose of religion is to prepare people to die; that when they have passed through a change of heart, become converted, then they are ready for glory at any moment and to dwell with the Father and the Son in the heavens to all eternity. This is a mistake; for they have to improve, become substantially changed from bad to good, from sin to holiness here or somewhere else, before they are prepared for the society they anticipate enjoying." Young thus rejects (or at least modifies) the evangelical emphasis on salvation as an act of dying to one's old life and being born again. Salvation for Young is more gradual, developmental, and joyful. Death is not the model; growth is.

Young was holistic in everything he did. He had to organize schools, recreation, and housing in Utah. Canals had to be built, water rights apportioned, and agricultural instruction begun. Self-sufficiency was the goal, and so Young avoided becoming reliant on financiers. In the early years he created his own currency using grains, seeds, and gold dust, finally issuing his own bank bills. Everyone was expected to do manual labor. He forbade mining for fear that any discovery of gold would bring a flood of non-Mormons to Utah, though Young eventually had to compromise with mining interests, and Mormons made a profit from gold seekers traveling to California.

Throughout all of these policies and activities, Young was careful to balance the need for individual initiative with the goal of communal cooperation. The more he became committed to capitalism, the more he recognized the drawbacks to keeping the church isolated from the outside world. That is why he petitioned for a national railroad, paid for the first surveys made through Utah, and became the chief contractor for the railroad's construction. The railroad brought in increasing numbers of non-Mormons, and in response, Young had to redouble his efforts to keep communal bonds strong. This led him back to increased regulation and government impositions on the economy, although always with an eye on economic growth. He established a cooperative to keep control of trade and price controls to limit profiteering. He also envisioned what he called the United Order, a utopian form of collectivism that had its roots in a revelation Joseph Smith had about the Law of Consecration. Started in 1831, the United Order was an attempt to create communities that would eliminate poverty, establish self-sufficiency, and reduce income inequality. In its early years, membership in the order was required for membership in the church. Participants would deed (consecrate) all of their property to the order, which would in turn assign a portion of it back to them for their stewardship. At the end of the year, any excess profit would be given back to the order. It was a short-lived experiment, but it demonstrates how far Young went to try to harmonize individual talents with the social good.

Many people today remain suspicious of the LDS Church's wealth and confused about its relationship to capitalism. From the very beginning of his ministry, Joseph Smith was more passionate about constructing a social world for his followers than a theological system of ideas. Young followed in Smith's footsteps but took a slight turn that made a profound difference for Mormon history. After Utah became a state and the Mormon Church gave up its political ambitions, Young's focus on teaching Mormons to be industrious and entrepreneurial came to the forefront of Mormon identity. By the twentieth century, Mormon enculturation took the form of fusing church and economics rather than church and politics.

Critics can be very harsh on the Mormon Church's business practices and investments, as with the recent opening of the City Creek Center, a megamall that sits directly across the street from the Salt Lake City Temple. Owned and operated by the Mormon Church, it has a dazzling retractable roof and a hundred stores, including a Tiffany's. To outsiders, this project can seem like a crass confusion of the religious and the secular. When Jesus said, "You cannot serve God and mammon" (Matt. 6:24), however, he meant that wealth should not be pursued for its own sake. The Mormon Church invests in businesses because it sees no contradiction between the spiritual and the material. The Mormon Church is, in this respect, like the Roman Catholic Church, which still controls a geographical territory called Vatican City and claims that land as a sovereign city answerable only to the pope. Many Christian churches today are much more involved in politics than the Mormon Church is. For Mormons, economic development is a better indicator of the building of the kingdom of God than political power. Prosperity, understood as developing the requisite self-sufficiency for one's family in order to be in a position to contribute to the church and to help others, is a reliable sign for Mormons that the ancient conflict between spirit and matter is being overcome.

PARLEY PRATT

If you ever wondered how the Apostles could have been so successful in spreading the Gospel so soon after the death of Jesus, you should study the life of Parley Pratt. Pratt's nearly superhuman vitality and unquenchable zeal surely provide a window onto the miracle of Christianity's early growth. Next to Joseph Smith, the founder, Brigham Young, his successor, and Orson Pratt, his brother, Parley Pratt was the most important Mormon of his day. He just might have been the greatest Christian adventurer, if you combine the distances he traveled with the intellectual terrain he surveyed and revised. His body and mind were in constant motion. When he was not building up the LDS Church, he was building his own homes, only to be led to abandon them by either forced expulsions or voluntary missionary callings. Parley Pratt was what they used to call "a man's man," and indeed, it was his zest for life that led to his tragic murder. Polygamy was one of the most hated social customs in America, and Pratt took it too far. He tried to exempt himself from the law of the land not only by marrying more than one woman but also by taking as a wife a woman who was not divorced from her husband, and he paid the ultimate price.

Pratt's fantastical life is the perfect illustration of Joseph Smith's fantastic ideas. He crossed the Atlantic six times, traveled to Chile with hardly a penny in his pocket, spent years on both American coasts, and was, in his own words, "received almost as an Angel by thousands and counted an imposter by tens of thousands." The sheer range, intensity, and ambition of his daily activities are exhausting to contemplate.

A recent biography by Terryl Givens and Matthew Grow calls him the Apostle Paul of Mormonism. The authors give three reasons for

this comparison. First, Pratt systematized Joseph Smith's revelations, in many cases pushing Smith in ways that forced the Mormon
Prophet to play catch-up. Smith scattered ideas like seeds, and Pratt
nourished their growth into full-fledged doctrines. This includes
the controversial Mormon teachings on the corporeality of God and
divinization as the form of salvation. (Orson, whose life was not
nearly as adventurous, was even more systematic and creative about
these ideas.) Second, like Paul, Pratt was a restless traveler who put
a small sect on the road to global growth. Third, Pratt too was persecuted for upsetting the conventional religious norms of his contemporaries. In fact, he drew comfort from being compared with Paul
when he spent eight months in a Missouri prison in 1838–1839. He
also proclaimed himself a martyr as he died in 1857, though that
claim is hard to justify.

Like many early Mormon converts, Pratt was first attracted to the
restorationist message of Alexander Campbell, founder of the church
that would become the mainline Disciples of Christ. The Campbellite
movement got thousands of Americans excited about the possibility of a real Christian revolution and thus prepared the way for
Joseph Smith's revelations. Campbell was an optimist about church
unity, but he was in no position to sympathize with Smith's brand
of restorationism. Campbell was an essentially conservative church-
man who thought the common-sense reading of the Bible could
unite Christians on the nation's frontier. Pratt, a restoration radical,
sought a stronger basis for religious authority than Campbell's irenic
rationalism would permit. Campbell wanted to simplify Christianity,
not complicate it. He had no interest, for example, in experiment-
ing with communal lifestyles to hasten the new millennium, while
Christianity for Pratt was all about extending family connections
outward to encompass and promote wider circles of social belonging.

Pratt joined Joseph Smith's movement a few months after its
founding. There he found not only an attempt to re-establish an
apostolic priesthood but also the practice of spiritual gifts such as
tongue speaking and healing. He was passionate about the Book of
Mormon in part because he grew up with romantic notions about

Native Americans and dreams of converting them to Christ. Most fundamentally, however, the Book of Mormon for Pratt was a sign that God was still speaking to those willing to listen for his voice. While Campbell was a postmillennialist (he thought that church reform would usher in a new age of national peace and prosperity) and thus comfortable with a slow and gradual Christianization of American society, Pratt's millennialism was much more urgent and complex. Pratt believed that the end time was near, but unlike those who abandoned worrying about this world in expectation of its imminent demise, Pratt combined a longing for Jesus' return with a great desire to begin building the kingdom of God here and now. In this he was inspired by Joseph Smith. Smith enflamed the desire for social reform by taking Zion literally as a place Christ would rule on earth when he returns. Every city should anticipate this holy place, and thus Smith thought that the practice of building the church was inseparable from the tangible act of building cities on the western frontier. The Saints were meant to be gathered in a single place, not just to wait upon the Lord's return but to experiment with social organizations that could pave the way for the earth's final transformation. The Saints thus practiced their own version of what historians call America's doctrine of Manifest Destiny.

Wherever Pratt went, he combined hard agricultural labor—splitting rails and sowing crops—with pedagogical fervor. Smith's vision of America's providential role in the reunification of Christianity required his followers to embrace higher education, especially the study of foreign languages. Pratt took to the task early, leading men in weekly outdoor classes that combined prayer and teaching. Pratt wrote at the time that "there has seldom, if ever, been a happier people upon the earth than the Church of the Saints now were."

Conflict, however, always shadowed Pratt's life. He usually traveled without "purse or scrip" (reflecting Jesus' teaching in Luke 22:35), and his efforts often went unrewarded. "I have preached the Gospel from Maine to Missouri," he once wrote, "for near eight years, and all I ever received, during my whole ministry, would not amount to the yearly salary of one of the lazy, extravagant loungers who under the name of Priests are a nuisance to the whole country." In his own way he lacked finesse and diplomacy as much as or more than Brigham Young. His physical strength and courage, however, were on full display in expeditions he led, during harsh winter months, through unexplored lands in southern Utah. As one of his traveling companions wrote about him, "I thought he was the best man I ever saw. I felt that I would like to stay with him all my life." Pratt even built a toll road in Utah that eventually became the route for Interstate 80.

Pratt often worked as a day laborer to pay his way and rarely let bouts with sickness slow his journeys, but he increasingly turned to writing and publishing to support his travels and his growing family. Anyone in the book and magazine business knows how hard that can be, and in fact, Pratt did not make much money for his voluminous efforts. Nonetheless, his writings, beginning with A Voice of Warning, were among Mormonism's most valuable treatises well into the twentieth century.

Smith hinted at new ideas, while Pratt fought for them like a barroom brawler. For Pratt, moral law (Aquinas) is not to be distinguished in any ultimate sense from the physical law of the cosmos (Newton). There is one law for all, whether animate, inanimate, or divine, because there is no spiritual realm hovering over matter. In a famous phrase that is often quoted by friends and foes of Mormonism alike but rarely attributed to Pratt, he stated that "God, angels and men are all of one species." This statement is somewhat misleading, I think, because Pratt sought to elevate humanity, not diminish deity. Indeed, he insisted that Christ's atonement entails "the salvation and durability of the physical world, the renovation and regeneration of matter, and the restoration of the elements to a state of eternal and unchangeable purity." Pratt humanized the cosmos in a way rarely before seen in Christian theology, but he did so because he thought that all of matter is organized to sustain, refine, and preserve the affections and loyalties that we experience here on earth. Infinity is the intensification of the finite, not its opposition or contradiction.

Eternity is unfathomable, but still, when we cross over into it, we will carry our bodies with us, which meant to Pratt that heaven cannot be absolutely different from earth.

Pratt was involved in more than just theological controversies. He got caught up in the Missouri Mormon War and was even accused, without much evidence, of shooting a member of the Missouri militia. After escaping a Missouri jail, he made several trips to England, where he wrote hymns, started newspapers, opened a bookstore, and even wrote Queen Victoria to warn her that "the world in which we live is on the eve of revolution, more wonderful in its beginning—more rapid in its progress—more powerful in its operations—more extensive in its effects—more lasting in its influence—and more important in consequences, than any which man has yet witnessed." There is no record of her reply.

Pratt's enthusiastic embrace of plural marriage led to his sad, complicated, and tragic death. He was at first a reluctant convert to the doctrine but went on to do his best to defend it to Mormons and non-Mormons alike. Some Mormon leaders spoke of "spiritual wifery," a concept they used to justify adulterous behavior. That put Pratt in the precarious position of figuring out how to "denounce unauthorized plural marriage...without condemning sanctioned polygamy." One of Pratt's wives, Belinda, wrote a pamphlet that made her the first Mormon woman to publicly defend the practice. She argued that, given the biological differences of the genders, polygamy is the best way to protect female chastity (because men who have more than one wife are less likely to stray) while also creating a community of sisterhood for the wives. Belinda also argued that, since there are more wicked men than virtuous, polygamy is the only chance most women have to marry a good man.

Pratt was as ambitious in his family life as he was in his travels and his theology. He fathered thirty children, with twenty-three living to adulthood (his last surviving child died in 1937). Only one of his wives divorced him (she remained a Mormon), and most of his children entered into polygamous families. As hard as he worked, his many missionary journeys left his children to be raised in poverty.

Visitors to his home in Salt Lake City, in fact, were always struck by the modesty of his material circumstances.

Pratt's marital overreach led to his tragic death. On a mission to San Francisco he befriended a convert who was estranged from her abusive and alcoholic husband. He made Eleanor his twelfth and final wife, even though she was not yet divorced. Pratt continued to travel outside of Utah even though the husband had publicly announced that he would track Pratt down and kill him. When the inevitable happened, Pratt's last words were, "I am dying a martyr to the faith." He was deeply mourned by all Mormons, although some Saints thought that he had acted foolishly in marrying Eleanor and fatalistically by not doing more to avoid crossing paths with her estranged husband. The media sympathized with the murderer, who bragged about his act and was never convicted of the crime. The scandal sealed the image of Mormon men as seducers for most Americans and the feeling of being persecuted victims for most Mormons. It also left Pratt's family destitute, with most of his wives being buried in unmarked graves in the pauper's section of the Salt Lake City Cemetery. Nonetheless, Givens and Grow, in their biography, estimate that his living descendants number between thirty thousand and fifty thousand. What a man indeed.

Chapter 6

How to Heal Modernity's Spiritual Breakdown

People in the ancient world did not think that they were living in primitive times, just as people in the medieval world did not think that they were living in a transitional period between (or in the middle of) the ancient and modern worlds. The ancients and the medievals thought that they were living in advanced societies that met complex challenges and offered opportunities denied to previous generations. They thought that they were, to use a modern word, modern. Unfortunately, we modern people tend to think that this word applies only to us. *Modern* derives from the Latin meaning "just now," and we need reminding, I suspect, that people throughout history have thought they were living in a momentous time that was on the edge of an unknown and open future. Nonetheless, there is something unique about the last several centuries of the Western world that sets them apart from all other historical epochs. The Protestant Reformation splintered the medieval synthesis of Christianity and Western culture, the Age of Enlightenment struggled to put reason on a foundation that did not overly depend on religion, scientific breakthroughs instilled confidence in the West that knowledge could be advanced without the aid of religion, and industrialization radically accelerated the pace of social change. Any one of these events would probably not be enough to cut us off from the past, but did their combination create something new?

All of these complex developments added up to what I think is the single most significant cultural revolution in the history of the world: the severing of the supernatural from the natural. That claim, I know, will be very contentious, especially for those who see little value in religion. Nevertheless, all cultures prior to the "modern" West have been deeply grounded in religion of some form. People prior to the rise of modernity took it for granted that knowledge, morality, and art (the true, good, and beautiful) were facets of humanity's relation to the divine and that cultural accomplishments, social order, and personal happiness were contingent upon religious beliefs and practices. Philosophers debated every question having to do with the nature of religion, but very few individuals doubted that God or the gods ruled the world and that pleasing the divine was an essential precondition for individual well-being and communal peace and prosperity.

Religion did not simply disappear in the modern world, although certain ideologies, like communism, tried to make that happen. Instead, the supernatural and the natural were separated like two chemicals that need to be kept in separate containers lest, coming into contact with each other, they ignite and explode. The Protestant Reformation unintentionally got the secular ball rolling with its attacks on papal authority. Martin Luther and company wanted religious freedom from Rome but ended up surrendering the church to the much greater power of the state. How did this happen? The trauma of the Reformation left Protestants and Catholics at each other's throats for over a hundred years, and though there were many causes for a series of wars that are often grouped together under the title of the European Wars of Religion (1524–1648), the slaughter and destruction left much of Europe open to the idea that governments should be in charge of religion, rather than religion being permitted to lead the charge of one nation against another.

Consequentially, Christianity became just another department of state, to be administered by the political, cultural, and economic elites for the good of the nation. Before modernity, Christianity pretty much ruled the West, or at least it tried to. After modernity, Christianity became a matter of individual choice and personal taste. Religion was removed from the public sphere of shared values and collective history and thus demoted to the private sphere of family values and individual piety. When Christians enter the public square today, they are typically asked to leave their faith behind. In a way, modernity forcibly returned Christianity to its earliest days, since the Christian faith came of age as an illegal sect in imperial Rome. Christianity spread in large part due to persecution, and Christians were always at their best as martyrs rather than rulers. In another way, however, Christianity has always been a deeply political religion—"Thy Kingdom come, on earth as it is in heaven," Jesus taught his followers to pray—and even when it is given its place on the margins of the modern world it cannot accept the total triumph of secularism. Christianity is never content to be one religion among many or just another source of commonly held values that could have been obtained elsewhere. Some people can separate Christian morality from its truth claims, but most Christians cannot.

When people complain about social fragmentation today, they are really talking about the quite literal dissolution of Western culture. The word *religion* comes from the Latin *religio*, which means the ties that bind a community together. Nationalism, sports, consumerism, or the unbridled pursuit of pleasure, power, or riches can take the functional place of religion for some people some of the time, but the resurgence of religion across the globe is prima facie evidence that religion is in a class of its own in terms of providing social solidarity and personal well-being. When the element that integrated all aspects of Western culture becomes just another part of that culture, there is no whole greater than the sum of its parts. Disintegration is the inevitable result. This breakdown is so thorough that no area of society has been left untouched.

Take the pursuit of knowledge. The astounding success of science in the mastery of matter has led to the triumph of a materialistic view of the world that leaves precious little space for religion. If everything can be explained by scientific theories, then religion is reduced to mere nostalgia and sentiment. The triumph of science is fueled by technology's seductive promise to alleviate the suffering that is so much a part of the human condition. The rewards of a longer and more pleasurable life have come to take the place of hope for a blessed afterlife. Hospitals provide chaplains for people who have exhausted their use of medical resources, but anything important to do with the human body is off limits to religious input. Christianity teaches that physical health matters little in comparison with spiritual health and that faith can make even the most terrible suffering meaningful and bearable. The aim of medicine, by contrast, is to eliminate suffering altogether. That laudable goal puts Christianity in an awkward position. Faced with the choice of eliminating their suffering or making it meaningful, most people are going to choose medicine over religion every time. Moreover, when Christian ethicists criticize the unlimited ambition of medicine, they risk appearing as though they have no sympathy for the universal desire for a better life. Of course, death is still unconquered, so there will always be room for priests and ministers to comfort the dying and reassure those left behind to mourn, but the success of medicine has made religion a bystander in some of the most important events in our lives. Religion means less and less as technology does more and more.

Science can prove its value to society by its obvious successes, which puts the pressure on religion to do the same. America is a deeply pragmatic country. We want to know how to get things done, and we want to see progress in all of our personal and social problems. Judged by those criteria, churches are pressured to deliver more goods and services and less doctrine and ritual. The result is disastrous for a religion like Christianity, which is based on a specific set of beliefs and ceremonies. Christianity requires faith, but it also requires the faithful to defend the truth of Christian beliefs. There are many ways to become a Christian, but even those who are "born again" in a sudden and emotional conversion go on to study the Bible and listen to countless sermons about what they should believe and how they should act. The modern world, by making Christian beliefs irrelevant to the pursuit of knowledge and the promise of social progress, cuts the connection between piety and education. Consequently, faith formation in the church becomes an afterthought to the schooling required for lifelong happiness and success. Going to church becomes a hobby, a choice some families make regarding how to spend their free time, and not a matter of urgent social concern like public education. Without social support and cultural validation, families that try to make church an integral part of their children's lives are fighting an uphill battle. Parents often find that it is hard enough to discipline children in a climate that promotes unlimited affirmation and approval of everything they do. When this life is so good, why long for another one? Indeed, the most striking theological aspect of the crisis that modernity creates for the church is the assumption, common nowadays even among the very devout, that the promise of heaven is irrelevant to the pursuit of happiness here and now.

The two traditions that have fought hardest against modernity are Protestant fundamentalism and Roman Catholicism, with questionable results. Many fundamentalist churches have joined their more culturally sophisticated evangelical brethren by adopting modern technology and popular culture to keep their young people entertained and engaged. Roman Catholicism rejected modernity from the very beginning of modernity's birth, but Vatican II opened Catholic doors to the modern world, and it rushed right in.

The case can be made that the most serious alternative to fundamentalism and Catholicism in terms of having the resources to turn back the tide of modernity is The Church of Jesus Christ of Latter-day Saints. The basis for my claim returns us to the issue of Mormon metaphysics. Mormons conceive of all life, from the heavens above to the earth below, as governed by one common law of spiritual development and material transformation. Time has no limit, no matter which direction, past or forward, you look, and space too is unbounded, with new and unimaginable worlds yet to be discovered. Through this grand and immeasurable scheme, the faithful can advance from strength to strength, with God ever before them but never in an absolutely transcendent beyond. All that people love here and now will be preserved and enhanced in the next life, which consists of many worlds without any foreseeable end. The more we come to know ourselves, Mormons wager, the more we will realize that our bodies are destined for a glory that our minds even now can begin to comprehend. Nature is already thoroughly supernatural right down to the smallest atom, and the supernatural is nothing more than nature in its most intense and concentrated form. In the next life, the supernatural will become our second nature, so that the deeper into the divine we go, the more we will become the best version of who and what we already are, right down to our most basic bodily functions. Heaven never looked so beautifully ordinary.

The early Christians were known to have remarkably positive views of the human body. Celsus was a second-century Greek philosopher who wrote the first book against Christianity (it was published around A.D. 178). In it, he called Christians a *philosomaton genos*, which means a "flesh-loving people." Celsus was amazed that Christians took their physical existence so seriously that they wanted to take their bodies with them to the afterlife. If we take Celsus's definition to heart, then Mormonism is the most characteristically Christian movement of all Christian traditions. The afterlife is more life for Mormons, not another kind of life altogether. The result is a branch of Christianity that is as fantastic and inventive in its doctrines and rituals as it is simple and even simplistic in its hopes and dreams. The whole point of the temple rituals (Mormons call them ordinances), for example, is to put back together the religious unity that the modern world, in a process that was already well under way during Joseph Smith's lifetime, has torn asunder. Indeed, one could say that the whole point of Mormonism is to affirm, celebrate, and seal the continuity between this world and the next.

Just the fact that Mormons have temples makes them the object of deep suspicion for many Christians. When Christianity emerged in the Roman Empire, many Christians were Jewish converts with firsthand experience at the Jerusalem Temple. After the Jewish temple was destroyed by the Romans in A.D. 70 and Judaism and Christianity began going their separate ways, temples were increasingly seen as a purely pagan institution. Even if the Jerusalem Temple had not been destroyed, Christians would have come to disassociate themselves from it. The main activity at the Jerusalem Temple, as at all temples in the ancient world, was the sacrifice of animals (though sometimes grains and wine were substituted for the animals). Christians interpreted the sacrifice of Christ on the cross as the most perfect and complete of all sacrifices. The cross thus put an end to the need for temples to the extent that they are associated with the spilling of animal blood. That is why Christians built churches and not temples. Nonetheless, many aspects of the Jewish sacrifice of animals were retained in Christian rituals, including the use of incense (which would have been used in temples to cover up the stench of the frightened and dying animals), an altar table, and references to Christ as the Lamb of God. Indeed, the Roman Catholic Church considers the Eucharist (what Protestants call the Lord's Supper or simply communion) to be a sacrifice in which the priest, invoking God's power, offers up the gifts of bread and wine, which God transforms (transubstantiates is the technical word) into the body and blood of Jesus Christ.

The Protestant Reformers wanted the Eucharist to be a meal of thanksgiving and remembrance, not an unsurpassable consummation of the Old Testament sacrifices. Most Protestant churches, therefore, dismantled all the ways in which the Lord's Supper resembled an animal sacrifice. Rather than having a priest entrusted with the sacred task of performing a sacrificial ritual, Protestants talked about a priesthood of all believers and began calling their priests "ministers" and "preachers." With no rituals to mark the church as a sacred space set apart from a profane world, Protestant churches became increasingly simple and plain. Today, many churches provide so many services to their members that they are built to look like community centers or public schools.

Mormons, as one might expect, do not fit neatly into this picture of Christian history. They have churches for weekly worship, but they also have temples. The first one was built in the 1830s, and now there are over one hundred in cities across the globe. Mormon temples have become even more imposing and attractive at the very time that most church design has gone in the exact opposite direction toward the efficient and functional. Significantly, Mormon temples reflect little or nothing of the historical association of temples with sacrificial ritual. There are altar tables in Mormon temples, but they are used as places to pray for guidance and make vows of dedication. Sacrifice at these altars is metaphorical, consisting of personal promises to Jesus Christ. Mormonism accepts the absolute sufficiency of Jesus' blood atonement on the cross and rejects the need for a special class of priests set apart for performing sacred rituals.

Nevertheless, they have priests! Yet, as one might expect, their understanding of the priesthood fits no previous categories. Churches typically have a priesthood only if they have sacred rituals to perform, like the transformation of bread and wine into the real presence of Jesus Christ. The priests who perform the Eucharistic transformation are thus heirs of the priesthood that performed the animal sacrifices in the Jewish temple. Mormons have a priesthood, but they do not treat the Eucharist, which they hold in their churches and not their temples, as a sacrificial ritual. Their Eucharist, in fact, is unadorned and ordinary: they use bread and water rather than bread and wine (or juice). Priests too are rather ordinary in the Mormon Church, since the priesthood, which is divided into two basic orders, the Aaronic and Melchizedek, is not reserved for only a small minority of Mormon men. Instead, these ranks are granted to all males who express a commitment to moral worthiness and regular church participation, beginning at age twelve. Rather than signifying expertise in performing rituals, the priesthood is a symbol of God's promise to grant believers an exalted and divine status in the afterlife. Instead of being a specially trained group set apart from other believers, Mormon priests are at the forefront of where the whole church should be heading. Mormonism thus follows Protestantism in democratizing the priesthood but follows Catholicism in associating the priesthood with increasing intimacy with Christ.

All of this might sound confusing, but it makes sense in the context of the life of Joseph Smith. One of the hallmarks of Smith's leadership was his readiness to confer authority on others. At the same time, he insisted on establishing and following formal rules of ordination, which included the laying on of hands. Ordination also had to be performed by the proper authority in order to pass on the physical power of the Holy Spirit. Smith even appointed a Quorum of Twelve Apostles, which continues to this day. He did all of this by appealing to the authority that comes from receiving revelations rather than, as in the Catholic Church, the authority that comes from a long line of ordinations that go back to the original apostles. Smith's commitment to careful church governance came early in his life, as demonstrated by the frequent passages in the Book of Mormon that speak of the need for proper ordination (see, for example, 2 Nephi 6:2 and Ether 12:10).

Smith was also a great devotee of ceremonialism. Critics often point out that many of the temple ordinances appear to be derived from Masonic initiation rites, and indeed, Smith joined the Freemasons in the early 1840s, the same time that he was developing the temple rituals. These criticisms miss the point. The origin of the rituals does not limit the purpose that Smith gave them. Besides, Smith had to borrow from various sources for his rituals because the Christianity of his day provided him with so few examples. He lived during a time of enthusiastic revivalism, which encouraged Christians to look inward at their emotions for evidence of their relationship to Jesus. The soul within was the sacred place where the believer met Christ. Protestants associated rituals with Roman Catholics, and anti-Catholicism was intense throughout Smith's lifetime. Somehow, Smith managed to blend Protestantism and Catholicism long before the two camps even dreamed of ecumenical dialogue.

He was able to break from the anti-Catholic prejudices of his day because of his view of the physical world. Most Protestants during Smith's lifetime thought that the material world was at best a bare reflection of the heavenly world to come and at worst a source of temptation that needed to be denied and overcome. For Smith, by contrast, physical matter already, here and now, participates in the supernatural. Rather than the supernatural and the natural being opposed to each other, the supernatural is nature intensified but not abolished. This view of matter also helps to account for the way in which Smith's theological imagination was geographically grounded. America was a sacred land, Smith taught, because Jesus had visited here and ancient peoples had left behind buried scripture. In his short life he was always looking for a new place to build his utopian version of Zion, God's city, and he even prophesied that the New Jerusalem that will come down from heaven at the end times will be located in Jackson County, Missouri.

The anti-Catholicism of Smith's social milieu went hand in hand with the dominance of Calvinism. John Calvin was a Protestant Reformer who built an austere and disciplined Christian community in Geneva, Switzerland. Calvinism is like Mormonism in being committed to a social expression of the Gospel (Calvinists, during their phase as Puritans, were the first to talk about America being a sacred land, a theme that deeply influenced Smith), but the similarities end there. Calvinism rejected adornment in every aspect of Christian life, and its critique of anything showy ran deep in American religion. For Calvinism, rituals are not appropriate means of mediating between this world and the next because every ritual focuses on an object of some sort and treats that object as sacred. Calvinists were always wary about the human instinct to worship things made by human hands. They preached that idolatry is the root of all sin, whether it gets expressed in the worship of money, beauty, oneself, or another human being. That is why Calvinists were so suspicious of anything that seemed flamboyant or flashy. They taught that our actions, just like our speech and dress, should be straightforward, direct, and understated. Rituals for Calvinists are inherently gaudy and ostentatious, distracting the believer from a properly inward relationship to the divine.

In some ways, it might seem that Smith would have been attracted to Calvinism. For example, he was not an affected or theatrical person. Eyewitness accounts show him to be a modest, rather conventional person. Even his name was ordinary! Those who have not read the Book of Mormon, his revisions of parts of the Bible, and his revelations collected in *Doctrine and Covenants* often assume that he must have had a grandiose view of himself, but in fact, his writings are so self-effacing that it is almost impossible to ascertain anything about his personality based on these writings alone. He was content to be a translator, not an author. His revelations are pronouncements in the voice of God and say nothing about the man who is receiving them. He was a pretty humble person for a self-declared Prophet!

Nonetheless, his love of ritual makes him decidedly un-Calvinistic. Why he was so attracted to rituals is hard to determine. Smith was a very private person, so there is little value to be found in speculations about his inner life, though it is important to note that he experienced plenty of pain and suffering. Four of his eleven children died at childbirth, and one died at fourteen months. He had difficult health problems, was tarred and feathered, was confined in jails best described as dungeons, and had many friends turn against him after the bank he started in Kirkland, Ohio, collapsed. Who can blame him for seeking rituals to heal such hurt? His metaphysics, however, cannot be ruled out as a source of his ceremonial creativity. Smith's materialism led him, contrary to the Calvinists, to embrace the inherent theatricality of humanity's social existence. Smith loved creating religious offices, organizing meetings, solving problems, and becoming deeply involved in the lives of his followers. He did not treat social roles as a burden and thus did not divide the public realm from the private. His life was the church he founded. He treated the roles we play in society as dress rehearsals for the even greater drama that is to come in the afterlife. Every relationship we have, he believed, will leave its mark on eternity. Everything we touch has something of the sacred in it.

The temple rituals are ways of making the transforming potential of faith vivid and real. Mormon temples are used not for sacrifices, which separate, rip, cut, and tear, but for rituals that bind, link, unite, and connect. If the supernatural and the natural are opposed, then to make a connection between this world and the one beyond requires a ritualized destruction or annihilation of something of great value. That is why animal sacrifices are so endemic in the ancient world. The gods are so far above us that they seek evidence that we are willing to destroy the valuable life of an animal in order to purchase the blessed life of eternity. Something in this world has to give if the immaterial world is to make an appearance. Only a cut in the fabric of life can open up a glimpse of the mystery of the divine. Smith had a radically different approach to ritual because he thought that the basic material constitution of this world would be preserved and elevated in the next. Christ gave himself as a sacrifice on our behalf so that nothing that we value needs to be destroyed to prove our loyalty to God. Everyone knows the saying "You can't take it with you when you go." Well, for Mormons, everything that God gives us in this world to cherish and use wisely will be a part of the world yet to come. We can take it all, and what we take when we go will become ever better when we arrive in the world to come.

The ordinances performed in the temple include baptism for the dead, endowments, and sealings. Most people know about the baptisms for the dead, which constitute most of the temple work and account for Mormon interest in genealogy. Some people even know that there is precedent for this practice in the New Testament, where the Apostle Paul refers to it: "Otherwise, what will those people do who receive baptism on behalf of the dead? If the dead are not raised at all, why are people baptized on their behalf?" (1 Cor. 15:29). Few people, however, stop to consider just how generous this practice is. Christianity, like most religions, does not have a single or simple position on the possible salvation of those who do not confess faith in Jesus Christ. Some Christians think that unbelievers will have an opportunity to affirm Jesus in the afterlife, while other Christians think that everyone who believes in God (regardless of what they think about Jesus) will be saved. Some Christians pray for those who are not saved, while some think that there is no hope whatsoever for non-Christians. Mormons do more than hope and pray for others. They volunteer to serve as proxies to be baptized in place of the non-Mormon dead. This does not mean that the dead person has all of a sudden become a Mormon. It means that the deceased will have an opportunity in the next life to affirm that baptism if he or she so chooses.

Why would anyone be offended by that? Baptism for the dead is incredibly controversial, but I think that those who condemn the practice, to be honest, have not given it enough thought. Many people have had the experience of having someone from a different faith offer to pray for them, and if the offer is genuine and heartfelt, most people do not find it offensive. People who travel abroad and get to know their hosts will sometimes receive a gift that has some kind of religious significance. A Hindu student of mine once gave me a statue of Shiva, a major Hindu deity. This statue portrayed him as the lord of the dance standing on the back of a tiny demon and surrounded by a ring of flame. Since I do not believe in Shiva, should I have asked him to take it back? Someone might say that it was only a work of art, but I know that it had religious meaning to my student, and when my wife and I visited him in India, we accepted all of his family's hospitality, even their prayers. The polite thing to do when given a gift is to say thank you, even if you do not attach to it the same meaning that it has for the giver—or any meaning at all.

Think about the following. Catholic families, especially before Vatican II, sometimes prayed for their ancestors, and this practice is not uncommon among non-Catholic Christians. Suppose that a young Catholic woman prays for her deceased mother, and suppose that her brother becomes Protestant and thinks that these prayers are not only useless but also downright sacrilegious. Should the brother be upset that his sister is trying to aid their mother in her afterlife? Of course, in this example, both siblings are Christians. It might be different if the brother had converted to Hinduism and now prayed for their mother to escape the nearly endless cycles of reincarnation. Should the sister be upset that her brother is offering Hindu prayers for their Catholic mother? Should atheists be angry that anyone at all prays for dead people?

As for the other ordinances, the endowment ceremonies involve a dramatization of various stages of salvation history (this used to be done by temple workers, but much of it now is accomplished by the use of films). The sealing ritual can take different forms, but it is a way of making the bonds that unite a family eternal. Smith drew his vision of sealing rituals from Matthew 16:19, where Jesus tells his disciples: "I will give you the keys of the kingdom of heaven, and whatever you bind on earth will be bound in heaven." The essence of all the temple rituals is a sealing together of the parts of life that we do not want ripped apart upon our death. Mormon couples have their weddings in temples, but converts or Mormons married in a civil ceremony can also have their marriage sealed there. Children and the dead can be sealed in family units as well.

Temple sealings bring us back to Smith's ambition to integrate everything that the world seems determined to disintegrate. It is as if Mormonism is fighting a rearguard action against the second law of thermodynamics, which states that even the most ordered parts of nature tend toward disorder. Matter, according to the theory of evolution, begins in randomness, and according to physics, it aims at dissipation. No matter how much we try to reserve our own energy, to say nothing of the planet's, scientists assume that just as every individual life comes to an end, the cosmos too will burn itself out (or freeze itself away). If entropy has the last word, the matter of the universe will eventually become completely homogeneous, and every form of energy will have been irrevocably spent.

For Smith, God is very much a part of this world even as he works from within it to oppose and overturn the apparent inevitability of entropy. Most traditional Christians interpret Christ's command, "Be ye therefore perfect, even as your Father which is in heaven is perfect" (Matt. 5:48), as a moral admonishment. Christ wants us to strive for moral perfection while keeping our vision fixed on the Father. For Mormons, perfection is not just a moral matter because it involves the whole person, including our bodies. It follows that deification is at odds with not just the human tendency toward sin but also the material world's inclination toward death and decay. God's power is an infinitely renewable source of physical as well as spiritual energy. Smith taught that in the end, "this earth will be rolled back into the presence of God, and crowned with celestial glory." His theology lets us hope that there is a law of renewal more deeply embedded in nature than the law of entropy. Orson Pratt, as we saw in chapter 3, tried to identify God's power with a physical force that invites all entities into a peaceful and harmonious space. Pratt's understanding of the Holy Spirit was rejected by the Saints, and such speculations are rare in Mormon thought today. Nonetheless, a physical interpretation of our spiritual journey toward God persists as one of the distinctive features of Mormon thought.

Smith clearly taught that the perfection of the faithful is a collective affair that crosses over the boundaries of time and space. This is most evident in his teaching about baptism for the dead: "And now, my dearly beloved brethren and sisters, let me assure you that these are principles in relation to the dead and the living that cannot be lightly passed over, as pertaining to our salvation. For their salvation is necessary and essential to our salvation, as Paul says concerning the fathers—that they without us cannot be made perfect—neither can we without our dead be made perfect" (D&C 126:15). What makes this ritual possible is "a power which records or binds on earth and binds in heaven" (D&C 126:9). The sealing of marriages and families in Mormon temples is not a token or nominal action. It is a participation in the literal power of God.

Indeed, the whole point of the temple ordinances for Smith is the empowerment of ordinary people to have the most extraordinary visions. In one of his revelations about the command from God to build a temple, Smith reported this saying from God: "Yea, and my presence shall be there, for I will come into it, and all the pure in heart that shall come into it shall see God" (D&C 97:16). According to Smith's way of thinking, God seems immaterial to us because we are weak in faith and thus in need of rites of purification and illumination. In the next life, he will appear as he really is, an embodied being of unimaginable glory. The point of the temple rituals, indeed, the point of being born on earth in the first place, is to begin preparing us for that moment. Those who see or hear God in this life really do experience who God is, not a mere token meant to stand in for God that has been given to us because of our epistemological limitations. In the next life our sight (and our hearing!) will be even clearer and stronger. Rituals of sanctification and dedication are meant to begin focusing our minds and strengthening our moral wills so that even in this life we can begin refining our physical sight in order to become open to spiritual dreams and visions.

God is a real person who occupies space, and heaven is a material place, so to draw closer to God, we need sacred places to inspire us to keep looking for what we will someday find in its ultimate fullness. If we are not used to entering into sacred spaces in this life, with all the moral repentance and transformation that temple attendance entails, how can we expect to get the full benefit of entering into heaven? That, in short, is why Mormons have temples.

Chapter 7

Two Decisions

Mormons need to make a decision about their own faith, and the rest of us need to make a decision about them. I am not the first to point this out, but I absolutely disagree with the way these decisions are usually formulated.

First, take the decision that many non-Mormon Christians think that Mormons need to make. This decision is usually framed as an either/or: Mormons need to decide whether they want to join mainstream, evangelical Christianity or to continue to follow their own eccentric path into a grotesque miasma of magical Christian polytheism. That is precisely *not* the decision Mormons need to make, as I will show in this chapter. Mormonism's strength lies in how it challenges many aspects of evangelical, Protestant theology. Mormonism *is* its metaphysics. A simpler message focused on a personal relationship with Jesus would betray what makes Mormonism special. Nevertheless, I want to suggest that there is room for a more explicitly Christological grounding of Mormon metaphysics.

Second, take the decision that the rest of us need to make about them. From the perspective of tolerance, pluralism, and multiculturalism, non-Mormons need to decide whether they will treat Mormonism with the respect that is due all religious traditions. That, of course, is a no-brainer, but the decision non-Mormon Christians need to make is of much greater magnitude. I have argued throughout this book that non-Mormon Christians need to decide whether to accept Mormonism for what it claims to be: a branch on the Christian tree. Now I want to take that argument one step further by suggesting that Mormonism presents a unique challenge and a breathtaking opportunity for American Christianity. The decision non-Mormon Christians need to make is about how open they want to become to the full intellectual richness of the Christian tradition. More specifically, Mormonism asks other Christians to come to terms with America's Calvinist heritage and to try to imagine what American Christianity might look like if it were to be freed from that debatable heritage once and for all.

In terms of the first decision—whether the Saints should trade in their metaphysics for a more conventional evangelical piety—I can speak only as an outsider to both camps, and my pro-metaphysical bias is obvious. The decision Mormons face is similar, I think, to the challenges Roman Catholics had to confront in the Second Vatican Council (1962–1965) and its liberalizing aftermath. In the United States, Vatican II had the effect of modernizing the church, which meant bringing it more in line with the dominant Protestant ethos. The rich culture of Catholicism was streamlined to the point where some distinctive Catholic practices, such as eating fish (or fasting) on Fridays, disappeared for all but the most devout. Vatican II came as a shock to many traditional Catholics in part because change of that magnitude is very rare in the Catholic Church. Mormons could follow suit by becoming more conventionally Protestant and less socially distinctive. The effect on the faithful, however, would be quite different from the impact of Vatican II. Mormons, who are led by a living Prophet, are used to (and indeed, expect) an ongoing evolution of their beliefs. So it is unlikely that Mormonism will experience any theological revolutions as dramatic as Vatican II, but it could experience a Vatican II of long duration.

Compared with most churches, Mormons are a very united bunch. As I observe the Mormon theological scene, however, I think that I can highlight two groups that want to take Mormonism in different directions, and in the long run, the Mormon future could look very different depending on which group exercises the most influence. One direction is metaphysical, and the other is evangelical. The metaphysical direction is best represented by the work of David Paulsen, a truly original and daring philosopher who would be better known if he were not Mormon. The evangelical direction is best represented by Robert Millet, an exceptional writer with a powerful theological voice and a genius for cutting away peripheral issues to get to what really matters. By singling out these two thinkers I do not mean to neglect others or to downplay the many scholars who influenced them. Scholars such as Hugh Nibley, B. H. Roberts, James Talmage, John Widtsoe, and Truman Madsen paved the way for Paulsen and Millet and are still essential reading for anyone interested in Mormonism. Contemporaries such as Terryl Givens, Richard Bushman, James Faulconer, Phil Barlow, Blake Ostler, and John Welch are exploring issues in history, exegesis, and philosophy in their own creative ways. Paulsen and Millet are representatives of two wings, but they are not the heads of any official schools of thought within Mormonism, and they are far from alone in pursuing the philosophical, historical, and textual credibility of Mormon beliefs and practices with the highest scholarly standards.

David Paulsen is the dean of Mormon philosophers. After earning a law degree from the University of Chicago and practicing law for several years, Paulsen returned to graduate school to earn a Ph.D. in philosophy from the University of Michigan and spent his career as a professor at Brigham Young University. He retired in 2011. Evidence of his impact on Mormon scholarship is the excellent collection of essays edited by Jacob Baker, *Mormonism at the Crossroads of Philosophy and Theology: Essays in Honor of David L. Paulsen*. Paulsen is a philosopher, and as such, he delights in both lofty speculation and rigorous analysis. He is also genuinely modest and intellectually generous with his time and energy. His spirit is as humble as his arguments are forceful. His many students over the years at Brigham Young speak of him with admiration bordering on adulation. It is no exaggeration to say that his impact on Mormon theological scholarship is second to none, and he has been a mentor to me in my own sojourn in Mormon studies. I can also testify that he is devoted to Mormonism precisely because it has brought him so close to the wonder and majesty of Jesus Christ.

One of his best-known essays, which is a testament to his wit and creativity, is entitled "Are Christians Mormon?" It is a play on the frequently asked question, "Are Mormons Christian?" In this essay he defends Joseph Smith from the charge of heresy on seven points: first, the reopening of the canon of the New Testament; second, the idea that God can experience human feelings like joy and suffering firsthand; third, a social model of the Trinity (which means that the three members of the Trinity, Father, Son, and Holy Spirit, are each individuals in their own right and thus make up a society, not a unity); fourth, the deification model of salvation; fifth, a place for a divine mother in heaven; sixth, the argument that God can change in the sense that God is able to surpass his own perfections by becoming ever greater; and seventh, a belief that persons after they die will have an opportunity to accept Jesus Christ as their Lord and Savior. Paulsen argues that all of these ideas have ancient roots, were once thought to be dead ends in the development of Christian theology, but now are back in play, with some being accepted by mainstream and traditionalist theologians. Paulsen concludes his essay with these words: "Charlatan or prophet? Heresy or truth? While the reactions to Joseph's doctrines remain clearly mixed, one thing is certain: the doctrines he proclaimed are not as 'unique' as they used to be."

Paulsen has put Mormon metaphysics front and center in contemporary debates about Joseph Smith's legacy. Indeed, it was Paulsen's work on divine embodiment in the *Harvard Theological Review* that jolted my theological imagination out of its immaterial slumber. He single-handedly put this topic back on the scholarly agenda by showing how the earliest theologians did not necessarily believe that God was pure (immaterial) spirit. In the light of his work, the idea that God has a body can no longer be dismissed as a peculiarly Mormon aberration.

Paulsen has also helped to frame the issue of restoration, a much contested concept that is very important in both Mormonism and Protestantism. Many Protestant churches teach that early Christianity lost its way sometime after the apostolic era. This belief is often couched in terms of an initial Christian purity and then a fall into pagan practices and foreign ideas. When Christianity grew in numbers and power in the Roman world, so the argument goes, it increasingly absorbed a Hellenistic worldview. Restoration is sometimes framed in very scathing and conspiratorial rhetoric, as if there was a single moment when a handful of church leaders decided to sell the faith for worldly fame and riches. There is no doubt that Smith and other early Mormon leaders were shaped by restorationist theology. The topic was all the rage throughout the nineteenth century, with preachers denouncing creeds as abominations and accusing Catholicism of venality and corruption.

Restorationism is typically little more than extreme Protestantism, a byproduct of the Reformation rebellion against the Roman Catholic Church's monopolistic regulations of Christian beliefs and practices. Creeds often carry the brunt of Restorationist criticism, but restorationists misunderstand their role in church history. Creeds, at their best, are not meant to provide final answers to Christianity's deepest mysteries. Creeds are meant to define a common vocabulary of theological terms and to clarify the theological grammar that allows that vocabulary to be used in productive ways. Creeds are the necessary condition for good theological conversations. Yet it is true that creeds can be misused, and church history is replete with examples of religious authorities using creeds to punish, silence, and persecute.

Significantly, Joseph Smith himself was remarkably free from prejudices against Roman Catholicism:

> The old Catholic church traditions are worth more than all you have said. Here is a principle of logic that most men have no more sense than to adopt. I will illustrate it by an old apple tree. Here jumps off a branch and says, I am the true tree, and you are corrupt. If the whole tree is corrupt, are not its branches corrupt? If the Catholic religion is a false religion, how can any true religion come out of it? If the Catholic church is bad, how can any good thing come out of it? The character of the old churches have always been slandered by all apostates since the world began.

This just might be the most pro-Catholic statement of any American Protestant church leader of the nineteenth century, and in it, Smith seems to accept the idea that Mormonism is a branch of the Catholic faith. It is true that Smith thought that The Church of Jesus Christ of Latter-day Saints is "the only true and living church upon the face of the whole earth" (D&C 1:30). That claim mirrors what Catholics have always said about their own church. (For Catholics, that claim rests on lineage and age, and for Mormons it rests on completeness and wholeness.) It is also true that Mormons have over the years used harsher anti-Catholic rhetoric than Smith. Early Mormons especially tended to interpret the reference in 1 Nephi 13:6 to "a great and abominable church" as a statement about Roman Catholicism, but that interpretation is no longer followed by Mormon authorities and scholars. It should never have been interpreted in an anti-Catholic light in the first place. The Prophet Nephi is relating a vision not unlike the apocalyptic message found in the Revelation of John, and both were warning Christians not to fall away from the truth. Nowhere does Nephi identify the general tendency of rebellion in human nature with Roman Catholicism in particular. Mormons did (and some still do) talk about a Great Apostasy, which can evoke an evil conspiracy of shady clerics intentionally betraying Jesus, but there has also been a concerted effort in recent years by young Mormon scholars to rethink the concepts of restoration and apostasy.

By emphasizing Mormonism's dynamic metaphysics, Paulsen helps us to see that Smith's version of restorationism goes forward rather than backward. Mormons are not nostalgic about the past. Joseph Smith was like a scavenger who sought opportunity where others saw nothing but waste and excess. Smith was a sifter and excavator who took a long view of church history. Everything is a process in Smith's thought, including the fall (and the restoration) of the church. Nothing can be blamed on any individual or group because, as Paulsen points out, the mistake of the developing church concerned metaphysics, not morality. This means that the restoration of the church cannot be simply a return to biblical fundamentalism.

Instead, an imaginative effort is needed to think through what Christianity might look like if Origen, Augustine, and others had not committed themselves to the philosophical immaterialism of Plato. Restoration in Paulsen's perspective is expansive, not contractive. Its energy goes onward and outward, not backward and inward.

Mormon restoration, in fact, is synonymous with the potential in all things to be united with God. Thus, Mormons are optimistic about the possibility of universal salvation, since they believe that all people, whether in this life or the next, will be given the opportunity to accept the Gospel. Mormons are also confident that the natural light of knowledge is given to all people as a grace of Jesus Christ. Even Brigham Young, who fought so hard for Mormon autonomy and self-sufficiency, believed that everyone has access to the truth: "I do not believe for one moment that there has been a man or woman upon the face of the earth, from the days of Adam to this day, who has not been enlightened, instructed, and taught by the revelations of Jesus Christ." This statement actually goes far beyond the issue of postmortem salvation. Young had such a vivid understanding of Christ's presence in the world that he dared to imagine that Jesus instructs every human being, whether they know it or not, in the ways of holiness and righteousness. Restoration, then, has nothing to do with the search for lost moral purity and everything to do with establishing the cosmic truth of Christianity.

What Paulsen has done for the reception of Mormon philosophy and theology Millet has accomplished in the areas of the Bible and Christology. Millet, a professor of ancient scripture at Brigham Young University, has been the leader, along with the Calvinist theologian Richard Mouw, of a series of meetings and a set of books dedicated to bringing evangelicals and Mormons closer together. He promotes mutual understanding and astutely avoids the temptation in religious dialogue of trying to score debating points or easy rhetorical victories. I first came across his work in a book he coauthored with Gerald McDermott, an outstanding Calvinist theologian, called *Claiming Christ: A Mormon–Evangelical Debate*. Staging a religious dialogue where people actually learn something and nobody's feelings are hurt is tricky business, but this book worked wonders with me. The two writers were honest and even combative without being arrogant or rude. They argued with each other only as friends could do. They could be daring and vulnerable because they wrote the book in an ethos of trust. Traditional Christianity's suspicion of Mormonism runs so high that taking Mormon theology seriously can require something like a spiritual if not intellectual transformation. The theology of the Latter-day Saints is soaked in Christology, and the experience of a non-Mormon Christian coming to recognize how much Mormons love their Savior in spite of some differences in how that Savior is described can be powerful. I confess that this happened to me in reading this book, but when I have told this to other theologians, they have warned me about the potential treachery of engaging Mormons in theological debate. There is an insistent suspicion that Mormons are secretive and that what they tell you publicly differs from what they practice privately. Millet is so intellectually honest and fundamentally transparent that he helps to put an end to such distorted constructions of the Mormon identity.

Millet is very open in this book (and other works) about the Mormon belief that Jesus Christ has a history that did not begin with the virgin birth. Jesus' personal growth and development extends far back in time. Traditional Christians believe that Jesus Christ was preexistent, of course, but what they mean is that the Son of God existed before he became a human person. Since the Son of God is absolutely equal to God, and God is immaterial, traditional Christians conclude that the human being Jesus Christ did not exist until he was born in Bethlehem. In other words, the Son of God experienced no drama before his birth as a human person. There is little point in talking about what the Son was like before he was born because he was identical to God and therefore did not undergo change in any way. There is no answer to the question of what he was doing before the creation of the world because there was no time before matter was made. Drama in the sense of a life that unfolds, deepens, and enlarges is limited to earth alone (if there; some traditional theologians deny that Jesus changed in any significant way even as he grew up from an infant to an adult).

Before the great ecumenical councils of Nicaea, Constantinople, Ephesus, and Chalcedon, speculations about the preexistent Jesus were actually pretty robust. A few theologians even made a strong case for the idea that Jesus had a body before his birth as a human being. This position is called Heavenly Flesh Christology, and there were many complex reasons why it was eventually rejected. Mormonism once again puts this position back on the theological table. It could be said, in fact, that Mormonism represents a kind of counterfactual historical reality, as if it shows what might have happened had the orthodox creeds not won the day. Mormonism is pre-Nicene theology in a post-Nicene world, the theological equivalent to discovering that dinosaurs are still living on some isolated island. Millet helped me see that Mormons have a more mythological view of Christ than many Christians today, who think of Jesus primarily in moral terms. The Saints, it could be said, have remythicized the history of Jesus, just as they have re-enchanted the physical world. How Jesus embodies perfect morality might be describable in static, abstract ways, but Mormons believe that his eternal existence as a real person—indeed, the most real person who ever lived—requires an epic narrative. For Latter-day Saints, Jesus is a heavenly figure whose history stretches across the eons of time. His life is too great to be contained in the years he spent in earthly ministry, no matter how much the incarnation perfectly epitomized his nature and character.

The long prehistory of the historical Jesus raises the obvious objection that Mormons do not put Christ on the same level as God, a view that is sometimes called subordinationism (the Son is subordinate to the Father) and sometimes called Arianism after the heretic Arius. There is some merit to this charge, since Mormons call Jesus a spirit child of God the Father and an elder brother to all human beings, but it is hard to make that charge stick because Mormons do not play by the rules of the ecumenical creeds. Millet downplays this charge by saying, "When he was God, he was God." He is right to say this, because the great majority of Mormons spend absolutely no time at all wondering what Christ was doing when he was not yet God. Yet there are important issues at stake. If a divine being can *become* divine, then being God is not all that traditional theists claim it is. If God became God, then everything in the world is subjected to a law of becoming, and there is no state of being that lies outside of space and time. In other words, there is no such thing as eternity (understood as timelessness) in Mormon theology. Everything that exists, including God, exists in a temporal realm and is thus subjected to the fact that life requires growth and change. From the perspective of the classical theism of the ecumenical creeds, the Father begot the Son only in a completely metaphorical way, since the Father is, was and always will be the Father of the Son. Their relationship is unchanging and, since it is one of equals, even the names Father and Son are metaphorical. Neither has precedent over the other. From a Mormon perspective, the Father truly is the Father of the Son, but since God the Father is a being who has grown into that role, saying that the Son has changed does not distinguish him from the Father. The Son and Father are both on the same level, even if that level is not the realm of changeless eternity. That is the crucial point. The Mormon Son of God is not subordinated to God the Father because both belong on the same level as beings who have achieved an absolutely divine status.

Classical theism, by putting God outside of time and making Jesus Christ identical with God the Father, has a hard time explaining how Jesus Christ is also identical with us. Explaining that is Mormonism's strong suit. Indeed, no other theology has ever managed to capture the essential sameness of Jesus with us in a more striking manner. To McDermott, this means that the Mormons have an essentially limited view of Jesus, since a Jesus who is too much like us cannot be sufficiently like God. Millet shows how Mormons agree that Jesus has all of the perfections of the divine but believe that one of those perfections is embodiment. The incarnation is thus not an afterthought to the creation of the world. Jesus had a spirit body from the very beginning, and it is that body that is the foundation of the created order.

The cosmic optimism in Mormonism originates in its under-standing of the role of Jesus Christ in the creation, sustenance, and guidance of all of nature. The idea that Christ was involved in the cre-ation of the world is deeply embedded in Christian theology, but it rarely receives any systematic treatment. Mormons affirm this idea wholeheartedly, which is why they can refer to Jesus as Jehovah. When the Old Testament talks about God, Mormons believe, it is often talking about Jesus Christ. Jesus Christ was the one who revealed himself to Adam and Eve, Enoch, Noah, Abraham, Jacob, Moses, and all the rest. The Book of Mormon explicitly teaches that "none of the prophets have written, nor prophesied, save they have spoken concerning this Christ" (Jacob 7:11). The Old Testament sacrifices were not just anticipations of the cross. Even those who lived before the incarnation had to call upon the blood of Jesus for salvation. Mormonism gives distinct roles to the Father, Son, and Holy Spirit in eternity, but in time everything is subordinated to the Son. Jesus Christ is the eternal God in the sense of being the begin-ning and end of this world and the only access we have to the world to come.

So how do we evaluate these two thinkers and the directions they want to take Mormon theology in? Paulsen's Mormonism looks like Roman Catholicism set free of Augustine, and Millet's Mormonism looks like Protestantism set free of Calvin. Or maybe Paulsen makes Catholicism look overly refined and cultured, while Millet makes Protestantism look restrained and timid. Together, Paulsen and Millet make Mormonism look like a creedless Catholicism joined to a nonliteralist Protestantism. Another way of thinking about these two thinkers is to imagine Millet as the representative of Mormon Sunday worship, with its roots in a Low Church ethos, and Paulsen as the Mormon of temple worship, with its High Church aesthetics and elaborate rituals. Is there a conflict?

There is certainly some tension between the positions these men represent, but there does not need to be any conflict—as long as metaphysics is permitted to do its work of providing the foundation for the Mormon worldview. To demonstrate the potential congruence of the metaphysical and evangelical wings of Mormonism I want to turn to one of the Saints' most surprising and provocative beliefs. It is a belief that is typically associated with the occult, because it has to do with the establishment of our personal identity in a time before our lives in this world began—indeed, in a time before the world itself was created. A fundamental Mormon doctrine is that our souls were in existence long before they were united to our bodies. Indeed, Mormons believe that what is essential about us is eternal and uncreated. Joseph Smith stated this in *The Doctrine and Covenants*: "Man was also in the beginning with God. Intelligence, or the light of truth, was not created or made, neither indeed can be" (93:29). The word *intelligence* in that statement has a special use. Because Mormons do not believe in an immaterial soul, they prefer to label the soul with the term *intelligence*. All people are originally intelligences that trace their lineage back as far as time can go. As intelligences developed, one of them became supreme, and this God created spiritual bodies for the others. Eventually, God united some of those spiritual bodies with physical bodies. Human nature, then, is composed of three elements: intelligence, spirit, and body. The physical world is only one stage in the cosmic drama of our evolution, but it is a very important stage, since it gives us opportunities to learn through pain and suffering the importance of making spiritual and moral progress toward God.

Even the best Mormon thinkers have trouble explaining in any detail how our preexistence actually works—and no wonder! We are dealing here with the mystery of the origin of human freedom and personality. We are also dealing with speculation about what happened before our world was even formed. Before throwing stones at this doctrine, however, traditional Christians should step back and take a look at their own belief in the immaterial soul.

Traditional Christians believe that our souls are created directly by God out of nothing, although there are different ideas about when that creation takes place (whether at conception or soon thereafter). Most traditional Christians agree with the Roman Catholic Church's position that souls are created at the moment of conception. Others, especially those who draw a close correlation between the soul and the mind, argue that humans do not have a soul until the fetus has most of the biological features of a human being (at least enough to support the initial formation of the brain). Regardless of these debates about when God implants the soul, traditional Christians agree about what the soul is. The soul is an immaterial entity that serves two functions. First, it distinguishes humans from all other animals by conferring upon its recipients the capacity to act freely and think analytically about the world. Second, it gives each human being a unique identity. The first function explains why our species is different from all other species, while the second explains why each member of the human species is different from every other member.

Needless to say, in today's climate of scientific advances and materialist philosophy the idea of the soul has been much criticized. In response to the first function of the soul, many scientists and philosophers today deny the uniqueness of the human species. Why think humans are unique when we know that we are a product of the same biological forces that shaped every other species? In response to the second function, many people think that science has explained why individuals differ from each other. Why posit the soul when we know that our genes (combined with environmental factors) make us who we are?

Christians who attribute individual identity to our souls have a serious *theological* problem to add to these scientific challenges. Most classical theists believe that we are born into sin, but if we inherit original sin as part of our basic human condition, where does it come from? The following dilemma seems unavoidable: If it comes from our souls, then God must have created sinful souls! If it comes from our misuse of freedom, then how can we be born into it? Either God is responsible for our sin, or sin is not original (it begins only when we are old enough to make bad decisions). Some early theologians tried to get around this problem by arguing that sin is passed down from generation to generation through the act of procreation, but the majority of theologians rejected this position. If sex is the means of transmitting sin, then sex must be bad, and celibacy should be everyone's goal. Sin as an inherited trait makes the material creation look like a mistake, not a good gift from God.

Moreover, the idea that the soul springs into existence when our bodies are first conceived has a serious *philosophical* problem. If human personality is not simply the product of social and biological forces, then the soul must play a crucial role in establishing our identity and character. But how does the soul do that if it is created out of nothing, with no history or background? Anyone who has spent time with infants and toddlers knows that they exhibit definite personality traits before they are old enough to know what they are doing. Children seem to come already packaged with a personality, and that personality grows on its own accord, no matter how hard parents try to shape it. When people look at babies, it is natural to discern something of the individuals they will become in the future. When Christians look at babies, they naturally see God's providentially planned destiny, not fate. Classical theists are thus forced to suppose that God creates each soul with its own inherent tendencies, tastes, and inclinations, which is why the mystery of personality is one of the most important impetuses behind the development of the doctrine of predestination in traditional theology. Predestination already has a problem in accounting for our freedom, but can the survival of this doctrine withstand the problem of imagining how God is the source of our personality? If God is responsible for the basic features of our character, is it fair that God gives some people better talents or a stronger will than others?

Mormons engage this debate by challenging the identity-conferring function of the soul. Mormon metaphysics is deeply in tune with the intuition that both freedom and character are already aspects of human life at its origins. Our personalities for Mormons, are not a product of our genes, social environment, or divine fiat. We are born with a character already formed, but it is the result of decisions we made and actions we took long before our birth. We inherit our personalities, but not from an external source. We inherit who we are from a past hidden in the depth of time. The preexistence of the soul is thus a welcome alternative to the puzzling and off-putting aspects of the doctrine of predestination.

Because all embodiment, including the incarnation, is a gift of the potential for greater glory, the Saints find the mystery of personal identity most concentrated in birth (the act of coming into the world), not death (the act of departure). Traditional Christians, drawing from the ancient wisdom of the Greeks, tie individual identity more closely to the moment of death. As the gateway from this life to the next, death is the time when people should take stock of their lives and determine who they have really been. Death for traditional Christians determines who we are both temporally and eternally. Decisions can be made on deathbeds that have the potential to reverse the entire history of an individual's existence. Mormons demure, arguing that birth is the real miracle. The person who is born has already had a life and has made the decisions that have brought that life to earth. Birth, not death, is the revelation of personality.

On the level of answering some of the perennial questions of human identity, the preexistence of the soul makes a lot of sense, but Mormon metaphysics should always be tightly grounded in Christology. Otherwise, speculation about worlds before we were born or worlds yet to come can become just that: ideas that are so enticing that they carry us away from their Christian roots. Notice, though, that there need not be a conflict between metaphysics (Paulsen) and biblical theology (Millet) on the preexistence of the soul. Mormons do not believe that our preexistent spirits were just floating around in the air before our birth. They believe that we were with Jesus. We have always been with Jesus. He is the firstborn of God the Father, and we are, in a very real way, his younger brothers and sisters. What this means on a practical level is that the moments when we are closest to Jesus are also the times that we are most true to ourselves. All people will someday worship Christ because we all carry his memory deep within us. It is Jesus, not our genes, that most determines who we are. We can turn to Jesus because we are returning to him when we acknowledge him as our Lord and Savior. We were with him before, and we will be with him again. That is the most important theological lesson we can derive from the idea that we existed before we were born. Mormon metaphysics and Christology thus ground each other and are inseparable.

Out of this synthesis of philosophy and theology comes a beautiful ethical outlook. Every child, no matter who the biological parents are, is adopted into this life—every child is literally a gift, on loan from an ancient past and intended for a glorious future—just as all Christians are adopted into the family of God and permitted to call Jesus friend and brother. Indeed, from a Mormon perspective, we are more literally the sons and daughters of God than we are the sons and daughters of our biological parents. We belonged to God for a lot longer than we belong to our earthly families because God gave us our first bodies (our spirit bodies) long before our parents gave us flesh, blood, and bone.

So much for the decision Mormons need to make about their own theology. What about the second decision—what non-Mormon Christians can learn from the Saints? To answer this question, I want to go back to the oldest theological movement in America, Calvinism. Calvinism has always been the default theological mode in American Protestantism, which is why so many American churches have rebelled against it. Curiously, it is back in fashion today and stronger than ever. There are several reasons for this revival of America's first intellectual worldview. Calvinism is clear, systematic, and principled in a way that most other theologies are not. Methodism, with its broad view of religious experience, and Lutheranism, with its roots in the more complex theology of Martin Luther, both have more adherents in America today but much less of an intellectual presence. Calvinism is also a theological movement that is easy to define: Calvinism is the product of John Calvin (1509–1564), the great Protestant Reformer who wrote *The Institutes of the Christian Religion* and established a model for how Protestants can change the world in the city of Geneva. The denominations that trace their roots to his influence are the Reformed and Presbyterian churches. Calvinism was summed up at the Synod (or Meeting) of Dort in 1619 in memorable fashion by the acronym TULIP: Total depravity, Unconditional election, Limited atonement, Irresistible grace, and Perseverance of the saints. Calvin himself did not use this formula, but it is a fair representation of what his theology became. Dort was convened to respond to Arminian theology, which argued that humans have freedom of will to accept or reject God's grace, so TULIP does not cover every aspect of Calvinism, although it does get to the heart of what makes Calvinism distinctive. Most of these phrases speak for themselves. Humans are totally depraved and thus can do absolutely nothing to draw nearer to God. God does it all, and when God elects someone for salvation, that election is not based on anything to do with what that person has done. Election, Calvin admits, appears from our perspective to be completely arbitrary. (It also appears arbitrary from God's perspective, because our souls have no prior existence to our bodies and thus we have no prehistory to justify God's eternal decree about our ultimate state.) We just do not know why some people believe in Jesus and others do not. It follows that Jesus Christ did not die for everyone. If he had, then everyone would be saved, but the power of the atonement, for Calvinists, is limited to those whom God elects to save. It also follows that grace is irresistible. If God chooses to save us, there is nothing we can do about it, and the same goes if God chooses not to save us. Finally, once we are saved, we will always be saved. We cannot fall away from our salvation because we did nothing to earn it in the first place. God's decisions are, in a word, final.

Although Calvinists are good at explaining these teachings, many people over the centuries have found them morally repugnant, and it is not hard to understand why. Calvin's God acts according to his own secret plans and hidden intentions, which would be bad enough if it were not also the case that Calvin's God is in complete control of every single event in the world. Calvinists define God's omnipotence as a direct and immediate causal determination of everything that happens in the world. The Holocaust is thus as much a part of God's plan as any other episode in world history. Taking this line of thought to its logical conclusion, Calvinists argue that the fall of Adam and Eve was as meticulously planned by God as the planting of the garden. It follows that our sinfulness is not really something we can control or be responsible for. And why does God orchestrate history so precisely and carefully? God exercises his power, Calvin firmly believes, for his own glory. That some souls are predestined for heaven and the others for hell is God's way of making sure that people pay him the proper respect.

Calvinists will say that my description of their position is a caricature, and there are plenty of extremely smart Calvinists in the world who can put a great spin on the great Reformer's ideas. In fact, the logical consistency of Calvinism has made it a sophisticated form of fundamentalism for conservative Protestant intellectuals. What I mean is that just as some Protestants think that every theological question can be solved by quoting a chapter and verse from the Bible, Calvinists think that every theological problem can be solved by referring to the Calvinist system.

So let me try to be a bit more neutral and just describe what all Calvinists agree is the starting point of their system. Logically, everything in Calvinism follows from the first principle of God's absolute sovereignty, a theme that Calvin never grew tired of emphasizing. This means—and Calvinists are delighted by this implication—that God is not like us, even though he loves us like parents love their children. God is essentially mysterious. An utterly transcendent God acts in ways that we will never understand precisely because he shares nothing with us. God has no nature because God is immaterial, but God does have a will, and his will is the source of all of his actions. What he wills (what he determines to do) is immediately what happens because there is nothing that impedes his wishes. For Calvinists, the key question to ask about any theology is whether it is God-centered or human-centered. There is no in-between. Either religion puts God at the center and recognizes that everything else exists for his glory, or religion puts humans at the center and teaches that humans are worthy of idolatrous worship. In other words, if God is in control, then we have to give up all efforts to pretend to be in charge of our own lives. We can only continually repent and constantly be grateful for what God has done for us. God needs nothing else from us. Indeed, if we think that we are cooperating with God's grace or helping to build God's kingdom, we are insulting God and doing much more damage than good in the world.

Mormonism, by portraying God as "one of us" and not an absolutely "other" sovereign whose will is unpredictable and unfathomable, is as far removed from Calvinism as any Christian tradition can be. For Calvinists, God is so unlike us that it was the most incredible miracle in the world for the Son of God to agree to bridge the gap by becoming a human being. For Mormons, the incarnation is the most amazing event in the history of the earth, but it is not the first time God had a direct experience of what it might be like to be embodied. The incarnation is a chapter, not the entire plot, in the life of Jesus Christ. Jesus is not the human face of an otherwise faceless deity. God has more than a will. God has a nature, just like we do, which is why God has many of the same hopes and feelings that we do.

There is a difference between God's nature and our own: God's nature is perfect, whereas our nature is not. Our nature leaves us prone to sin, but God's nature is to be perfectly loving as well as powerful and all-knowing. Far from being unpredictable, the Mormon God is the most consistent, steady, and dependable being imaginable. God's will is infinitely stronger and God's mind is infinitely more consistent than our own, since God has been acting to organize matter from the very beginning of the cosmos. God's nature, in fact, is that of a father, and as a father, God predictably always wants what is best for his children. And the gift that God cherishes the most for us is the freedom to make choices and take responsibility for our own actions. Without that freedom, we cannot grow in faith in this life, let alone expand our possibilities for sharing with God in the life to come.

My criticisms of Calvinism are not meant to call into question the Christian commitments of any particular Calvinist. On the contrary, Calvinists, in my book, are just as fully Christian as Mormons. Indeed, both traditions ground their faith in intellectually daunting worldviews and morally serious lifestyles. Christianity is big enough for both of them, even though they are opposites in many ways. With such fundamental differences, however, one might expect a Calvinist, of all Christians, to have a very hard time understanding Mormonism, and this is exactly what we find in a recent book by Richard Mouw, *Talking with Mormons: An Invitation to Evangelicals.* In raising some criticisms of this book I am certainly not criticizing Mouw's theological credentials or his standing, demonstrated by his leadership of Fuller Theological Seminary, as one of the prominent leaders in evangelical Christianity. Moreover, I completely agree with about half of what Mouw says in this book. He has two goals. The first is to persuade non-Mormon Christians to be kinder to and more tolerant of the Saints. Indeed, he admits that many Christians demonize the Saints, and he implores them to stop. It is his second goal that I have problems with. That goal is to persuade Mormons to be more Calvinist in their theology.

Mouw's plea for tolerance is persuasive, though he does not base it on the supposition that Mormons are as fully Christian as any other Christian tradition. He bases it on the biblical demand to love thy neighbor, which applies to everyone, including Mormons. For me, I am convinced that we should take Mormons at their word and acknowledge the sincerity of their conviction that Jesus Christ is their Lord and Savior. By this point in church history Christians should know better than to judge fellow followers of Jesus by the quality of their philosophical speculations rather than the fruits of their faith. Before long, we may hope, religious prejudices against Mormons will go the way of the once widespread prejudices against Roman Catholics. Mouw's book, written by an evangelical insider who can speak with authority to Mormon-despisers, should help to bring that about.

Mouw's second goal is a different story. That he—as a Calvinist—would like to see Mormonism become more Calvinistic is hardly surprising, but the two traditions make a very odd couple. The Mormon imagination is edgy and expansive, while Calvinism is restrained and ascetic. Mormonism is a compendium of every nineteenth-century religious movement, including restorationism, social utopianism, hermeticism, and even a healthy dose of liberalism. It is almost as

catholic as the Roman Catholic Church—and that, for Mouw, is precisely its problem. After all, both Mormons and Catholics believe in
the historical development of doctrine, divinization as the form of
salvation, the need for centralized religious authority, the beauty of
ritual, the connection between faith and love, and the existence of a
heavenly Mother.

Calvinism, by contrast, is theologically lean and clean. Calvinism
teaches "that God is sovereign and totally 'other' than the creation;
that human beings are depraved sinners who are desperately in need
of rescue by God; and that salvation is by grace alone." Mormons fail
the Calvinist test because they believe that, as Mouw puts it, God and
humans are "of the same species ontologically." Mormonism went
wrong not with the Book of Mormon but with a flawed metaphysics.

Mouw and I agree that metaphysics makes all the difference
between Mormons and the rest of the Christian world, but where
I see Mormon metaphysics as providing a much needed corrective to
Western philosophy, Mouw sees Mormon metaphysics as the reason
for its departure from historical Christianity. Mouw argues that a
"metaphysical gap" between God and us is essential to Christian faith
and that Calvinism offers the best protection against any attempt to
close that gap: "Judaism and Christianity have been united in their
insistence that the Creator and creation—including God's human
creatures—are divided by an unbridgeable 'being' gap." Mouw means
that God's existence is so different from our own that it can be said
that God is beyond being altogether. Put another way, God is so
"other" that God cannot even be said "to be." Minding the gap is the
best way to honor God's uniqueness.

To me, that sounds like Mouw is asking Mormons to swal-
low Calvin with a big helping of Plato thrown in for good measure.
While it is true that the Church Fathers treated Plato as an honor-
ary Christian, many theologians these days try to overturn the
Platonic heritage of a dualism between spirit and matter, soul and
body, and the transcendence and immanence of the divine. For these
theologians, Mormons can be seen as companionable explorers of a
post-Platonic Christianity. In any case, the Saints seek to close the

metaphysical gap between God and us only as a means to bridging any spiritual gap that separates the modern world from the divine.

At one point in his book, Mouw identifies an unexpected affinity between Mormonism and Calvinism: "It has often struck me," he writes, "that [the Mormon] view of their later scriptures is much like my own view of the Calvinist creedal documents that I subscribe to." This confession surprised me, and I was eager to hear him develop these parallels further. After all, Mouw regards the Heidelberg Catechism, the Belgic Confession, and the Synod of Dort to be decisive "explanations and clarifications" of the Bible, which is, he says, how Mormons treat the *Doctrine and Covenants*. What Mouw says is revealing. "If I come across someone—as I often do—who teaches something that conflicts with the system of thought set forth in these documents, I regard that teaching as less than fully biblical." In other words, the Synod of Dort is not an explanation or clarification of scripture. It is the system of thought (and the only such system) entailed by scripture. This is radically different from the way that the Saints treat the ongoing and evolving authority of prophetic revelation. Calvinism can certainly provide a solid framework for rigorous apologetics, but it can also become an intellectual idol that leads to a defensive and arrogant mindset. Its danger lies in its logical neatness, which makes Calvinists think that every question can be answered according to a precise scheme of rational theologizing.

Ironically, given Mouw's proselytizing, Mormonism was born from frustrations over aggressive and antagonistic argumentation. The young Joseph Smith was overwhelmed by the dissension and strife of the different denominations battling for his attention. Smith turned to visions and prophecy for new answers (just as today many Protestants are returning to Rome for more theological authority and sacramental mystery), but Mouw wants Mormons to return to the strict Calvinism that had already, in Smith's day, fragmented into a thousand competing sects. Offering Calvinism to Mormons is like giving the victim of a dog bite the dog as compensation. Calvinism, for all of its intellectual achievements, can hardly be a source of healing for the fragmentation that it has helped to cause.

And yet, for all of his Calvinistic crusading, Mouw ends his book on a warmly pietistic note. He recommends that evangelical theologians treat Mormonism the way Charles Hodge, the great nineteenth-century champion of Calvinist orthodoxy, treated Friedrich Schleiermacher, the father of liberal theology. Schleiermacher undercut the infallibility of the Bible, but Hodge admitted that Schleiermacher's "personal faith in Christ was real." In the end, it is enough for Mouw that Mormons love Jesus: "People can have a defective theology about Christ while still putting their trust in the true Christ." With those words, Mouw sounds much more like an evangelical than a Calvinist (and demonstrates how far apart the two really are), although he still resists acknowledging that Mormons theology (in contrast to Mormon piety) is indeed directed toward Christ. Evangelicals are willing to let love reach out and heal where logic tries to divide and conquers.

As a fairly recent convert to Roman Catholicism, I think of both Mormonism and Calvinism as branches on the Christian tree. Calvinists will protest that surely they are closer to the trunk, but Mormonism actually goes deeper in trying to restore neglected practices and overlooked beliefs from ancient Christianity. I think of Calvinism as a sturdy, singular, and perfectly gray branch that extends straight out from the tree. It has one crook in it (divine sovereignty) that is well made for sitting or attaching a rope for swinging. When I try to imagine Mormonism, I think of a branch that extends precariously up rather than out, with countless twisting twigs cluttering its many-hued bark. The Calvinist branch is more familiar to me, and its closeness to the ground makes me think I could jump up and grab it, although I would probably need help. The Mormon branch, however, looks a little bit dangerous, yet it is enticing in the way that it extends upward, challenging me to consider how far I could climb out on it. Both branches, as far as I can see, bear good fruit, and both return ample nourishment to the tree's roots, but I must admit that the Mormon branch looks to me like it begins closer to the center of the tree and that it is reaching farther toward the light. I would go so far as to say this: No other branch of the Christian tree is so entangled in complex and fascinating ways with the earliest and most neglected doctrines of the church, and no other branch extends so optimistically and brazenly upward as it stretches toward a horizon bound only by the cosmic significance of Christ.

To drop the tree image, if I had to choose between Smith and Calvin, I would unhesitatingly choose Smith. A Calvinist could not begin to fathom all the riches in Mormonism, although a Mormon can go a long way toward understanding and sympathizing with Calvinism. Mormonism is just a bigger set of ideas than Calvinism. It is capacious and expansive, with plenty of intellectual room to grow. Roman Catholicism, of course, is bigger yet in terms of institutional size and geographical reach. Mormonism embraces the material cosmos as the locus of an astounding metaphysics focused on Christ. Catholicism embraces the whole expanse of church history with a fidelity to the legacy left by those early Christians who survived the persecutions of the Roman Empire and made the church a worldwide movement. Many Mormons, in my experience, are too committed to being part of the Protestant world to recognize just how close to Catholicism they come. Perhaps it is time to recognize that Mormonism's cosmic metaphysics and Catholicism's elaborate history have room to accommodate, inspire, and teach each other, all to the goal of deepening the truth of Jesus Christ.

Of course, Mormonism's metaphysics has significant implications for church history, just as Catholicism's rich history is replete with metaphysical arguments. Mormons can remind Catholics of the high price the church has had to pay for uniformity of belief and practice. Indeed, it could be said that Mormonism fulfills all the hopes and dreams of the myriad groups in church history who were swept from its pages, either because they were accused of heresy or because their ideas did not prevail in the intellectual marketplace. Perhaps it is time for Catholicism to recognize, reconsider, and even reclaim some of the theological pluralism and metaphysical complexity that were lost in the church's march toward creedal consensus.

Catholics, of course, believe that popes, kings, and bishops, in all of their fallen humanity, were guided by the Holy Spirit to do the best they could to protect and promote the mystery of God and the majesty of Jesus Christ. If God did not abandon Christianity for the whole sweep of time between the first Apostles and Joseph Smith's First Vision, then the Catholic Church is still Mormonism's elder brother in the faith, and Mormons have much to learn about the development of doctrine and the practice of rituals that guided the whole of Western Christianity for so many centuries.

Joseph Smith accomplished much precisely because he was free of much nineteenth-century anti-Catholic bias, which makes me wonder what would have happened if he had been personally acquainted with more Catholics or had known more about the Catholic tradition, which had its own fullness of the Gospel hidden in plain sight. That question is for the historians, but perhaps theologians can be excused for wondering what Mormonism would look like in the future if it were stripped completely free of any remaining remnants of that bias. The result, surely, would be a truly universal church.

APPENDIX A

Two Theological Problems Mormonism Solves

Mormon metaphysical materialism can help solve two theological puzzles. The first concerns the body of Jesus Christ (and by implication our bodies as well), while the second concerns the Roman Catholic understanding of the Eucharist (what Protestants call the Lord's Supper or simply communion). To demonstrate my claim requires some technical language and logical analysis, but that is what makes philosophical theology so much fun!

The first puzzle actually involves a set of problems that are grouped around the nature of the body of Jesus Christ during the three days of his death (called in Latin the *triduum mortis*). How is it that this body did not experience decay or decomposition? The Gospels are not specific about this point, but the Acts of the Apostles is. Peter, on the Day of Pentecost, gave a speech to his fellow Israelites, saying that "David spoke of the resurrection of the Messiah, saying 'He was not abandoned to Hades, nor did his flesh experience corruption'" (Acts 2:31). It has always been a part of Christian tradition to affirm that the body of Christ in the tomb did not decompose. When the German artist Hans Holbein the Younger painted the body of Jesus in a grotesque and twisted position, with his skin showing the early stages of putrefaction, he stirred up a major controversy. Dostoevsky found the image so repugnant that he had his character Prince Myshkin, in *The Idiot*, say that the painting had the power to make anyone viewing it lose his or her faith. So the question is this: Assuming that a miracle took place, can traditional Christian metaphysics account for it?

Christianity traditionally teaches that Jesus had a human soul like our own and that his soul and body were united with the Word or Logos, the second person of the Trinity. That view of the incarnation—that Jesus Christ was wholly human and wholly divine—is called Chalcedonian Christology after the council that took place in Chalcedon in 451. Classical theism also teaches that it is the soul that makes our bodies living, organic material and that at our death our soul is separated from our body. That is what death means: the departure from our flesh of the very thing (or immaterial substance) that makes us living beings. The soul, to use Thomas Aquinas's language, is the form of the body. Without the soul, our bodies immediately begin to undergo putrefaction and decomposition. They become formless.

If Jesus' human soul gave his flesh life, and he was really dead in the tomb, with his soul separated from his flesh, how was it that Jesus' body did not suffer any of these insults and horrors? Can the metaphysical assumptions of Chalcedonian Christology explain this phenomenon? Without a human soul to keep it intact, the flesh of Jesus, if it did not decay, must have been immediately and directly connected to its owner, so to speak, who is the Son of God (or *Logos*, a Greek word meaning reason, plan, or word). The Logos must have kept his own flesh pure and pristine, since this was the flesh that God the Father would glorify in Jesus' resurrection and that he, the Logos, would be united with for all of eternity in heaven. That is indeed the position of Thomas Aquinas in the third part of the *Summa Theologica*, Question 50, Article 2. (He bases his position on a creedal literalism: that the Son of God died and "was buried," which means, for Aquinas, that the Son was identical to the dead body that was buried.) If so, during these three days the divine was united with a corpse, not a human being. That is actually a fairly grotesque image: the Son of God united not to a human person but to a soulless body. It is not even clear whether such a thing makes any sense, whatever your metaphysics is. Sure, God can take the temporary form of inanimate objects, as when he speaks to Job out of the whirlwind or the Holy Spirit appears as a dove at the baptism of Jesus, but this sounds like a parody of the incarnation: God is, for a time, a dead body.

Moreover, since the soul descended into Hades (there are debates about where Jesus went, but most scholars think the Bible implies that he went to the place where unsaved [perhaps holy] souls await the final judgment), the Son must have been united to the human soul while he was united to the dead body. (This, again, is Aquinas's position.) Since the soul is what makes human flesh human, then neither the human body nor the human soul is a human being when separated by death. The Son of God therefore must have been simultaneously a bodiless soul and a soulless body. (This was the clear teaching in the authoritative Catechism of the Council of Trent.) Although there are complex ways of understanding this mystery, it seems to suggest that there are two hypostatic unions (the permanent and intimate union of the Logos with Jesus Christ), with the Logos split into two entities, neither of which is a person in any reasonable definition of that term.

Mormons have a much easier way of dealing with these questions, and to see that, we have to begin with their belief that humans have a spirit body rather than an immaterial soul. (There is some debate in Mormon literature about whether the spirit body is synonymous with the soul or whether it is the unifying principle of the soul and the body, in which case it is not identical to the soul. To me, it seems not to be identical to the soul because the spirit body inhabits a *human* body, which must therefore already be animated by a soul.) This spirit body coincides with our physical bodies even though it too is composed of matter, albeit matter of a more refined kind. While traditional Christians believe that souls are created and united with bodies when those bodies are conceived (or soon thereafter), Mormons believe that our spirit bodies were created by God before our physical bodies were conceived. (Mormons also believe that some essential part of what we are, called intelligence, is eternal, but our spirit bodies are not eternal. They were created by God prior to the creation of the material world, presumably out of the same basic substance that God shaped into the world. What Mormons call intelligence is more like what classical theists call the soul than is the spirit body.) When Jesus was born, his spirit body entered his physical body in the same manner that happens for every human being, but his spirit body was quite different from ours. Jesus' spirit body was divine in his premortal existence, which means that his physical body was also different from our physical bodies. Having a divine spirit body gives Jesus' physical body greater protection from not only decomposition in the tomb but also disease and imperfections during his life. According to traditional Christian theology, Jesus had a body just like our own. He suffered, experienced hunger and desire, and aged just like everyone else. According to Mormon metaphysics, Jesus' flesh had a high level of incorruptibility even before his resurrection. The Mormon view does a better job of accounting for Jesus' miracles (he has a mastery over material existence, calming storms, walking on water, and healing diseases) than the traditional view. It also accounts for how Jesus' flesh, if it was not joined directly to Christ during his death, did not decompose in the tomb.

There is another reason why Mormons believe that Jesus' earthly body, though mortal, was already much closer to the divine than any other human body. Mormons believe that Jesus was born of a union between Mary and God the Father. Now let me pause to explain that. Mormon critics sometimes claim that Mormons deny the virgin birth of Jesus, but that is not exactly correct. The details of the virgin birth are surely inscrutable, biologically and supernaturally, under the best of interpretive circumstances, and the Blessed Virgin Mary is deserving of our discretion in these discussions. Nonetheless,

APPENDIX A

lucidity does not have to be lurid. Minimally, the doctrine of the virgin birth states that Jesus had no natural father, which is usually taken to mean that Mary was not inseminated by any male seed. Mormons believe that Jesus was begotten by an immortal (but not immaterial) heavenly father. Mormonism has no authoritative doctrine about how this conception occurred, but Mormons do have ways of understanding this mystery that preserve Mary's antepartum virginity. Still, placing the origin of at least some aspect of Jesus' body in God the Father seems to deny the traditional teaching that Jesus was conceived *solely* by the power of the Holy Spirit. On the positive side, Mormon belief brings new insight to the idea that God was preparing a body for Christ prior to the moment of conception (Heb. 19:5). Moreover, the Mormon position is certainly not any more obscure than the traditional position that the humanity of Jesus proceeded from Mary *exclusively*. The important point for my purposes is that Mormons have a theory for why the body of Jesus was incorruptible during his earthly life *and* the three days he spent in the tomb. Jesus was born out of a holy union between Mary and God. Mary is the Mother of God, although not all of the material of Jesus' body came exclusively from her. God the Father is literally (in the sense of contributing to Jesus' material substance) the father of Jesus Christ.

A related problem for Chalcedonian Christology involves the question of how Jesus descended into hell (or some part of it), where he preached to (perhaps only a portion of) the unsaved before being resurrected from the tomb and ascending into heaven. This traditional belief comes from Peter: "He was put to death in the flesh, but made alive in the spirit, in which also he went and made a proclamation to the spirits in prison, who in former times did not obey, when God waited patiently in the days of Noah, during the building of the ark, in which a few, that is, eight persons, were saved through water" (1 Pet. 3:8–20; also see Eph. 4:8–10). There is a general consensus about this event in Christianity, although there are interesting debates about whether Jesus went all the way into hell itself or only to the forecourt where the righteous who lived before Christ dwelt. There are also debates concerning what precisely Jesus did there. Nevertheless, scripture and tradition are clear that his soul left the tomb. Classical theists argue that Jesus went to Hades only with (or as) his soul, but how, then, could he have experienced solidarity with the damned, and how did he preach and minister to them? It makes better sense to imagine Jesus in Hades with his spirit body (and not just his soul), actively revealing himself to the unsaved.

The second puzzle that Mormonism solves has to do with what Catholics call transubstantiation. Even though Mormons do not believe in transubstantiation in the same way that Catholics do, their metaphysics is better able to explain how it happens. (I know that this sounds a bit odd, but as I argued in chapter 2, Mormons have their own version of transubstantiation, even though they do not apply it to communion.) It is hard to imagine another theological topic that so clearly demonstrates the incompatibility of metaphysical immaterialism with the Christian faith. Catholics take literally the statement from Jesus regarding the bread and wine: "Take, eat; this is my body" and "Drink from it, all of you; for this is my blood of the covenant which is poured out for many for the forgiveness of sins" (Matt. 26:26–28). This happens in the Eucharist, the Catholic Church explains, because when elements are consecrated, God changes their substantial form (the bread and wine), not their accidents (their taste, shape, color, and so on). The body of Christ is not present on the altar in the manner of being available to the senses, but it is substantially present nonetheless, so in this one particular instance, the accidental properties of a substance appear without the substance they are ordinarily attached to (the taste of bread presents itself to us without the nature of bread remaining in the object that looks like bread). (This perplexity is brilliantly analyzed in Marilyn McCord Adams, *Some Later Theories of the Eucharist. Thomas Aquinas, Giles of Rome, Duns Scotus, and William Ockham* [New York: Oxford University Press, 2010]).

How can something material become something divine if the divine is defined according to its immateriality? For a classical theist like Aquinas, the answer is obvious: It does not. In fact, change does not really happen in the instantaneous act (not process!) of transubstantiation, since God is capable of simply annihilating the material substances of the bread and wine and replacing them with the body and blood of Jesus Christ. The result or product of this miracle is actually invisible and undetectable. Whatever is different about the bread and wine is evident only on a spiritual, not material, level. There are so many problems with this view that it is hard to know where to start. For one thing, the bread and wine material of the elements is now missing, yet the elements continue to behave as if that is not true. What, then, spoils or turns to vinegar? What is causally active in our stomachs? Does the material substance of Christ now act like the bread and wine in order to test our faith? (Does it take on the causal properties of the material elements so that our senses tell us that nothing has happened and thus we have to blindly believe transubstantiation has taken place?) Moreover, what aspect of Christ's body is on the altar? Aquinas argues that it is only the substance of Christ's body, not the fullness of it, as if Christ's body has a prime material substructure that can be isolated by stripping away its accidental properties. Aquinas makes this argument because he does not want to think that we consume Christ's body in an ordinary sense, but then he is left without explaining how it is we consume Christ's body even in an extraordinary sense. The idea that Christ is composed of a new kind of prime matter is certainly attractive, but Aquinas's immaterialism does not permit him to speculate about that.

In fact, much of the medieval debate about transubstantiation was driven by two competing concerns. First, the church wanted to give the Eucharistic elements as much reverence as possible, even to the point of worrying about mice eating the consecrated bread or the host being contaminated by the mouth of a communicant who had not confessed his or her sin; and second, most theologians did not want to encourage people to think that they were literally consuming the body and blood of Jesus. The medieval schoolmen were appalled by the thought that Christ's incorruptible body could be subjected to the corruptions of the digestive system. Christ's body is not literally torn by the teeth and so on. These concerns go in opposite directions and thus place an impossible pressure on Eucharistic theory. Somehow, Christ has to be bodily present without being materially accessible. Recipients eat the signs of his body and digest the accidents of his substance but do not consume his literal flesh and blood! Transubstantiation, in Aquinas's hands, is thus a very elaborate attempt to walk a middle way between Christ being materially and metaphorically present. The attempt fails because Christ's body and blood end up even less real than prime matter. They are, to coin a term, the immaterial matter of the consecrated elements, but do they take the place of their original prime matter? Without any concept of gradations of matter, Christ's body, even in its perfect, heavenly state, cannot mix with our own.

The effort of medieval schoolmen to fit the Eucharist into an Aristotelian framework endures as a historical monument to the ingenuity of these masters of logic. Inevitably, at the end of these mind-boggling exercises lay the appeal to divine omnipotence—God could make it work because God is all powerful—which was the prelude to modernity's rejection of God altogether. Who wants to worship a tyrant who changes the rules of nature on a whim? How credible is a ritual that defies not only natural law but also metaphysical elaboration? As even Aquinas's supporters admit, theories of transubstantiation grounded in Aristotelian metaphysics always dissolve into negative theology, which heroically tries to turn ignorance into a virtue. It is easy to see why the Protestant Reformers concluded that the change in the elements is all in our heads and thus the Eucharist is really a matter of rumination and memory, not the material presence of God. A defender of the classical view might reply that God sees that the elements are different after the consecration even though we do not. This suggests that reality is whatever God wants it to be, regardless of how we experience it. That conclusion is a high price to pay for defending classical theism.

The only way out, it seems to me, is to rethink the nature of matter. Matter, for the ancient Greeks, is unknowable in itself because it is known only through its form. In fact, matter is close to being nothing at all, since it has no reality apart from the form it takes. Christians believe that matter is good and that the Son of God assumed a human person, body and soul, and made that flesh his own. Yet Christian theologians adopted Platonic (and Aristotelian) metaphysics and its low estimation of matter. That adoption is fraught with difficulties, because from a Platonic perspective, matter does not have enough "existence" to convey the divine in any way, shape, or form. If matter is purely passive and contributes nothing to what an object is, how could matter, like the body of Jesus, ever become divine? Indeed, how could our bodies become glorified and immortal in heaven?

From the perspective of Mormon metaphysics, matter is one of the characteristic perfections of the divine. All of matter is active, self-moving, and directed toward God, and the material of God's body reveals matter in its most perfect form. Since matter has a goal built into it, prime matter is not a homogeneous and empty substance. Matter has multiple depths that can be differentiated according to their closeness to the divine. Here an analogy might be helpful. The relation of Mormon metaphysics to traditional metaphysics is analogous to the relation of quantum physics to classical physics. Quantum mechanics has overturned not only classical physics but also the classical metaphysics that grounds it. We now know that properties are related to their substances in indefinite (not necessary) ways, that the state of an object is not something that belongs to that object alone, and that causation is not confined to events that share the same basic location. The quantum approach to matter can help us to see how Christ's body can assume properties not ordinarily associated with it, how it can be in many places at the same time, and how the substance of his body can be causally active even as it remains in heaven. Mormon metaphysics and quantum physics make a natural pair, and together they can make sense of how we can participate in Christ's body through the Eucharist by demonstrating that we too are composed of matter that is not bound by the restrictions of classical physics.

Grounding matter in an analysis of the implications of the incarnation that is mediated by quantum physics and Mormon metaphysics can better account for the mystery of transubstantiation than the philosophies of Plato and Aristotle. An Aristotelian interpretation of transubstantiation is not the only way to understand the Eucharist. After all, the term *transubstantiation* was used prior to Aristotelianism's acceptance in the West, and not even the Council of Trent says explicitly that only an Aristotelian interpretation of this elemental change is valid. A materialist metaphysics, far from denying church dogmas, makes transubstantiation rational without diminishing its miraculous character. Bread and wine can become Jesus' body and blood because the body of Jesus is matter in its perfect state, and that state is the destiny of everything that exists, including something as simple as the food we eat.

APPENDIX B

Some Puzzles Regarding Thomas Aquinas's Understanding of Matter

Mormon metaphysics is radically ambitious in its attempt to overthrow all of Western philosophy and theology. Is it also logically consistent and systematically coherent? On the face of it, Roman Catholicism has the obvious and overwhelming advantage of being guided by one of the most careful and inventive thinkers in the history of philosophy. Thomas Aquinas was as clear and precise in his appropriation of Aristotelian logic as Mormonism is free of philosophical jargon and colorful with concrete images. Aquinas is the best representative of what is often called classical theism, which is the belief that God is eternal, unchanging, omniscient, omnipresent, and so on. But before we rush to the judgment that Aquinas would surely win any and every debate against a whole team of Who's Who in Mormon theology, we need to think through Aquinas's central metaphysical commitment to immateriality as it relates to the body of Christ. That will give us a better sense of what metaphysical standards Mormonism must live up to.

Aquinas has what I call a "place problem." Aquinas thought that Jesus Christ could not have descended from heaven because the Son of God was not in any place from which he could descend: "One can say pertinently of the Word of God that He descended, not by some local motion, but by reason of the union to a lower nature" (Thomas Aquinas, *Summa Contra Gentiles*, bk. 4: *Salvation*, trans. Charles J. O'Neil [London: University of Notre Dame Press, 1975], p. 166 [chap. 34]; hereafter cited as *SCG*). The Word (or Logos) occupied space for the first time when he became incarnate. If it moved to occupy that space, then it would have withdrawn from a previous place, but such a thought is frivolous given God's omnipresence (*SCG*, p. 156 [chap. 30]). Yet Aquinas accepts the idea that Christ ascended to heaven in the form of his resurrected body: "To ascend into heaven plainly belongs to Christ" (*SCG*, p. 166 [chap. 34]). This asymmetry is inelegant at best, given Aquinas's systematic proclivities, but it also indicates a bothersome inconsistency in the life of the Son. What Christ is at the end of time is utterly distinct from what he was from time's beginning. To maintain the coherence of his immaterialism, it seems, Aquinas must sacrifice consistency in the life of Christ. Aquinas's metaphysics keeps the spiritual and the material essentially separated, but Christ's resurrected body awkwardly straddles the line.

The same can be said for our own resurrected bodies. Aquinas knew about theological positions that try to imagine the resurrection of the body in terms of a metamorphosis of the body from its earthly state to a higher and finer grade of matter. He vigorously denies that this is possible: "Things do not change into one another unless they have matter in common" (*SCG*, p. 322 [chap. 84]). There are two problems with this denial. First, he bases his analysis of the possible modes of union between two natures solely on Aristotle's *On Generation and Corruption*. He rejects the continuum or convertibility of spirit and matter by drawing from what the ancient Greeks knew about natural phenomena (His interest in this topic, by the way, is driven by his rejection of Monophysite Christology which, he argues, confuses the two natures of Jesus Christ.) Second, he presupposes the conclusion he wants to reach. If there is such a thing as refined matter, then our earthly bodies do have some kind of "matter in common" with our resurrected bodies. The question is whether all matter is of one homogeneous kind.

Not only will our heavenly bodies not be spirit-bodies for Aquinas. They will also not be composed of a celestial substance. Aquinas bases this denial on the idea that celestial bodies, following Aristotle, are perfectly spherical and, besides, celestial bodies do not change and thus do not have tangible experiences. Our resurrected bodies will be higher than celestial bodies, yet they will still be bodies that "one can handle, composed of flesh and bones" (*SCG*, p. 321 [chap. 84]; for his argument about celestial bodies, see p. 323). We will be resurrected as flesh-and-bone human beings, with the same material substance we had on earth, but without the corruption that belies our bodies in our sinful state. The material of our bodies will not change, but the relation of that matter to our soul will (our souls will be empowered by God to exercise complete authority over our bodies).

Does Aquinas's position make sense? Let me raise four questions. First, if God the Father is beyond all space and above having to move from one place to another, how could Christ reign in heaven in his glorified body while sitting at the Father's right hand? Of course, one can say that such language is metaphorical, but the metaphor in this case must point to a real place— heaven—if Christ rules it and we, in our resurrected bodies, will worship him there. Conversely, if heaven is material in some way, what form will God the Father have in it?

Second, is Christ's resurrected body a merely temporary and tentative form of his divinity, or is it really who he is? Could it be something that he might give up some day, shrugging it off like an old set of clothes? Or is it the case of "once incarnated, always incarnated"? The dilemma I am trying to expose in this set of questions is the following: If Christ really is joined to his body in heaven, and he does not experience it as some kind of restraint, then he must have had at least the potential for becoming embodied from the beginning, and moreover, he must have identified with that body as the consummation of his full identity; yet how can that be the case for Aquinas, who has defined the Word as essentially (but not, evidently, eternally) immaterial?

Third, and related to the second point, if Christ's heavenly, resurrected body is a glory to him, then how is the Son not more than the Father— unless, that is, the Father himself is also material in some way? Moreover, if the Son increases in glory as he becomes embodied, what does that say about Aquinas's understanding of divinity as unchanging? It is precisely this dilemma that forced Joseph Smith to argue that God the Father is embodied, since Smith believed that bodies are a blessing and God the Father does not lack what the Son has.

Fourth, if immateriality is the true nature of the Son, then his visible presence in heaven will not reveal God to us. Indeed, it is hard to know on Thomistic grounds why Jesus Christ will retain his body and what he will do with it. Aquinas typically depicts heaven as a state in which the faithful enjoy the beatific vision, which has all the hallmarks of Aristotle's contemplative ideal. There will be no rituals in heaven because the faithful will be united to God by a simple and translucent cognitive intuition. Matter there will be, but it will not share any of the properties that we associate with matter in this life. It follows that matter will become, for all practical purposes, immaterial. Our souls will govern our resurrected bodies effortlessly, but our bodies will not perform any acts of governance, because there will not be enough world in heaven to give us anything to accomplish. For example, there will not be plants to tend or animals to befriend. In fact, the motion of the heavens will cease altogether (SCG, chap. 97). The elements, the stars, and human bodies will remain, but there will be no chemical interactions or molecular motion of any kind, since all movement has a goal and all goals will have been met. It goes without saying that there will be no generation, since perfection, for Aquinas, means that nothing is missing, and thus there will be no need for any additions to heaven's fullness. There will also be no eating—just recall how deleterious digestion is for the body and blood of Jesus Christ in the Eucharist! This sounds like less of a consummation of human flourishing and more of a cessation of human experiencing.

I suppose that a defender of Aquinas will say that there will be intellectual movement in heaven (of our soul toward ever greater awareness and love of God, which involves an intensification of subjectivity), but how, then, is that movement not a stripping away of every last remnant of the meaning of matter? If heaven is physical, won't we need to transcend heaven in order to know and worship God more fully? Doesn't that mean, however, that we will need to get "out" of heaven in order to get "into" the divine? Isn't there something wrong with a theology that seems to suggest that we will need to be saved from heaven?

Aquinas raises these kinds of questions because, on the face of it, he appears to both accept and undermine the absolute gulf between immaterial spirit and physical bodies. God is not material, and yet the Son's reign is embodied. Matter and spirit cannot be mixed together, yet our resurrected bodies will be far superior to the stuff of the stars (the objects that occupy the celestial region). It is no wonder that Aquinas is not consistent on the issues of place and motion.

He acknowledges that our resurrected bodies will have a place, but it will be a place above the stars and thus outside of space altogether. Our bodies will be "lifted up above every body whatever" (SCG, p. 328 [chap. 87]). We will be perfectly agile, but that is because we will not be limited by space, not because our bodies will be transformed into a spiritual substance. Yet Aquinas admits that we will need to pass through the celestial bodies in order to achieve this place beyond time and space, and at the same time he anticipates critics who will wonder how our bodies will be able to pass through the celestial bodies of the stars: "For the divine power will bring it about that the glorious bodies [our resurrected bodies] can be simultaneously where the other bodies are" (SCG, p. 328 [chap. 87]). That this is no minor point is demonstrated by the evidence he posits for his claim. The resurrected Christ, he reminds his readers, was able to pass through shut doors (John 20:26). Confusingly, though, Aquinas says that Christ's ability to walk through walls (and exit the tomb with the stone still blocking the opening as well as come forth from the Virgin without harming her) was not the result of a quality proper to Christ's glorified body. Instead, it was the power of his divinity working through his resurrected body. Likewise, our ability to pass through the celestial sphere will not be a property of our bodies but a product of divine omnipotence. The liberation of our heavenly bodies from their earthly limits only goes so far, it seems. The idea of physical entities that can occupy a space already occupied by another entity is nothing new to the quantum world of modern physics, but it certainly defies the logic of Aristotelianism, even given how much Aquinas revises Aristotle. The bottom line is that Aquinas wants to hold matter and spirit apart, even when he sees that they are forever united in heaven. The two substances cannot be mixed together because even in heaven they will have nothing in common

APPENDIX C

Three Philosophical Problems Mormonism Needs to Solve

Criticizing classical theism as represented by Thomas Aquinas is one thing, but trying to overthrow it is another thing altogether. Those who seek to undermine it need to be reminded of its staying power, its intellectual beauty, and the formidable logical training of its many defenders. Indeed, in my lifetime, the number of philosophically trained classical theists has been growing, not shrinking, and their critics tend to make them even more forceful. Anyone entering into these debates should have a strong dose of humility and a healthy case of fear and trembling. Mormon scholars such as David Paulsen and Blake Ostler, in this respect, can serve as role models for all of us who dare to go down this path. My own version of Christian materialism, as developed in my book *Jesus Christ, Eternal God: Heavenly Flesh and the Metaphysics of Matter* (New York: Oxford University Press, 2012), pursues a way around immaterialism that strictly follows what I call a "maximal Christology." The whole person of Jesus Christ, including his body, should function as the warrant and measure of every theological claim about matter.

From that perspective, let me raise some of my hesitations about Mormon thought (keeping in mind that they could say as much about my own intellectual limits as they say about potential challenges in Mormon theology). More specifically, I want to reflect on three aporias (apparently unsolvable riddles or deep puzzles) of Mormon theology. These aporias, which concern God, humanity, and nature, are more than creative tensions but less than outright contradictions. All of them have to do with the fascinating way that Mormonism affirms both radical freedom and a thoroughgoing materialism.

These aporias are genuine puzzlements that appear to leave thought at an impasse, yet, unlike simple contradictions, they persistently invite further meditation. They emerge from a thorough examination of the consistency involved in holding together several of the fundamental presuppositions of Mormon metaphysics. As the etymology of *aporia* suggests, these dilemmas offer no safe passage in the realm of theory, yet they point to mysteries that demand more rigorous and creative thought.

The first aporia concerns the relation between Mormonism's view of a material God and its commitment to an eternal law that governs both spirit and matter, which includes, presumably, the spiritual material of God. Mormons believe that God is a free person, just like we are. Mormons also believe that there is an eternal law that governs how intelligences (or spirits) become exalted to the status of the divine. Another way of putting this is to say that since matter is eternal, the law that governs it is also eternal and thus also applies to God. The coherence of each of these ideas, considered independently, is, of course, open to debate; good arguments can be made for and against them. Their combination, however, raises a conceptual conundrum. If God is the master of matter, then no matter how God has come to be God, God's ability to form the cosmos out of preexisting matter is a sign of God's freedom from material constraints. After all, according to Mormon metaphysics, God is who he is precisely because he has exercised his freedom in the most maximally powerful and creative manner. God has come to understand the eternal law so well (indeed, coming to understand it is what makes him God) that he is not, whatever path he has taken to the status that we know him to have, bound by it. It would seem, then, that God is both free from and subjected to the same law.

Mormons typically do not want to say that God is free from the eternal law because if God governs the cosmos by being the source of its law, then God stands outside of time and space, and that makes God look like the immaterial divinity of traditional Christian theism. They also do not want to say that God is bound to the law because God is the supreme instance of personhood, and what it means to be a person for Mormons is to be free to make decisions without any causal constraints. One possibility is that God voluntarily submits to the eternal law. That preserves God's freedom and the law's ongoing validity, but why would God do that? Moreover, if God can submit to the law, then does not God have the power to overthrow the law or to create another law to takes its place? Perhaps then God submits to the law out of necessity. If the law is able to compel God's submission, then God must be a bystander in the process that culminates in him. If so, then the eternal law must be identical with the teleological movement inherent in physical matter. That makes eternal law a kind of impersonal karma that regulates all action, physical and spiritual. The result is a law that is something like a God above God—an active power or (impersonal?) force that holds the universe together (like the Higgs field). What makes this problem difficult for Mormon metaphysics is that Mormons do not have the luxury of believing that God is identical to the eternal law. That is the position of Thomas Aquinas, who thought that the eternal law is nothing more (or less) than the nature of God. God for Aquinas is absolutely simple, which means that God can have a law without being subjected to it, which raises its own aporia regarding what it means for God to *have* a nature. In any case, the Mormon God is not simple, has a nature, and is thus subjected to the law that governs all of nature, even as he is free to impose his will on nature.

The second aporia concerns Mormonism's optimistic anthropology and its continuity view of the afterlife. The preexistence of the human soul as well as the divinization view of soteriology are central tenets of Mormon belief, but if we descended once from a superior realm, we can do so again (and again). This is especially true if the afterlife is going to be more of this life· richer and better but not qualitatively different from what we already know. In other words, is there enough transformation in the Mormon view of heaven to justify Mormonism's optimistic anthropology, or is heaven so much like earth that Mormons end up with a cyclical, rather than linear, cosmology? The answer seems to be obvious: the making of gods is a process of elevation that necessarily entails the possibility of demotion as well. Up is not the only moral direction intelligences can go. The more dynamic the Mormon view of heaven is, the less assured we are that the afterlife will be better than this life. Indeed, with greater power in heaven comes greater moral risks as well.

The second aporia can be sharpened by comparing Mormonism's view of freedom with its critique of dualism. All dualisms of any kind begin in the ultimate dualism of spirit and matter, and critiques of dualism typically aim to uncover a pervasive unity that overcomes that division. Mormonism teaches that people are absolutely free. So is God, who could, if he wanted to, turn his back on us and everything he has made. Everything depends on the steadiness of his (and our) purpose. Only God's constantly renewed dedication and hard work can keep the disintegration of the cosmos at bay, just as our hard work is needed to keep social disintegration at bay. Freedom here has no shape or form (it is not grounded in nature), which suggests that it has no ultimate goal other than its own realization. In philosophical terms, this is a libertarian view of freedom taken to an extreme. Mormonism is thus dangerously close to treating freedom as little more than power. One might hope, of course, that this power will be used, by God and people alike, creatively, but if freedom is an end in itself, then its destructive exercise could be just as enjoyable as its responsible use. The metaphysical muddle here is that libertarian freedom is born out of a dualistic understanding of the will's independence from the constraints of the body, but that is precisely one of the problems of classical metaphysics that Mormonism seeks to overcome.

The third aporia concerns the relationship between matter and divinization. Mormons view matter as eternal and thus, relatively speaking, unchanging, but they view humans as material beings who undergo significant, indeed unimaginable, changes. To understand how problematic this is, we need a brief overview of the metaphysics of matter. The orthodox Christian doctrine that God created matter out of nothing, while impossible to picture in any way, served to save the dignity of matter from the malady of the various dualisms that plagued ancient philosophy and religion. Putting an absolute beginning on matter made it not only good (its origin is in God's will) and manipulable (it is finite) but also absolutely subordinate to the divine will. What is new about Mormonism is not its belief in the eternity of matter. The ancient Greeks shared that belief, but they could not go beyond equating the eternity of matter with an unbounded chaos. Mormonism is also not new in subjecting the divine to the basic laws that govern the material world. The Greeks too could not grasp how God could be exempt from the eternal law, which is why the God of Plato and Aristotle is like a mind that cannot be bothered with his body. The Greek God is different from the Mormon, of course, in that his activity is one of self-contemplation rather than self-surpassing creativity, but in both cases God is not infinite and thus is essentially *not* mysterious. It was theologians, not philosophers, that made God infinite. Both Greeks and Mormons reject the infinity of the divine without simply reducing God to the world, but they do so in different ways: the Greeks could contrast God to the material world only by making God a pure mind, incapable of being bothered by matter, while Mormons locate that contrast in God's capacity to use matter for ever greater states of joyful and loving relations. What is new about Mormonism, then, is its combination of the eternity of matter and the materiality of God. Matter is thus both chaotic (eternally in need of being formed, organized, and shaped—this is the Platonic side of Mormonism) and good (it is the very stuff of the divine— this is, with different justification, the Christian side of Mormonism). That matter is both chaotic and good is surely as good a candidate for an aporia as they come. One could say that Mormonism thus wants to have its (very material!) cake and eat it too: it wants all the rights and benefits belonging to the early church's achievement in overcoming the Platonic heritage (of dark, mysterious, and somewhat evil-inclining matter) while having nothing to do with the doctrine of creation out of nothing.

Let me be a bit clearer about this. When Mormons are being Platonists, they treat matter as a force or energy that is in dire need of control. For Plato and some of his Neo-Platonic heirs (but not Iamblichus), matter is of questionable ontological moral status. It exists only in a state of pure potentiality; it *is* insofar as someone makes something of it, and it resists being made into anything of lasting permanence. Consequently, matter must be continually made and remade. Mormonism agrees with this view when it treats matter as instrumental for the evolution of divine personhood. Matter is only what we make of it, and if we do not make anything of it, then it is very close to being nothing at all. This instrumental view of matter leaves a trace of dualism between mind and body lurking within the heart of Mormon soteriology. How can we progress to becoming more like God, to the point of sharing God's power and even, in a sense, becoming gods ourselves, without having our intelligence outstrip our bodies? Already in this life and on this planet scientists are trying to overcome every limit imposed on us by matter. When people become gods, what will stop them from completing this project by developing the tools to exercise an absolute mastery over everything, including their own bodies? If this happens, then the material constraints of our bodies that make life on earth so meaningful will disappear. The material place of heaven, that is, will become increasingly dematerialized. If that is true, then matter is not nearly as foundational to existence as Mormonism's materialism suggests.

Those are the implications of Mormon belief when Mormons are being Platonists. When Mormons are being more Christian in their view of matter, they affirm its goodness, and they actually go much further than creedal orthodoxy on this point. By attributing matter to the divine, they also end up thinking of matter as having its own motion and, within that motion, its own direction. Matter moves inexorably toward the divine on its own accord, since it is ruled by the same law that governs God and us. Matter, after all, is just another name for everything and anything. Even souls and angels, not to mention God himself, are merely organized forms of matter too complex (or too perfectly singular) for us to presently analyze. If this is the case, then what is the potential for divinization that is born into matter? We could think of that potential as a kind of act and call it transcendence, but transcendence is typically another name for spirit, which takes us right back to spirit-matter dualism. For matter to be able to transcend itself and remain material, there must be gradations of matter, but would not the highest gradation of matter be, for all theoretical purposes, immaterial? (It would have none of the limits of the lowest forms of matter.) And if that highest gradation is the source of matter's movement, would not it have all the characteristics of a personal agent who inspires, guides, and satisfies every kind of transcendence? This immaterial person, of course, the more perfect he is, starts looking an awful lot like the God of classical theism. Could it be that Mormon theology ends up with Aquinas's God, with the difference being in the route it takes to get there (or that there is a route at all)?

Perhaps these aporias will be resolved by Mormon thinkers in the future, and perhaps they could be resolved by reference to the eternal body of Jesus Christ, not an eternal law of increase or transformation. That, however, is a project for another time and place.

SOURCES AND SUGGESTED READING

Introduction: The Mormon Ecumenical Moment

The quotation about the "larger cup" comes from Truman G. Madsen, *Eternal Man* (Salt Lake City: Deseret Book Company, 1970), p. iv. I was honored to be invited to give the Fifth Annual Truman G. Madsen Lecture sponsored by the Wheatley Institution at Brigham Young University on November 15, 2012. I want to thank Richard Williams, James Faulconer, and Emily Reynolds (Truman Madsen's daughter) for their warm hospitality, encouragement, and constructive responses to my work. I read *Eternal Man* when I first started a serious study of Mormonism, and it was unlike any theology I had ever read before. Indeed, I did not think that such theological views were even possible, let alone that they could be delivered in inspiring and engaging prose.
A good rejoinder to the resurgence of atheistic materialism among some philosophers and scientists has been written by Ian S. Markham: *Against Atheism: Why Dawkins, Hitchens, and Harris Are Fundamentally Wrong* (Malden: Blackwell, 2010). For my review of one of the best books on the restoration movement, see Stephen H. Webb, review of William R. Baker, ed., *"Evangelicalism and the Stone-Campbell Movement,"* *Encounter* 64, no. 1 (Winter 2003): pp. 106–108. In that review I point out that the restorationist emphasis on baptism for the remission of sins set the Stone-Campbell movement apart from the evangelical emphasis on having a born-again experience. Interestingly, Mormons too focus on baptism as the means of salvation and also tend to avoid born-again language.
Statistics about Mormon growth and other aspects of the Latter-day Saints can be found in Brandon S. Plewe, ed., *Mapping Mormonism: An Atlas of Latter-day Saint History* (Provo: Brigham Young University Press, 2012).

Chapter 1: Mormon Envy

All of Joseph Smith's works can be found on the official website of The Church of Latter-day Saints at http://lds.org. This includes the *Doctrine and Covenants*, which is mainly a collection of revelations received by Joseph Smith, and the famous King Follett Sermon. Context is everything in the study of Joseph Smith, as has been pointed out by the historian who knows Smith the best: "To a large extent, Joseph Smith assumes the character of the history selected for him. The broader the historical context, the greater the appreciation of the man" (Richard L. Bushman, "Joseph Smith's Many Histories," in *The Worlds of Joseph Smith*, ed. John W. Welch [Provo: Brigham Young University Press, 2006], p. 4).

For more of my reflections on the evangelical culture of the church of my youth, see Stephen H. Webb, "Recalling: A Theologian Remembers His Church," in *Falling toward Grace: Images of Religion and Culture from the Heartland* (Bloomington: Indiana University Press, 1998), pp. 70–76; and for my analysis of church traditions in terms of what I call their theoacoustical soundscapes, see Stephen H. Webb, "Silence, Noise, and the Voice of Jesus Christ," in *Developing Ears to Hear: Listening in Pastoral Ministry, the Spiritual Life, and Theology*, ed. Aaron Perry (Lexington, Ky.: Emeth Press, 2011), pp. 29–35.

An insightful examination of the role sincerity plays among the Saints has been written by Laurie F. Maffly-Kipp; see "Tracking the Sincere Believer: 'Authentic' Religion and the Enduring Legacy of Joseph Smith Jr.," in *Joseph Smith Jr.: Reappraisals after Two Centuries*, ed. Reid L. Neilson and Terryl L. Givens (New York: Oxford University Press, 2009), chap. 11. Saints often appeal to enduring and heartfelt experiences to confirm their religious beliefs.

For an analysis of what he calls Mormonism's "selective literalism," see the important book by Philip L. Barlow, *Mormonism and the Bible: The Place of the Latter-day Saints in American Religion* (New York: Oxford University Press, 1991), p. 32.

The quotation from the mental health expert is from John Watkins, *Hearing Voices: A Common Human Experience* (Melbourne: Michael Anderson Publishing, 2008), p. 5. For more on the research of Henry Sidgwick, see T. M. Luhrmann, *When God Talks Back: Understanding the American Evangelical Relationship with God* (New York: Alfred A. Knopf, 2012), esp. chap. 8.

For the quote from Terryl Givens, see his excellent book, *By the Hand of Mormon: The American Scripture that Launched a New World Religion* (New York: Oxford University Press, 2002), p. 221. The quote from Alexander Campbell comes from the same book, p. 232. I am grateful to Givens for advice and inspiration in writing this book.

Bible quotations are from the New Revised Standard Version except when the context makes it appropriate to use the King James Version. There are many editions of William James's classic *The Varieties of Religious Experience*.

No understanding of anti-Mormon prejudices would be complete without reading J. Spencer Fluhman, *"A Peculiar People": Anti-Mormonism and the Making of Religion in Nineteenth-Century America* (Chapel Hill: University of North Carolina Press, 2012).

Chapter 2: The Magic of Being Mormon

For a fascinating history of magic, see Keith Thomas, *Religion and the Decline of Magic* (New York: Penguin Books, 1971).

Both Plato quotations are from his dialogue *Theaetetus*. See *The Collected Dialogues of Plato*, ed. Edith Hamilton and Huntington Cairns (Princeton: Princeton University Press, 1961), p. 881 (176b) and p. 860 (155d). Plotinus's last words were recorded by Porphyry in his "Life of Plotinus." See the first volume of the A. H. Armstrong translation of the *Enneads* in the Loeb Classical Library (Cambridge: Harvard University Press, 1966), p. 7. For the argument that the theurgist becomes his own demiurge, see the important book by Gregory Shaw, *Theurgy and the Soul: The Neoplatonism of Iamblichus* (University Park: Pennsylvania State University Press, 1995), p. 56. I have also learned much from Algis Uzdavinys, *Philosophy and Theurgy in Late Antiquity* (San Rafael: Sophia Perennis, 2010); and John Dillon, *The Middle Platonists, 80 B.C. to A.D. 220* (Ithaca: Cornell University Press, 1977).

More philosophers are beginning to recognize that philosophy traditionally was (and still should be) a spiritual discipline. See, for example, Pierre Hadot, *Philosophy as a Way of Life*, trans. Michael Chase (Malden: Blackwell Publishing, 1995).

For John Brooke, see his book *The Refiner's Fire: The Making of Mormon Cosmology, 1644–1844* (Cambridge: Cambridge University Press, 1994). An excellent survey of various receptions of this book can be found in Jan Shipps, *Sojourner in the Promised Land: Forty Years among the Mormons* (Urbana: University of Illinois Press, 2000), chap. 10.

The Iamblichus quotation is from *Iamblichus: On the Mysteries*, trans. with intro. and notes by Emma C. Clarke, John M. Dillon, and Jackson P. Hershbell (Atlanta: Society of Biblical Literature, 2003), p. 169 (III.19).

The quotation from Jeffrey Holland, a member of the Quorum of the Twelve Apostles of The Church of Jesus Christ of Latter-day Saints, is from a devotional address, "Of Souls, Symbols, and Sacraments," that he gave on January 12, 1988, at the Marriott Center while he was president of Brigham Young University. It can be heard on YouTube at http://www. youtube.com/watch?v=e5PBqxwlfHI, and it was printed as a pamphlet by Deseret Book Company in 2001.

An insightful discussion of LDS–Roman Catholic relations can be found in Michael G. Reed, *Banishing the Cross: The Emergence of a Mormon Taboo* (Independence: John Whitmer Books, 2012).

Chapter 3: What's Up with Mormons and Matter?

For further discussion of the Messalian movement, see my review of Paul L. Gavrilyuk and Sarah Coakley, eds., *"The Spiritual Senses: Perceiving God in Western Christianity,"* Reviews in Religion and Theology 19, no. 4 (September 2012): pp. 452–455. Joseph Smith's Book of Moses is considered scripture by Latter-day Saints and is included in a selection of his other works under the title *Pearl of Great Price*. As further evidence that Smith taught the doctrine of a spiritual sense, Erastus Snow recalled him saying that "the Holy Ghost or Spirit of the Lord underlies all of the natural senses, viz., seeing, hearing, smelling, tasting, and touching. This spirit communicates with the spirit of man, and enlivens all the other senses" (quoted in Truman G. Madsen, *The Sacrament: Feasting at the Lord's Table* [Provo: Amalphi Publishing, 2008], p. 136). Rather than limiting the spirit sense to the eyes, Smith understood spirituality as a deepening of all of our senses toward their ultimate synesthetic consummation in heaven. For my own interests in synesthesia, see Stephen H. Webb, *The Divine Voice: Christian Proclamation and the Theology of Sound* (Eugene: Wipf and Stock Publishers, 2011).

All the quotations from Orson Pratt are from David J. Whitaker, foreword, *The Essential Orson Pratt* (Salt Lake City: Signature Books, 1991). The best book on Orson Pratt's scientific and metaphysical speculations is Erich Robert Paul, *Science, Religion, and Mormon Cosmology* (Urbana: University of Illinois Press, 1992). Paul associates Joseph Smith's thought with what he calls "astronomical pluralism" (p. 75) or, in Smith's own words, a belief in "worlds without number" (Moses 1:33). For Paul, Smith's ontological heterogeneity (being itself is plural) follows upon his fascination with astronomical multiplicity. Paul also associates Pratt with the occult: "In contrast to the mechanical requirement of inert particles, however, Pratt's atomistic ontology admitted particles that possessed self-volition. Thus his ontology of nature was a curious mixture of the occult with the mechanical" (p. 130). Paul helps us to see the connections between "multiple worlds" astronomy and Smith's view of God's embodiment and the role of propagation in heaven. The cosmos has to be big enough for all of these gods-in-the-making! Smith stretched the imagination of the universe to make the world large enough to include God. Mormon thinkers like Pratt did not take Smith's astronomy in the direction of natural theology because their materialism inspired them to seek a more immediate connection between doctrine and science.

There is also a fine discussion of Orson Pratt in Craig James Hazen, *The Village Enlightenment in America: Popular Religion and Science in the Nineteenth Century* (Urbana: University of Illinois Press, 2000), chap. 1. The only biography of Orson Pratt is Breck England, *The Life and Thought of Orson Pratt* (Salt Lake City. University of Utah Press, 1985).

Lynne McTaggart's book is *The Field: The Quest for the Secret Force of the Universe* (New York: Harper, 2008). For an excellent investigation of how quantum mechanics is changing theology, see Kirk Wegter-McNelly, *The Entangled God: Divine Relationality and Quantum Physics* (New York: Routledge, 2011). I refer to this book in my own critique of *creatio ex nihilo*, forthcoming from Routledge in a volume edited by Thomas Oord. John Durham Peters has written a creative and accessible essay on some of these issues: "Reflections on Mormon Materialism," *Sunstone Magazine*, March 1993: pp. 49–52.

Chapter 4: Branches on the Family Tree: Relatives or Impersonators?

This chapter is a thoroughly revised expansion of an essay that originally appeared as "Mormonism Obsessed with Christ," *First Things*, February 2012: pp. 21–23; with my reply to letters in the April 2012 issue, pp. 9–15. I am very grateful for the dozens of e-mails I received from readers, most of which were helpful suggestions and encouragement from Mormons. I especially learned from an informative and gracious letter from Elder Bruce D. Porter.

Very few books about Jesus Christ written by non-Mormons begin with his prehistory. The only one that I know of is the exceptional work Leonard Sweet and Frank Viola, *Jesus: A Theography* (Nashville: Thomas Nelson, 2012). Chapter 1 is entitled "Christ before Time." Note this comment: "Consequently, the incarnation should not be seen as a single temporal act in history. But the divine emptying that it embodied began before creation, continued into the incarnation, and further than that" (p. 4).

Richard Lyman Bushman is the author of a grand biography of Joseph Smith that has significantly shaped my thinking: *Joseph Smith: Rough Stone Rolling* (New York: Vintage Books, 2005).

All of Robert Millet's books are instructive and helpful. In particular, see Robert L. Millet, *A Different Jesus? The Christ of the Latter-day Saints* (Grand Rapids: William B. Eerdmans Publishing Company, 2005). Philosophers have become interested in analyzing "vague concepts" (concepts whose extension is unclear), but theologians have not; theologians still treat vagueness as a debility that must be corrected. Millet introduces the idea that the chasm between humanity and God is "almost infinite" (p. 117), which sounds to me like a perfectly good vague concept.

Chapter 5: Mormon Overreach? Brigham Young and Parley Pratt

For the quotation from Turner, see John G. Turner, *Brigham Young: Pioneer Prophet* (Cambridge: Harvard University Press, 2012), p. 2. Several of the quotations from Young are from Turner's book, while the rest can be found in *The Essential Brigham Young*, foreword by Eugene E. Campbell (Salt Lake City: Signature Books, 1992), available at the publisher's website: http://signaturebookslibrary.org/.

The section on Brigham Young is a revised and expanded version of my review of John Turner's book: "A Many-Sided Man," *Books and Culture*, September/October 2012: pp. 30–31.

The section on Parley Pratt is also revised from a review forthcoming in *Books and Culture*. I am extremely grateful for that journal's editor, John Wilson, for all of the support he has given my writing over the years and for encouragement in my pursuit of Mormon studies. John is an incredibly generous reader and supporter of writers.

All of the quotations from the Pratt section are from Terryl L. Givens and Matthew J. Grow, *Parley P. Pratt: The Apostle Paul of Mormonism* (New York: Oxford University Press, 2011). I have also benefited from Gregory K. Armstrong, Matthew J. Grow, and Dennis J. Siler, eds., *Parley P. Pratt and the Making of Mormonism* (Norman: University of Oklahoma Press, 2011).

I have not given much discussion to the significant role that millennial expectation played in early Mormonism, primarily because I believe that apocalypticism in all of its forms is a type of religious experience that collapses and minimizes the distances of time, while the Saints developed their spiritual perception in a different direction: their materialism crosses and dissolves the great distances of space.

There are many ways of viewing early Mormon polygamy. The most helpful, I think, is to see it as a product of a premature eschatological enthusiasm. It was also an attempt to recover not just an Old Testament practice but the New Testament's emphasis on how the church should have a creative impact on restructuring the nature of the family. Finally, it must have seemed to early Mormons a natural implication of Joseph Smith's vision of human spirits being, before the creation of the world, the literal offspring of God the Father. Propagation for Mormons is the primary means by which acts of creation take place, and thinking of spirits as propagated by God is a way of drawing all creatures into an intimate portrait of God's love. Smith basically reorganized discourse concerning God's relationship to the world along the lines of family ties. That so many non-Mormon Christians find a sexualized eternity both in prehistory and in heaven offensive is a good issue to ponder. It presupposes not only God's embodiment but also the speculation that there is a Mother God along with God the Father. One of its theological benefits is that it gives stronger meaning to the phrases "Son of God" and "God the Father."

Chapter 6: How to Heal Modernity's Spiritual Breakdown

The quotation from Joseph Smith regarding the earth being crowned with glory is from Joseph Fielding Smith, ed., *Teachings of the Prophet Joseph Smith*, first published in 1938 and available on the Web at http://www.boap.org/LDS/Joseph-Smith/Teachings/T1.html.
The best brief explanation of Mormon baptism for the dead that I know of is provided in James E. Talmage, "Missionary Labor among the Dead Was Inaugurated by the Christ," in *Jesus the Christ: A Study of the Messiah and His Mission according to Holy Scriptures Both Ancient and Modern* (Salt Lake City: Deseret Book Company, 1983), p. 627. Jesus tried to save the dead, so why should not Christians follow suit?
The indisputably great work of the Old Testament Temple scholar Margaret Barker is just beginning to be assimilated by Mormon (and other) scholars. See Margaret Barker and Kevin Christensen, "Seeking the Face of the Lord: Joseph Smith and the First Temple Tradition," in *Joseph Smith Jr.: Reappraisals after Two Centuries*, ed. Reid L. Neilson and Terryl L. Givens (New York: Oxford University Press, 2009), chap. 10.

Chapter 7: Two Decisions

For the quote from David L. Paulsen, see his "Are Christians Mormon?" *BYU Studies* 45, no. 1 (2006): p. 280. For the book dedicated to his work, see Jacob T. Baker, ed., *Mormonism at the Crossroads of Philosophy and Theology: Essays in Honor of David L. Paulsen* (Salt Lake City: Greg

Kofford Books, 2012). I draw his understanding of apostasy from his review of Roger Olson, *"The Story of Christian Theology,"* BYU Studies 39, no. 4 (2000): pp. 185–194. There is a great need to publish Paulsen's collected papers. Miranda Wilcox is editing an excellent book on apostasy: *Standing Apart: Mormon Historical Consciousness and the Concept of Apostasy* (forthcoming).

Parts of this chapter are a revision of my Web article "Talking with Mormons: A Catholic Looks at a Calvinist Looking at Mormons," posted in 2012 on the *Books and Culture* website: http://www.booksandculture. com/articles/webexclusives/2012/may/talkingmormons.html. See also Richard J. Mouw, *Talking with Mormons: An Invitation to Evangelicals* (Grand Rapids: William B. Eerdmans Publishing Company, 2012). I also borrow from my review of Robert L. Millet and Gerald R. McDermott, *Claiming Christ: A Mormon–Evangelical Debate* (Grand Rapids: Brazos Press, 2007), *Reviews in Religion and Theology* 15 (July 2008): pp. 426–429.

For Blake Ostler's groundbreaking work in systematizing Mormon doctrine, see his *Exploring Mormon Thought,* vol. 1: *The Attributes of God;* vol. 2: *The Problem with Theism and the Love of God;* vol. 3: *Of God and Gods* (Salt Lake City: Greg Kofford Books, 2001, 2006, and 2008).

For an excellent discussion of The Book of Mormon and anti-Catholicism, see Stephen E. Robinson, "Nephi's 'Great and Abominable Church,'" *Journal of Book of Mormon Studies,* 7 (1998), pp. 32–39.

A marvelous book on the often hidden history of Western affirmations of preexistence is Terryl L. Givens, *When Souls Had Wings: Pre-mortal Existence in Western Thought* (New York: Oxford University Press, 2010). Also see the beautifully written book Terryl L. Givens and Fiona Givens, *The God Who Weeps: How Mormonism Makes Sense of Life* (Pleasant Grove, Utah: Ensign Peak, 2012). It is a standard belief in Mormonism that God the Father held a council before the creation of the earth to determine the plan of our salvation, and our premortal spirits were there. On the way Joseph Smith's experiences of the deaths of loved ones shaped his thought, see Samuel Morris Brown, *In Heaven as It Is on Earth: Joseph Smith and the Early Mormon Conquest of Death* (New York: Oxford University Press, 2012).

There is a growing number of Mormon scholars who advocate for an a-theological approach to Mormonism. They affirm and celebrate Mormonism's freedom from the obsession in traditional theology for system building and logical completeness. The leading voice in this movement is James E. Faulconer. See his fine collection of essays, *Faith, Philosophy, Scripture* (Provo: Neal A. Maxwell Institute for Religious Scholarship, 2010): "Perhaps the most important reason that Latter-day Saints have done little toward giving an intellectual clarification of revelation is that our experience of religion is fundamentally practical and, so, does not lend itself readily to systematic theological reflection" (p. 64). This position has not stopped Faulconer from becoming one of the most insightful Mormon thinkers writing today. His analysis of the Mormon view of transcendence, which puts it into dialogue with the philosophy of Emmanuel Levinas, is outstanding (it appears in Jacob T. Baker, ed., *Mormonism at the Crossrouds of Philosophy and Theology* (Salt Lake City: Gregg Kofford Books, 2012), chap. 13). Following in his footsteps, in a more self-consciously (and even systematically!) postmodern way, is Adam S. Miller, *Rube Goldberg Machines: Essays in Mormon Theology* (Salt Lake City: Gregg Kofford Books, 2012).

INDEX